Shakespeare & the Ethics of War

Shakespeare &

Series Editors:
Graham Holderness, *University of Hertfordshire*
Bryan Loughrey

Volume 5
Shakespeare & the Ethics of War
Edited by Patrick Gray

Volume 4
Shakespeare & Creative Criticism
Edited by Rob Conkie and Scott Maisano

Volume 3
Shakespeare & the Arab World
Edited by Katherine Hennessey and Margaret Litvin

Volume 2
Shakespeare & Commemoration
Edited by Clara Calvo and Ton Hoenselaars

Volume 1
Shakespeare & Stratford
Edited by Katherine Scheil

Shakespeare & the Ethics of War

Edited by
Patrick Gray

berghahn
NEW YORK · OXFORD
www.berghahnbooks.com

Published in 2019 by
Berghahn Books
www.berghahnbooks.com

© 2019 Berghahn Books

Originally published as a special issue
of *Critical Survey*, volume 30, number 1.

All rights reserved. Except for the quotation of short passages
for the purposes of criticism and review, no part of this book
may be reproduced in any form or by any means, electronic or
mechanical, including photocopying, recording, or any information
storage and retrieval system now known or to be invented,
without written permission of the publisher.

Library of Congress Cataloging-in-Publication Data

Names: Gray, Patrick, 1978– editor of compilation.
Title: Shakespeare & the ethics of war / edited by Patrick Gray.
Other titles: Shakespeare and the ethics of war | Critical survey (Oxford, England)
Description: New York : Berghahn Books, 2019. | Series: Shakespeare &; vol 5 | "Originally published as a special issue of Critical Survey, volume 30, number 1."—Title page verso. | Includes bibliographical references.
Identifiers: LCCN 2019026281 (print) | LCCN 2019026282 (ebook) | ISBN 9781789202618 (hardback) | ISBN 9781789202625 (paperback) | ISBN 9781789202632 (ebook)
Subjects: LCSH: Shakespeare, William, 1564–1616—Political and social views. | War in literature. | Politics and literature. | Literature and history.
Classification: LCC PR3017 .S258 2019 (print) | LCC PR3017 (ebook) | DDC 822.3/3—dc23
LC record available at https://lccn.loc.gov/2019026281
LC ebook record available at https://lccn.loc.gov/2019026282

British Library Cataloguing in Publication Data

A catalogue record for this book is available from the British Library

ISBN 978-1-78920-261-8 hardback
ISBN 978-1-78920-262-5 paperback
ISBN 978-1-78920-263-2 ebook

Contents

Introduction **Shakespeare and the Ethics of War** *Honour at the Stake* Patrick Gray	1
Chapter 1 **Shakespeare in Sarajevo** *Theatrical and Cinematic Encounters with the Balkans War* Sara Soncini	26
Chapter 2 **John of Lancaster's Negotiation with the Rebels in *2 Henry IV*** *Fifteenth-Century Northern England as Sixteenth-Century Ireland* Jane Yeang Chui Wong	46
Chapter 3 **Shakespeare's Unjust Wars** Franziska Quabeck	68
Chapter 4 ***Sine Dolore*** *Relative Painlessness in Shakespeare's Laughter at War* Daniel Derrin	83
Chapter 5 **The Better Part of Stolen Valour** *Counterfeits, Comedy and the Supreme Court* David Currell	101
Chapter 6 **Hamletism in the Spanish Civil War, 1936–39** Jésus Tronch	118

Chapter 7 137
   Where Character Is King
   Gregory Doran's Henriad
   Alice Dailey

Index 158

Introduction
Shakespeare and the Ethics of War
Honour at the Stake

Patrick Gray

My first memory of any kind of political event was the fall of the Berlin Wall in 1989. I was eleven years old, and I failed to grasp its importance. I could not understand why the teacher had stopped class simply to watch people on TV tear down chunks of grey, graffiti-spattered concrete and cheer. As I was about to graduate from high school, however, seven years later, I thought I had understood it. The 'Evil Empire' had collapsed; in the words of Francis Fukuyama, we had arrived at 'the end of history'. For several generations, the men in my family had served in the military, and I assumed I would do the same. I would join the Marines; I knew that they would cover the costs of a college education, and I imagined that running around playing soldier would be harmless, even fun. I had not been keeping track of events in the Balkans; the only warfare I had really registered in my own lifetime was the first Gulf War, a short-lived, triumphant joyride across Mesopotamia, supported by a near-unanimous global

Notes for this section begin on page 22.

alliance. 'What could go wrong?', I thought. Communism lies in ruins. The time for war is over. Being a Marine would be a bit of a lark, like an extended Boy Scout camping trip. The worst that could happen would be some sort of clean-up operation, with yours truly as one of the good guys, the sheriff in the white cowboy hat (metaphorically speaking). To my surprise, however, as I was trying to figure out how to enlist, I was awarded a generous scholarship to attend Chapel Hill, one that I could not combine with the ROTC (Reserve Officers' Training Corps). The offer was too good to pass up. Plus, I figured I could go to OCS (Officer Candidate School) after I graduated, if shooting rifles and so on still seemed enticing at that point.

Once I actually got to college, my interests changed. Shakespeare began to consume my attention. Even so, I thought I might begin with this anecdote – a story of my own 'road not taken' – as a preamble to reintroducing some of the unforeseen events of the past two decades. Over time, these conflicts have begun to feel familiar. Yet they represent an ongoing and perhaps insurmountable challenge to what were once commonly held expectations about international relations. Progressive accounts of history have come under duress; in the wake of 9/11, Iraq, Afghanistan, the Ukraine, Syria and North Korea, not to mention Brexit, as well as the election of Donald Trump, the hypothetical 'arc of the moral universe' towards global peace, prosperity and justice no longer seems as plausible as it once did, in the years immediately following the end of the Cold War. I want to recover our initial reactions of incredulity, shock and lingering confusion, as that dream-vision began to dissipate, the sense of surreal disorientation that continues, still today. Looking back now more than twenty years, I feel an eerie chill when I think how casually I assumed at the age of eighteen, never even once having travelled overseas, that the world was well on its way to Kant's 'perpetual peace', that joining the military, once the USSR had been defeated, would not be likely to involve any actual combat. Yet I was hardly the only one caught off-guard.

In the academy, as in the world at large, the turning point seems to have been the September 11 terrorist attacks in 2001.[1] In the 1980s and 1990s, Shakespeare studies in the United States had been dominated by the aims, assumptions and methods of New Historicism. From an American perspective, these decades were a time of relative peace; perhaps for this reason, as Nick de Somogyi observes, 'despite its obsession with violence and power', New Historicism 'neglected the subject of early modern war'.² The omission was perhaps inevitable, given the premises of this school of thought. A predetermined narrative in which the existing hegemon always triumphs is easier to reconcile to a seemingly unipolar world such as the one the so-called 'Pax Americana' provided at the time, as the Soviet Union began to come unglued, than it is to a shifting, multipolar balance of powers such as seems to be emerging at the moment, still less a 'hot' or 'shooting' war with an uncertain outcome, such as we saw in WWI and WWII, and now again in places such as Iraq, Afghanistan and Syria. Likewise, the New Historicist template is easier to apply to desultory political unrest or doomed, disorganized uprisings such as Jack Cade's rebellion than it is to cataclysmic civil wars such those which overturned the Roman Republic. The Cultural Materialism that sprang up in the United Kingdom in the same decades, the close of the twentieth century, is more accommodating in this respect, insofar as it leaves the trajectory of political change an open-ended question.

Part of the attraction of New Historicism has always been that by accepting the determinism latent within French antihumanism, especially the claims of Foucault, its theoretical underpinning provides a consoling explanation for the perceived failure of various earnest, radical, sometimes violent attempts in the 1960s and 1970s to reshape society into a kind of secular paradise.³ What is to be done, when there turns out not to be a beach beneath the pavement? At what point does it become acceptable for a would-be rebel to give up and sell out? The utopian, Hegelian version of Marxism proposed by Henri Lefebvre and enacted, even if only briefly, by his students in the riots in Paris in May 1968 proved unsustainable, or at least much more difficult to believe in, over time, than had been supposed.⁴ So, it was exchanged for the more sinister, Stalinist Marxism of Louis Althusser, together with what Lee Patterson aptly describes as Foucault's 'nightmare': a 'totalizing vision of an entrapping world organized not primarily but exclusively by structures of domination and submission'.⁵ It was not anyone's fault that the revolution did not succeed; it never could have in the first place. The powers-that-be always win; subversion is always contained. Precisely in those assumptions that distinguish it from other types of historicism, New Historicism is curiously, conveniently hopeless. As such, it always struck me, even at its height, back when I was an undergraduate, as a form of what Sartre would call 'bad faith'. New Historicism styles itself as an act of courage, peering past the veil of 'ideology' into the Nietzschean 'abyss'. But it always seemed to me more like self-exculpatory therapy. Like other forms of antihumanist 'critique', it is the comfortable, default interpretive mode of what Nietzsche calls 'the last man', reconciling himself to the modern state.

As it happens, probably the best-known example of a New Historicist approach to Shakespeare's plays does touch upon war, if only indirectly. In his essay 'Invisible Bullets', Stephen Greenblatt undercuts critics such as William Hazlitt who see *Henry V* as 'ironic', as well as those such as Norman Rabkin who see the play as 'radically ambiguous'. The problem with the play's 'apparent subversion of the monarch's glorification', Greenblatt argues, is that 'the very doubts that Shakespeare raises serve not to rob the king of his charisma but to heighten it'.[6] 'Actions that should have the effect of radically undermining authority turn out to be the props of that authority.'[7] In *Shakespeare Recycled*, Graham Holderness pushes back against this alignment of Shakespeare with Foucault. Tracing changes in interpretation and performance of Shakespeare's English history plays from WWII up through the Falklands War and after, from Olivier's *Henry V* to Branagh's, Holderness demonstrates that these plays 'make themselves available for reactionary *or* progressive reproduction'.[8] 'Discrete and alternative positions of intelligibility' reflect 'forces of liberty' as well as 'forces of oppression'.[9]

Taking up and elaborating upon Holderness's approach, research on the wartime reception of Shakespeare has become increasingly international in scope. The collection *Shakespeare and War*, edited by Ros King and Paul Franssen, includes sections on 'translation and adaptation', as well as 'wartime interpretation', focused on the effects of twentieth-century conflicts.[10] In their collection of essays, *Shakespeare and the Second World War*, editors Irena Makaryk and Marissa McHugh and other contributors consider the impact of WWII on productions of Shakespeare's plays in Germany, Italy, Palestine, Greece, Poland, Russia, Japan, China, Britain, the United States and Canada.[11] In a special issue of *Shakespeare*, 'Shakespeare and the Great War', editor Monika Smialkowska and other contributors examine the 'cultural mobilization' of Shakespeare for nationalist and imperialist purposes during WWI, as well as 'challenges to such appropriations'.[12]

In her chapter for this volume, 'Shakespeare in Sarajevo: Theatrical and Cinematic Encounters with the Balkans War', Sara Soncini looks closely at three productions that draw upon Shakespeare as a framing device for representation of the ethnic violence that broke out in the Balkans War: Katie Mitchell's staging of *3 Henry VI* (1994), Sarah Kane's play *Blasted* (1995) and Mario Martone's film *Rehearsal for War* (1998). As Soncini points out, none of these works actually show the Balkans War directly on stage or screen. Yet they each use Shakespeare's plays as a 'powerful conceptual aid to universalize the conflict', as well as to address 'their discursive positioning as outsiders and its problematic implications'. Mitchell's staging of *3 Henry VI* deliberately reduces the Wars of the Roses to a 'matter of personal vendettas', an 'unheroic turf war', akin to a present-day 'low-intensity conflict'. By aligning her British 'audience's "here"' with 'the Balkan "elsewhere"', Mitchell undercuts 'Balkanism': 'the systematic process of othering whereby, following the end of the Cold War, the Balkan region was constructed as an antitype of civilization'. Inspired by Shakespeare's depiction of pagan England in *King Lear*, Sarah Kane, too, tries to 'shatter' British 'political complacency': 'the belief that the "tribal" bloodshed of ethnic conflict could never happen in a civilized country'. Martone's documentary-style film, *Rehearsal for War*, is more metafictional; Shakespeare's *Taming of the Shrew* serves as a foil to Aeschylus's *Seven Against Thebes* in a symbolic reflection on the practicality and ethics of responding to crises such as the Balkans War artistically from afar, as Martone himself, like Mitchell and Kane, hopes might be possible, despite the attractions of escapism.

As Holderness argues in *Shakespeare Recycled*, changes in the adaptation and appropriation of Shakespeare's plays over time help to reveal the variety of perspectives latent within their structure. Understanding those 'potentialities', however, requires some familiarity with their original context. Reception history cannot be separated from 'the originating moment of a text's production'. 'Those formal and ideological characteristics and capacities inserted into it by the specific determinations and liberties bearing on its initial construction, are all that the activity of reproduction has to work on.'[13] Insofar as we know, Shakespeare himself never went off to war. So, what were his sources? How does his depiction of warfare compare to the military theory and practice of his contemporaries? Paul A. Jorgensen wrote a pioneering book in the 1950s, *Shakespeare's Military World*, which sought to juxtapose Shakespeare's 'concept of war' with the 'military treatises and newsbooks' published in England during his own lifetime.[14] During the Cold War, nonetheless, this field of inquiry fell fallow. Starting in the late 1990s, however, with the Balkans War, and with increasing frequency since 9/11, historicist critics have returned to the question. How did warfare in Shakespeare's own immediate context affect his representation of it on stage?

Like Jorgensen several decades earlier, in *Shakespeare's Theatre of War*, Nick de Somogyi's 'chief aim', as he says, is 'to allow a series of the period's non-"literary" texts both generally and in detail to further the interpretation of its drama'.[15] As Patricia Cahill observes, 'Between 1575 and 1600, some fifty military treatises, both original works and translations of classical and Continental texts, were published in London, and several went through multiple editions'.[16] Given, as he explains, that 'Shakespeare's was an era of siege warfare rather than mobile warfare', de Somogyi is particularly interested in analogies between military practices and stagecraft, real and fictional 'theatres of war'.[17] Nina Taunton's *1590s Drama and Militarism* is more tightly focused; Taunton considers the actions of the earls of Essex and Northumberland at the time in light of theoretical debates about the 'ideal general' in manuals on the 'art of war', as well as contemporary military correspondence, then turns to Marlowe's Tamburlaine, Shakespeare's Henry V, and Chapman's Henri IV. Their inadequacies, she argues, reveal 'hunger for a national military hero, a lion who would lead his army to glorious deeds and victory'.[18] She draws analogies between 'erosions of the masculine self' on stage and 'anxieties' about 'the erosion of national boundaries'.[19]

Since the 1950s, historians of early modern Europe have debated the nature and scope of what Michael Roberts in a seminal article describes as 'The Military Revolution, 1560–1660', a paradigm shift driven, he argues, by the introduction of portable firearms.[20] As Andrew Hiscock explains in his recent review essay, 'central areas of discussion' within this ongoing and contentious field of research include 'the increasing centralization of European states and the growth in their schemes of military expenditure; changing practices of recruitment, organization, and training of large-scale armies; proliferation in publications and manuals devoted to military practice; and, especially importantly, technological advances in firearms, fortifications, and logistics in this period'.[21] One index of Shakespeare's sense of this historical sea-change is his depiction of old-fashioned warriors such as Coriolanus, Mark Antony, Hamlet Senior, Hotspur and Talbot. Their reckless, straightforward pursuit of individual martial honour is depicted as glamourous but obsolescent and at times more than a little pig-headed, leading to predictable, sometimes outright foolish self-destruction. The political order that these 'alpha males' represent is seen as on the wane: they and their kind are being replaced, slowly but surely, by cunning, cautious, slightly contemptible courtiers, as well as monarchical masterminds.

Drawing on the same kinds of sources as Jorgensen, de Somogyi and Taunton, and in keeping with the concept of an early modern 'military revolution', Patricia Cahill in *Unto the Breach* traces the emergence of 'military science' as a 'modern discipline' in early modern England. 'By exploiting the power of the stage to shape the cultural imaginary', plays such as Shakespeare's English history plays, Cahill maintains, 'helped to produce and circulate new regimes of rationality and abstraction'; 'new military rationalities' regarding 'the ordering of space, the disciplining of bodies, and the regulation of populations' led to 'new understandings of personhood and of the body politic', anticipating 'nineteenth-century efforts to standardize, quantify, and appropriate the productive energies of workers'.[22] Yet the stage, Cahill goes on, also registered 'profound cultural ambivalence toward this new way of knowing the world'.[23] Drawing on theorists such as Cathy Caruth and Dominick LaCapra, Cahill argues that the late Elizabethan experience of militarization was traumatic and that the theatre provided a reprieve, 'a public space for the collective re-enacting of the incomprehensible and, with that, the possibility of a cultural "working through" of what might otherwise resist psychic assimilation'.[24]

In an article on *Henry IV*, Tom McAlindon connects the fifteenth-century rebellions it depicts to the Northern Rebellion of 1569–70, as well as the earlier Pilgrimage of Grace (1536). As McAlindon explains, 'the Pilgrims were defeated in a notorious piece of treachery', carried out by a trusted, temporizing deputy of the king; following the suggestion of historian Penry Williams, McAlindon sees an allusion to this incident in Shakespeare's depiction of Prince John's treatment of the rebels at the end of *2 Henry IV*.[25] In her chapter for this volume, 'Prince John's Negotiation with the Rebels in *2 Henry IV*: Fifteenth-Century Northern England as Sixteenth-Century Ireland', Jane Yeang Chui Wong discerns another such analogy, this time more immediate. Prince John's violation of his promise to the rebels is a shocking episode, which Wong argues is best understood as 'part of Shakespeare's exploration of an immensely delicate system of exchanges between ruler and ruled'. More specifically, John's double-dealing demonstrates the precariousness of the relationship between the king and his more distant subjects, given the long distances that separated more far-flung regions from the central government in London. Wong contends that English kings worked to destabilize local lords in order to consolidate their own authority. As an illustration, she looks closely at English efforts to undermine kinship ties between Irish chieftains, and in particular the fraught negotiations between Irish rebel Hugh O'Neill and representatives of Queen Elizabeth. As in *2 Henry IV*, the royal emissaries argue that because the rebels broke their oaths of allegiance, they are not required to deal with them in good faith. The separation between royal seat and distant representatives allows them to break their word without impugning the honour of the monarch.

Turning to the legalities of war in Shakespeare's plays, the scholar who has written the most on the subject, Theodor Meron, brings to bear unrivalled and indeed rather astonishing professional expertise. In addition to his side-line as a Shakespeare enthusiast, Meron is Professor of International Law at New York University, Counselor on International Law to the US Department of State and Israeli Foreign Ministry, former President of the International Criminal Tribunal for the former Yugoslavia, Presiding Judge of the Appeals Chambers of the International Criminal Tribunal for Rwanda, and current President of the International Residual Mechanism for Criminal Tribunals of the UN General Assembly. In his first book on Shakespeare, *Henry's Wars and Shakespeare's Laws*, Meron uses *Henry V* as 'a vehicle to analyse the issues of war that governed, or should have governed, that conflict [the Hundred Years War] and to develop an intertemporal, historical perspective on the law of war and its evolution'.[26] In his second book, *Bloody Constraint*, subtitled *War and Chivalry in Shakespeare*, Meron explores the medieval development of a chivalric code that would in theory govern knightly behaviour, featuring ideals such as 'honour, loyalty, courage, mercy, commitment to the community, and the avoidance of shame and dishonour'.[27] He also acknowledges with dismay how these values were often violated in practice. Turning to Shakespeare's plays more specifically, he concludes with the contentious claim that Shakespeare himself was a pacifist.

In keeping with most international law regarding war today, Meron draws heavily on just war theory, as it emerged in the Middle Ages out of scholastic reflections on St. Augustine's *City of God*, as well as Cicero's account of Roman law regarding warfare in his treatise *On Duties*. Paola Pugliatti explains this tradition and builds on

Meron's legal analysis of Shakespeare's *Henry V*, turning to a myriad of other plays as well, in *Shakespeare and Just War Tradition*, as does Franziska Quabeck in *Just and Unjust Wars in Shakespeare*.[28] In her chapter for this volume, 'Shakespeare's Unjust Wars', Quabeck calls into question critics such Steven Marx and R. S. White who present Shakespeare as a thoroughgoing pacifist, as well as those such as Norman Rabkin who see his opinions about war as 'undecidable'.[29] Instead, she argues, just war theory provides Shakespeare with 'a general framework for evaluating the ethics of war case by case'. What constitutes a worthy cause for declaring war (*jus ad bellum*)? What determines, morally speaking, how a war should be conducted (*jus in bello*)? Should a military response, for example, necessarily be proportional to its cause? Quabeck gives particular attention here to the problem of proportionality in *Troilus and Cressida*, as addressed in the debate between Hector, Diomedes and Troilus. Seen through the lens of just war theory, Quabeck explains, almost all of the wars Shakespeare depicts are 'unjust', in one sense or another, with the notable exception of Richmond's deposition of Richard III, as well as Malcolm's of Macbeth.

In his chapter, '*Sine Dolore:* Relative Painlessness in Shakespeare's Laughter at War', Daniel Derrin considers the problem just war theory is designed to address – the tension between Christian moral precepts and self-defence – but from the perspective of psychology, rather than legality. 'How does a Christian society balance the need and means for war against a duty neither to exult in it nor to enjoy constructing an "honourable" selfhood through the destruction of others?' The Christian soldier's dilemma, as Derrin points out, is that he must somehow bravely engage in war without at the same time stooping to take satisfaction in 'the pleasures of self-definition that military "honour" can afford'. Derrin sees Shakespeare as working towards this balance through 'criticizing laughter', a form of poking fun that allows an emotional distance from what might otherwise prove troubling, even horrifying. Derrin locates the laughable in a moral deformity or deviation from 'nature' that exists *sine dolore*, because it is without any serious consequence. The butt of the joke demonstrates 'wilful ignorance of what is commonly known and recognized', in this case in terms of moral norms. Comic distortions of the ideal balance between martial efficacy and Christian scruple, taken as normative, reveal by contrast how a Christian soldier should behave. As examples of various kinds of misjudgement, Derrin juxtaposes Coriolanus's slaughter of enemy soldiers with his son's killing of a butterfly; Hotspur's insatiable desire for honour with Falstaff's cowardice; and Parolles' betrayal of his comrades-in-arms with Bertram's infidelity to his wife. In each case, what prompts laughter is the disparity between the moral ignorance of the character in question and the audience's common-sense awareness. Using foils drawn from opposite ends of the spectrum of deviation from the norm, Shakespeare implies a viable, admirable middle ground between Christian compassion and the demands of martial honour, in keeping with Aristotle's doctrine of virtue as a mean between extremes, as well as St. Augustine's compromise concept of the 'just war'.

Is Henry V an ideal king? Or is he, as Hazlitt says, an 'amiable monster'?[30] One way to make sense of his ethical ambiguity is to see him as attempting to navigate between the incongruent claims of two rival ethical systems, on the one hand Christianity, on the other a political order driven by imperatives of honour. 'If it be a sin to covet honour', he confesses, 'I am the most offending soul alive' (4.3.28–29). The fascinating word in that admission is 'if'. Can the nobleman's traditional pride in force of arms be reconciled to Christ's admonition to turn the other cheek? Perhaps not. If a soldier takes no satisfaction, however, from success on the battlefield, how effective, if at all, is he likely to be, if he should find himself, willy-nilly, face to face with a determined enemy? Falstaff is good for a laugh, but a worse than incompetent commander; his indifference to achieving any kind of victory with the soldiers who serve under his command proves just as deadly to them, in the end, as Hotspur's recklessness would have been. Too little desire for honour is just as dangerous as too much.

Like most of us today, Shakespeare seems to be deeply suspicious of the notion that the pursuit of martial honour in and of itself could ever be considered adequate grounds for taking any kind of military action. Men like Homer's Achilles raid and plunder without pretext or compunction. To conquer is glorious, without further complication. For Shakespeare, however, as for Virgil, any honour that accrues to those victorious in battle must be weighed against the suffering which made that triumph possible.[31] There must have been some sort of injury, or at least some sort of threat, what in just war theory would be called a *casus belli*. Whether or not an effort to regain lost territory qualifies as such is debatable; the scene in *Henry V*, in particular, in which the Archbishop of Canterbury tries to convince Henry V that his claim to France is legitimate is often played for laughs. But I often wonder if we are today too quick to dismiss his argument. Queen Elizabeth's legitimacy depended, in part, on the same kind of discrediting of misgivings about women inheriting the throne that the French Salic law represents.

In any case, it is possible to imagine other, more obviously worthy causes, at least from the perspective of an early modern Christian. In *King John*, Salisbury grieves to find himself taking up arms with the French against an English king, even for a cause – the restoration of papal authority – that he sees as just. 'O nation, that thou couldst remove', he cries, 'unto a pagan shore, / Where these two Christian armies might combine / The blood of malice in a vein of league, / And not spend it so unneighborly!' (5.2.33, 36–39). Even Erasmus, for instance, who is for the most part an outspoken pacifist, makes an exception for armed resistance to Ottoman expansion. Henry points up this possibility in his marriage proposal to Katherine. 'Shall not thou and I', he says, 'compound a boy, half French, half English, that shall go to Constantinople and take the Turk by the beard?' (5.2.203–6). As in the case of the Crusades which Henry's father, Henry IV, hopes in vain to join, many of Shakespeare's countrymen, as well as, perhaps, even Shakespeare himself, would have considered the restoration of greater Christendom in the Holy Land, if it could be done, a paradigmatic example of a legitimate justification for military action. Honour itself, however, especially at the cost of other Christians, was suspect.

Shakespeare's clearest attack on the intrinsic value of honour as a cue for war appears in *Troilus and Cressida*. Hector argues with considerable force that the Trojans should not support Paris's adultery, then abruptly resolves, nonetheless, 'to keep Helen still' for the sake of 'our joint and several dignities' (2.1.191–93). Troilus agrees. 'I would not wish a drop of Trojan blood / Spent more in her defence' (2.1.197–98). 'But', he goes on, 'she is a theme of honour and renown' (2.1.198–99). The volte-face in their reasoning is meant to be dubious; it is the same kind of self-deceptive casuistry Shakespeare often explores in his soliloquies.[32] Shakespeare's own perspective can be discerned in the ironic prologue, as well as the general tone of the play, undercutting and de-glamorizing the legend of the Trojan War at every conceivable turn. 'The princes orgulous', the prologue proclaims, 'their high blood chafed' (2); 'orgulous' is deliberately over-the-top diction, setting up the anti-climax of 'chafed'. The same pattern of deflation holds throughout. 'The ravished Helen, Menelaus' queen, / With wanton Paris sleeps, and that's the quarrel' (9–10). 'Quarrel' is a bathetic punchline; the end in this case, Shakespeare suggests, does not measure up to the means.

Shakespeare's most extensive criticism of violence in the name of honour can be found, however, in his depiction of ancient Rome. In *Coriolanus* and *Titus Andronicus*, the imperatives of honour lead to ongoing conflict between Rome and its neighbours, the Volscians and the Goths. In *Julius Caesar* and *Antony and Cleopatra*, as well as *Coriolanus*, dissatisfaction with anything less than absolute *imperium*, absolute individual command, leads to civil war within Rome itself. Enobarbus, for example, simply dismisses out of hand the very idea that Antony and Octavian might peacefully coexist. After Lepidus, a would-be peacemaker, fails and is disposed of, Enobarbus dryly remarks, 'World, thou hast a pair of chaps, no more; / And throw between them all the food thou hast, / They'll grind the one the other' (3.4.13–15). In like vein, St. Augustine uses Rome's founders, Romulus and Remus, as a paradigmatic example of the 'fratricide' which he sees at the heart of what he calls 'the earthly city'. 'Both desired to have the glory of founding the Roman republic, but both could not have as much glory as if only one claimed it; for he who wished to have the glory of ruling would certainly rule less if his power were shared' (15.5).

In his depiction of ancient Rome, Shakespeare echoes St. Augustine's critique of the Romans in his *City of God*, which itself draws on the more secular Roman history of Sallust. At the beginning of this account of the war with Catiline, Sallust claims that ambition first entered the world with the Persians, Athenians and Spartans. These empires, he says, were the first 'to subdue cities and nations, to make the lust for dominion [*libido dominandi*] a pretext for war, [and] to consider the greatest empire the greatest glory' (2.2). Citing this passage (3.14), St. Augustine seizes on Sallust's concept of *libido dominandi* and recasts it as the defining feature of the Roman character. It is this quality, he argues, not Christianity, that was the cause of Rome's inevitable self-immolation, as well as its initial, dazzling success. Elaborating on Sallust's history, St. Augustine proposes that 'the state [of Rome] grew with amazing rapidity' on account of its 'desire for glory' and love of 'domination' (5.12). Eventually this 'vice', however, led Rome into interminable civil wars (3.14). 'This craving for sovereignty [*libido ista dominandi*]', he concludes, 'disturbs and consumes the human race with frightful ills'. 'How shall I speak in detail of the same wars, so often renewed in subsequent reigns, though they seemed to have been finished by great victories; and of wars that time after time were brought to an end by great slaughters, and which yet time after time were renewed by the posterity of those who had made peace and struck treaties?' (3.14; cp. 19.7; cp. 15.4).

In his retelling of the history of medieval England, as well as ancient Rome, Shakespeare presents something very like the problem of recurrent civil war which St. Augustine emphasizes in his *City of God*. Secular civilization as St. Augustine describes it there is by nature trapped in an incessant cycle of violence: 'the earthly city is divided against itself' (15.5). As Freud says in *Civilization and Its Discontents*, *homo homini lupus*: man is a wolf to man. A slightly more hopeful perspective can be found, surprisingly, in Thomas Hobbes' early treatise, *On the Citizen*: 'There are two maxims which are surely both true: *Man is a God to man* and *Man is a wolf to man*. The former is true of the relations of citizens with each other, the latter of relations between commonwealths'.[33] The development of international law in the wake of WWII was intended to repair this incongruity; the record since then of deific international cooperation, however, has been mixed, at best. The phrase 'forever war' first came to prominence in the 1970s, in connection with America's involvement in Vietnam.[34] The ongoing conflict in Afghanistan, however, has proved even longer in duration, long enough for two generations of soldiers, perhaps in time even a third, now that President Trump has decided to maintain an American military presence in the region. A recent headline from *The Onion*, a satirical newspaper: 'Soldier excited to take over father's old Afghanistan patrol route'.[35] A recent headline (not a joke) from the US military newspaper, *Stars and Stripes*: 'After years apart, military father and son catch up in Afghanistan'.[36]

St. Augustine would not be surprised. In our postlapsarian condition, he would say, peace is a rare and precarious state, constantly reverting back to internecine conflict. War is the norm, not peace, here in the City of Man. Shakespeare would probably agree. As Paul Jorgensen explains, 'In Shakespeare's usage peace tends to describe a political condition, a social atmosphere, more troubling and more provocative of human drama than its customary associations of concord and tranquillity'. Peace 'tends to prevail as the play opens', usually in 'a decadent or unsound form'. War, in contrast, 'comes almost always late in the play, and comes as an agent of resolution rather than unrest'.[37] Working through a wide variety of contemporary sources, Jorgensen shows that this perspective on the relative merits of peace and war was far from exceptional. 'In thus giving peace a frequently ominous or unwholesome connotation, Shakespeare was but sharing with his countrymen a pessimism induced by current political writings and events'. Like 'most Elizabethans', Jorgensen hastens to add, Shakespeare 'did not like war'.[38] His point is, rather, that Shakespeare's fundamental vision of history is more Augustinian than utopian. To put it in present-day parlance, Shakespeare is on the side of John Gray, rather than Steven Pinker.[39] *Pace* the Beatles, as well as the Whigs, everything is not getting better all the time. As Gray writes, 'Liberal civilization is not the emerging meaning of the modern world but a historical singularity that is inherently fragile'.[40]

Gray's unspoken target in this case is most immediately Francis Fukuyama. 'Civilization', Gray insists, 'is not the endpoint of modern history, but a succession of interludes in recurring spasms of barbarism'.[41] In a hugely influential, still-controversial essay in *The National Interest*, written in the wake of the collapse of the Soviet Union, then later reworked into a book, *The End of History and the Last Man*, Fukuyama argues that we are approaching the 'end of history', in which liberal democracy is the only intellectual option that appears legitimate, having triumphed over erstwhile rivals such as hereditary monarchy, fascism and communism. Since then, the rise of radical Islam, including the suppression of the Green Revolution in Iran, the general failure of the Arab Spring, and the ongoing antidemocratic, Islamist turn in Turkish politics has, to say the least, made things more difficult for those who would defend Fukuyama's thesis. Nevertheless, his more general sense of how history works, one that he derives from Hegel, does provide some useful insights into Shakespeare's keen awareness of the connection between war and concepts of 'honour'.

In brief, Fukuyama helpfully aligns three different ways of talking about more or less the same emotion. The part of Henry V that, as he says, leads him to 'covet honour' is the same faculty of the soul that Plato describes as *thymos* and which he personifies in his *Republic* as a dedicated military caste. Fukuyama defines it as 'man's sense of self-worth and the demand that he be recognized'.[42] That last word, 'recognized', is especially important; it reflects Fukuyama's sense that what Shakespeare calls honour is a desire for what Hegel would call 'recognition' (*Anerkennung*). In keeping with Hegel, as well as other, latter-day Hegelians such as Charles Taylor and Axel Honneth, Fukuyama sees our desire to have our sense of ourselves acknowledged by other people as an innate, ineluctable and very powerful human drive.[43] Our effort to validate our own self-esteem is nothing less than 'the motor of history'.[44] What Axel Honneth calls the 'struggle for recognition' is more important, in particular, than the social and economic conditions Marx calls 'relations of production'.[45] What people want most, more than any material sustenance, more than what Agamben calls 'bare life', is to feel respected; this desire for 'recognition' (*Anerkennung*) is or should be the bedrock, the most fundamental ground, of all historicist explanation of human conflict.

In his chapter for this volume, 'The Better Part of Stolen Valour: Counterfeits, Comedy and the Supreme Court', David Currell focuses on the 'counterfeiting of military identity by an imposter who misappropriates the honour due to the valorous'. In the case of *United States vs. Alvarez*, Currell finds a modern counterpart to Shakespeare's Falstaff or Pistol, who themselves reprise the classical figure of the *miles gloriosus* (braggart soldier). Within the United States, the Stolen Valor Act of 2005 had criminalized falsely claiming to have been awarded US military honours. In 2012, however, the US Supreme Court struck down on the Act on the grounds that it violated the defendant's right to free speech, in keeping with the First Amendment to the US Bill of Rights. Currell takes the opinions of the justices as a starting point to consider how honour is defined in Shakespeare's plays, as well as classical sources such as Homer's *Iliad*, Aristotle's *Nicomachean Ethics* and Plautus's *Miles Gloriosus*. In the ancient world, honour 'cannot be shared without division'. Martial glory is a zero-sum accolade; one wins it at the cost of someone else. Community recognition of military accomplishment, understood in this light, leads to proportional material as well as emotional rewards. Fraudulent claims jeopardize the delicate balance of this system, which the state must maintain, in some guise or other, in order to keep its military motivated. Honour is a valuable form of social capital; early modern England protected and policed its allocation through shaming, as we see in Shakespeare's comic treatment of figures such as Parolles and Falstaff. In the case of the United States, after the Stolen Valor Act was struck down as unconstitutional, it was amended to allow false claims to military honours and instead criminalize gaining any kind of tangible benefit from such imposture. In effect, Currell concludes, 'the dissenting and majority opinions in *United States vs. Alvarez* contest the question of whether the civil repercussions of US militarism belong to epic or comedy'.

As Hegel observes, the desire for recognition cannot be eradicated from the human psyche. No-one can be self-sufficient in that sense, not even Shakespeare's Coriolanus, despite his strenuous efforts to escape his own need for validation. We all want honour of one kind or another.[46] The key problem of politics, then, as Fukuyama suggests, is not to get rid of what Plato calls *thymos* altogether, but instead to channel it in a direction that is as conducive as possible to peace. To help explain what he means, Fukuyama invents two terms. *Isothymia* is the desire to be recognized as equal and is compatible with peaceful coexistence. *Megalothymia* is the desire to be recognized as superior, and eventually, inevitably leads to violence. For Fukuyama's former supervisor, Samuel Huntington, the paradigmatic example of what Fukuyama would call a megalothymotic society in our own time is the Muslim world. As Huntington notoriously notes, 'Islam has bloody borders'.[47] For Shakespeare, in contrast, as for St. Augustine, the paradigmatic example of what Fukuyama would call a megalothymotic society is ancient Rome. Fukuyama's neologism, *megalothymia*, is essentially interchangeable with St. Augustine's concept of *libido dominandi*, as well as perhaps Nietzsche's not-unrelated concept of 'the will to power'.

In his *City of God*, St. Augustine defends Christianity against pagan accusations that it was the reason for the ongoing, alarming collapse of the Roman Empire. As St. Augustine sees that decline, Rome fell prey to its own unreconstructed will to power, torn apart and fatally weakened by internecine civil wars. In the Enlightenment, however, Edward Gibbon took up the pagan charge anew. By discouraging Romans' traditional valour and ruthlessness, he argues, Christianity left them unable to resist the onslaught of various German tribes. Christian doctrines of 'pusillanimity' led the once-indomitable Romans to become, as he says, 'indolent' and 'effeminate'. In his depiction of the Wars of the Roses, Shakespeare seems to set up a similar clash of possible interpretations. Why did England descend into civil war?

One answer can be found in the contrast between Henry V and his son, Henry VI, the two kings at the centre of Shakespeare's two tetralogies of English history plays. Of the two, Henry V tends to draw more attention. For the last several decades, stage productions of *Henry V* have tended to use the play as an occasion to agitate against Western military involvement overseas, casting Henry in an unflattering light. If we want to understand Shakespeare's own perspective, however, I would suggest that we hold off on criticism of Henry, unless we also address the manifest failure of his son, Henry VI, as well as the various fatal mistakes of another peace-loving, pious royal heir: Hamlet. Otherwise, we run the risk of blaming Henry V personally and perhaps excessively for what Shakespeare himself might well see instead as the imperfect, fallen nature of the world itself: to read the context of Henry V, the political arena in which he exists, as if its evils were somehow products of his own particular character.

Within the Christian tradition, it is not an exaggeration to say that secular government is sometimes represented as the special province of the devil. When Christ is tempted in the wilderness, Satan offers him, as if they were his own to give, 'all the kingdoms of the world, and the glory of them' (Matt. 4:8). In keeping with this vision of 'the earthly city', for St. Augustine, any postlapsarian political order inevitably will fall short of the kingdom of heaven. Even at its best, for it to function at all, for it simply to exist, a secular state will require incessant, off-putting moral compromise. The measure to keep in mind is up from anarchy, Hobbes's *bellum omnia contra omnes*, rather than down from Kant's 'perpetual peace'. In light of this pessimistic, Augustinian view of secular politics, as opposed to present-day progressive optimism, Henry VI's efforts at diplomacy seem quixotic, and his abstemious aversion to any kind of violence comes across as short-sighted, inadequate to the task of maintaining a viable peace. As Lord Clifford is dying, he lays the blame for England's civil war squarely on its child-like, mild-mannered king.

> Henry, hadst thou swayed as kings should do,
> Or as thy father and his father did,
> Giving no ground unto the house of York,
> They never had then sprung like summer flies!
> I and ten thousand in this luckless realm
> Had left no mourning widows for our death. (*3 Henry VI*, 2.6.14–19)

Shakespeare depicts the reign of Henry VI, in other words, in much the same way that unsympathetic historians of American foreign policy now tend to describe the presidency of Jimmy Carter, back in the 1970s, and perhaps in time may come to describe the more recent presidency of Barack Obama. Pious progressive naïveté about human rights and international norms, emerging out of an over-optimistic secularization of Christian principles, found itself caught off-guard, in the end, by ruthless Russian and Iranian *Realpolitik*.[48] Henry VI, like Jimmy Carter, makes a category error: he treats the City of Man as if it were the City of God, and it blows up in his face.

In his *Decline and Fall of the Roman Empire*, Gibbon describes 'the contempt and reproaches of the Pagans', who, he explains, confronted by the rise of Christianity, 'very frequently asked, what must be the fate of the empire, attacked on every side by barbarians, if all mankind should adopt the pusillanimous sentiments of this new sect?' (1.15). We today tend to be concerned about the danger of what Fukuyama calls *megalothymia*, which we see writ large in the figure of Shakespeare's Henry V. It is also possible, however, to see cause for concern in the political implications of its polar opposite, a timid and retiring *microthymia*. What happens if an individual, or a nation, lacks the *thymos* necessary for effective self-defence? 'I am pigeon-livered', Hamlet complains, 'and lack gall / To make oppression bitter' (2.2.512–13). In his *Nicomachean Ethics*, Aristotle criticizes what he calls *micropsychia* ('smallness of soul', 'undue self-denigration'). In his *Moralia*, Plutarch introduces a parallel concept, *dysōpia* (lit., 'lack of [inner] resources').[49] We might call it 'fecklessness'. It denotes an inability to stand up for oneself; to resist importunity; to fight rather than concede. In his *Life of Brutus*, for instance, Plutarch complains that some men 'dare deny nothing'.

This charge of *dysōpia*, 'fecklessness', seems fitting for Henry VI, and it is perhaps just as dangerous, if not more so, in its own more indirect fashion, as Henry V's war to win back English territory in France. At least, Shakespeare seems to think so. A refusal to engage in power politics creates a power vacuum which is not necessarily an improvement; we might look, for instance, to present-day Iraq, Syria and Libya. In Shakespeare's first tetralogy, the chaos which Henry VI allows to consume the nation leads in time, and not by chance, to the rise of less-scrupulous, genuinely frightening figures such as Richard III. For all his talk of the 'end of history', Fukuyama for his part does worry, as his argument draws to a close, that efforts to excise all interest in military engagement from the moral universe of liberal democracies will leave them defenceless, in the end, against abiding enemies. The 'last men of history', he warns, will not survive if they allow themselves to become 'men without chests'. As explanation, he cites Nietzsche's Zarathustra: 'For thus you speak: "Real we are entirely, and without belief or superstition". Thus you stick out your chests – but alas, they are hollow!'[50]

With this problem of *thymos* in mind, it was fascinating to me to see how frequently former US President Barack Obama was compared to Hamlet, when he was in office, as a way of criticizing his approach to foreign policy.[51] The analogy could be found across the entire spectrum of opinion, left to right, foreign and domestic: Mitt Romney ('This is not the time for Hamlet in the White House'),[52]

The Guardian,[53] The Huffington Post,[54] National Review,[55] The Weekly Standard,[56] Commentary,[57] Russia Today,[58] The Times of Israel,[59] Al Arabiya[60] and so on. In his chapter for this volume, 'Hamletism in the Spanish Civil War, 1936–39', Jésus Tronch considers a similar case of political appropriation. During the Spanish Civil War, in newspaper articles, theatrical productions and a novel by Paulino Masip, *The Diary of Hamlet Garcia,* Republican provocateurs sought to counter the perceived 'Hamletism' of intellectuals: 'ineffectuality, vacillation, or irresolution in social and political commitment'. The newspaper *La Vanguardia*, edited by Masip, sought to 'stir the "inertia" of some citizens' and to 'dispel the moral qualms and problems of conscience which the "revolution" posed to them'. José Bergamin in *Hora de Espana* tried to persuade them that 'the essence of intelligence is in the faculty of deciding rather than hesitating'. A production of *Hamlet* in Valencia in 1937 tried to 'hold the mirror' up to its own audience, critiquing them for their neglect of 'urgent affairs'. Finally, in his novel *The Diary of Hamlet Garcia,* written in retrospect from exile in Mexico, Masip reflects upon the defeat of the Republican cause, brought about in part, he suggests, by intellectuals like his protagonist opting out of political engagement.

The accusations, like Masip's, brought against President Obama that he was too akin to Shakespeare's Hamlet are all the more interesting when weighed against the equally pervasive tendency to compare his predecessor, President George W. Bush, to Hamlet's polar opposite, Henry V.[61] What journalists criticized Obama for was not simply indecision, but more specifically a lack of 'fire' or 'passion' – I would say, a lack of *thymos*. They wanted, that is, the same kind of flashing-eye, fire-in-the-belly, impulsive, even reckless emotional engagement that they had criticized, not long before, in President Bush. Perhaps they were right on both counts. In any case, it is interesting to observe their ambivalence about the role of indignation in foreign policy, as well as their use of Shakespeare's characters as a kind of shorthand. Given the change Fukuyama describes – the tendency of liberal democracies to attempt to tame or even eradicate *thymos* – we no longer have a shared framework for thinking clearly and explicitly about the role of honour in international relations.[62] Journalists turn, therefore, to Shakespeare, and to an age in which it was more acceptable to talk about honour openly. Shakespeare's kings, like the US presidents themselves, serve as helpful personifications of different approaches to managing, reconciling and stabilizing our collective human desire for recognition.

In her chapter for this volume, 'Where Character is King: Gregory Doran's Henriad', Alice Dailey reflects on her experience of attending the Royal Shakespeare Company's recent 'mega-event', 'King and Country: Shakespeare's Great Cycle of Kings', a production of all four plays of the second tetralogy in Stratford, London, China and New York, directed by Gregory Doran and headlined by David Tennant in the role of Richard II. Dailey finds the productions surprisingly 'modest, intimate', 'less interested in a conceptual engagement with politics or monarchy than in an exploration of character'. The Histories Cycle directed by Doran's predecessor at the RSC, Michael Boyd, a decade earlier, which included both tetralogies, 'made elaborate use of conceptual casting, stylized battle scenes, trapeze, prop recycling and ghostly reappearance to create thematic coherence'. Doran, in contrast, eschewed 'design-driven staging' and 'conceptual intervention' in favour of an emphasis on 'subtle characterization' and 'ensemble acting'. This decision, Dailey observes, helps to clarify 'the inadequacy of conventional literary-critical hermeneutics for describing theatrical performance', in keeping with the concerns of performance scholars W. B. Worthen and Andrew James Hartley, as well as Rebecca Schneider's sense of the limitations of archival evidence, which inevitably tend to foreground 'design or concept'. In the case of 'the Richard-Aumerle kiss scene' in Doran's *Richard II*, for example, 'the ephemeral, emotive present' is 'the essential content of the production', a form of 'subtle character work' which it is difficult, perhaps impossible, to record on video or in still photos.

Other choices about characterization, however, Dailey argues, proved less effective. Dailey questions young actor Alex Hassel's 'nice-guy portrayal of Henry V' as 'figuring out his warrior-king role on the fly', especially his performance of the 'I know you all' speech from *1 Henry IV* as an 'epiphany', as well as his representation of Henry's dismissal of Falstaff as an anxious, hurried, reluctant recitation of a set speech the king has learned by rote. Dailey sees this interpretation as too incongruous with her own sense from the text itself of Prince Hal as calculating, cold-hearted and cynical. 'By suggesting Henry's spontaneous discovery of his role, the production attempted to sanitize the character of premeditation or strategy.' In light of this perceived 'dissonance' between text and performance, Dailey sees some limitations to Doran's approach. 'What hampered the cycle's presentation of Henry was its prioritization of emotional immediacy over the production script's built-in formal mechanisms for constituting character, such as typology, structural juxtaposition, and the diachronic accretion of habitual action'.

Is Henry V a 'good guy' or a 'bad guy'? The debate has become in practice a synecdoche for a larger question: was Shakespeare a pacifist? More broadly speaking, was Shakespeare a progressive? Steven Marx argues that Shakespeare changes his mind; he starts out pro-war in his early plays and ends up anti-war in his late plays. Like Quabeck, however, I think it is possible to discern a fairly consistent compromise position on the ethics of war running throughout all of his plays, akin to and perhaps informed by the positions typical of contemporary just war theory: a reconciliation of the real and the ideal grounded in the Christian doctrine of the Fall of Man, as well as Aristotle's sense of ethics as inherently and at best only approximate and circumstantial.[63] According to this perspective, which in Shakespeare's context would have been the norm, war is at times a necessary evil. War is on occasion the least-worst solution, given the fallenness of human nature.

To use the technical language of law, as well as theology, the ethics of war as Shakespeare sees it is an ethics of equity. Calvin develops this concept in his early commentary on Seneca's *De Clementia*, in which he distinguishes equity, the individual application of a law, from *summum ius*, the fullness or strict letter of law. Christian theology does tend to present pacifism as an ethical ideal. In keeping with the principle of equity, however, Christian theologians also grant that violence is sometimes acceptable, even necessary; magistrates have a responsibility to protect the innocent from injury. In his *Institutes*, for example, Calvin writes, 'both natural equity [*naturalis aequitas*] and the nature of the office dictate that princes must be armed not only to restrain the misdeeds of private individuals, but also to defend by war the domains entrusted to their safekeeping, if at any time they are under attack' (4.20.11).

As St. Augustine explains in his *City of God*, 'the wise man will wage just wars'; 'wrongdoing of the other party' sometimes compels him to do so. Nevertheless, he will 'lament' the 'necessity' of any violence he brings to bear (19.7). Wars bring the Christian soldier grief, insofar as they are a manifestation of man's persistent wickedness, his more general propensity for sin. This perspective casts Shakespeare's Henry V in a different light. As Peter Phialas writes, 'the king is not the ruthless Machiavellian that some critics take him to be'. Henry 'has no choice in the rejection of Falstaff or the execution of the traitor'. 'It does not follow', therefore, that he 'fails to experience real pain in passing judgment'. 'Actions on the king's part are made to underscore the tragic element in Shakespeare's – and King Henry's – conception of the royal dilemma'.[64] Seen from this Augustinian perspective, Shakespeare's Henry V, like his father before him, ends up isolated and sad, not because he is evil, but because Shakespeare sees politics as inherently tragic. There is no hidden, progressive solution; no better alternative that Henry somehow missed; no escaping from the grim necessity of moral compromise. We today tend to want to believe otherwise. But I am not sure Shakespeare would share our optimism.

Patrick Gray is Associate Professor of English Studies at Durham University. He is the author of *Shakespeare and the Fall of the Roman Republic* (Edinburgh University Press, 2018), co-editor with Lars Engle and William M. Hamlin of *Shakespeare and Montaigne* (Edinburgh University Press, 2020), and co-editor with John D. Cox of *Shakespeare and Renaissance Ethics* (Cambridge University Press, 2014). His essays have appeared in *Textual Practice*, *Shakespeare Survey*, *Shakespeare Jahrbuch*, *Comparative Drama*, and *The Journal of Medieval and Early Modern Studies*.

Notes

1. See Matthew Biberman, ed., *Shakespeare Yearbook* (2011), 'Shakespeare after 9/11: How a Social Trauma Shapes Interpretation'.
2. Nick de Somogyi, *Shakespeare's Theatre of War* (Aldershot, UK: Ashgate, 1998), 5.
3. On the historical context of New Historicism, see esp. Stephen Greenblatt's preface to the second edition of Greenblatt, *Renaissance Self-Fashioning: From More to Shakespeare* (Chicago: University of Chicago Press, 2005; 1st edition 1980), xi–xvii.
4. For a comparison of Shakespeare and Lefebvre, see Patrick Gray and Maurice Samely, 'Shakespeare and Henri Lefebvre's "Right to the City": Subjective Alienation and Mob Violence in *Coriolanus*, *Julius Caesar*, and *2 Henry VI*', *Textual Practice*, http://dx.doi.org/10.1080/0950236X.2017.1310755 (accessed 28 September 2017).
5. Lee Patterson, *Negotiating the Past: The Historical Understanding of Medieval Literature* (Madison, WI: University of Wisconsin Press, 1987), 66.
6. Stephen Greenblatt, *Shakespearean Negotiations: The Circulation of Social Energy in Renaissance England* (Berkeley, CA: University of California Press, 1988), 62–63.
7. Ibid., 53.
8. Graham Holderness, *Shakespeare Recycled: The Making of Historical Drama* (Hemel Hempstead: Harvester Wheatsheaf, 1992), 231.
9. Ibid., 228–29.
10. Ros King and Paul J. C. M. Franssen, eds., *Shakespeare and War* (New York: Palgrave Macmillan, 2008).

11. Irena R. Makaryk and Marissa McHugh, eds., *Shakespeare and the Second World War: Memory, Culture, Identity* (Toronto: University of Toronto Press, 2012).
12. Monika Smialkowska, ed., 'Shakespeare and the Great War', *Shakespeare* 10, no. 3 (2014).
13. Holderness, *Shakespeare Recycled*, 228.
14. Paul A. Jorgensen, *Shakespeare's Military World* (Berkeley: University of California Press, 1956), viii.
15. De Somogyi, *Theatre of War*, 5.
16. Patricia A. Cahill, *Unto the Breach: Martial Formations, Historical Trauma, and the Early Modern Stage* (Oxford: Oxford University Press, 2009), 16.
17. De Somogyi, *Theatre of War*, 104.
18. Nina Taunton, *1590s Drama and Militarism: Portrayals of War in Marlowe, Chapman, and Shakespeare's Henry V* (Aldershot, UK: Ashgate, 2001), 29.
19. Ibid., 16.
20. Michael Roberts, 'The Military Revolution, 1560–1660' (inaugural lecture, Queen's University of Belfast, 1956), reprinted in Clifford J. Rodgers, ed., *The Military Revolution Debate: Readings on the Military Transformation of Early Modern Europe* (Oxford: Westview Press, 1995), 13–36.
21. Andrew Hiscock, '"More Warlike than Politique": Shakespeare and the Theatre of War – a Critical Survey', *Shakespeare* 7, no. 2 (2011): 221–47, here 227–28. For another very helpful review essay, see Paola Pugliatti, 'Visible Bullets: Critical Responses to Shakespeare's Representation of War', *Lingue e letterature d'Oriente e d'Occidente* 2 (2013): 489–503.
22. Cahill, *Unto the Breach*, 4–8.
23. Ibid., 73.
24. Ibid., 139.
25. Tom McAlindon, 'Pilgrims of Grace: *Henry IV* Historicized', *Shakespeare Survey* 48 (1996): 69–84, here 70; cp. Penry Williams, *The Tudor Regime* (Oxford: Clarendon Press, 1979), 316–17, cited in McAlindon, 'Pilgrims of Grace', 69n2.
26. Theodor Meron, *Henry's Wars and Shakespeare's Laws* (Oxford: Clarendon Press, 1993), 211.
27. Theodor Meron, *Bloody Constraint: War and Chivalry in Shakespeare* (Oxford: Oxford University Press, 1998), 11.
28. Paola Pugliatti, *Shakespeare and the Just War Tradition* (Aldershot, UK: Ashgate, 2010); Franziska Quabeck, *Just and Unjust Wars in Shakespeare* (Berlin: de Gruyter, 2013).
29. Steven Marx, 'Shakespeare's Pacifism', *Renaissance Quarterly* 45, no. 1 (1992): 49–95; R. S. White, *Pacifism and English Literature: Minstrels of Peace* (Basingstoke: Palgrave Macmillan, 2008), 139–77; Norman Rabkin, 'Rabbits, Ducks, and Henry V', *Shakespeare Quarterly* 28, no. 3 (1977): 279–96.
30. William Hazlitt, *Characters of Shakespeare's Plays* (London: C. H. Reynell, 1817), 203–14.
31. On Shakespeare and Virgil, see Patrick Gray, 'Shakespeare and the Other Virgil: Pity and Imperium in *Titus Andronicus*', *Shakespeare Survey* 69 (2016): 30–45.
32. On Shakespeare's soliloquies as studies in self-deception, see Patrick Gray, 'Choosing between Shame and Guilt: Macbeth, Othello, Hamlet, Lear', in *Shakespeare and the Soliloquy in Early Modern English Drama*, ed. A. D. Cousins and Daniel Derrin (Cambridge: Cambridge University Press, forthcoming).
33. Thomas Hobbes, *On the Citizen*, ed. Richard Tuck and Michael Silverthorne (Cambridge: Cambridge University Press, 1998), 3–4.

34. Cp. Joe Haldeman, *The Forever War* (New York: St. Martin's Press, 1974).
35. The Onion, 'Soldier Excited to Take Over Father's Old Afghanistan Patrol Route', 22 August 2017, http://www.theonion.com/article/soldier-excited-take-over-fathers-old-afghanistan--56731 (accessed 28 September 2017).
36. Phillip Walter Wellman, 'After Years Apart, Military Father and Son Catch Up in Afghanistan', *Stars and Stripes*, 19 April 2017, https://www.stripes.com/news/after-years-apart-military-father-and-son-catch-up-in-afghanistan-1.464271#.Wc1juY9SyUk (accessed 28 September 2017).
37. Paul A. Jorgensen, 'Shakespeare's Use of War and Peace', *Huntington Library Quarterly* 16, no. 4 (1953): 319–52, here 350.
38. Ibid., 320.
39. John Gray, 'Stephen Pinker is Wrong about Violence and War', *The Guardian*, 13 March 2015, https://www.theguardian.com/books/2015/mar/13/john-gray-steven-pinker-wrong-violence-war-declining (accessed 28 September 2017); cp. Steven Pinker, *The Better Angels of Our Nature: Why Violence Has Declined* (New York: Viking Books, 2011).
40. John Gray, 'The Anomaly of Barbarism', *Lapham's Quarterly*, https://www.laphamsquarterly.org/disaster/anomaly-barbarism (accessed 28 September 2017).
41. Ibid.
42. Francis Fukuyama, *The End of History and the Last Man* (New York: Simon and Schuster, 2006), 181.
43. Cp. Charles Taylor, 'The Politics of Recognition', in *Multiculturalism: Examining the Politics of Recognition*, ed. Amy Gutmann (Princeton, NJ: Princeton University Press, 1994), 25–73.
44. Fukuyama, *End of History*, xix.
45. Axel Honneth, *The Struggle for Recognition: The Moral Grammar of Social Conflicts*, trans. Joel Anderson (Cambridge: Polity Press, 1995).
46. For more detailed analysis of doomed attempts at autonomy in Shakespeare's Roman plays, see Patrick Gray, *Shakespeare and the Fall of the Roman Republic: Selfhood, Stoicism, and Civil War* (Edinburgh: Edinburgh University Press, forthcoming).
47. Samuel Huntington, *The Clash of Civilizations and the Remaking of World Order* (New York: Simon and Schuster, 1996). In a note to a later edition (2011), Huntington dryly observes, 'No single statement in my *Foreign Affairs* article attracted more critical comment than "Islam has bloody borders". I made that judgment on the basis of a casual survey of intercivilizational conflicts. Quantitative evidence from every disinterested source conclusively demonstrates its validity'. In an op-ed in *The Guardian*, published one month after the 9/11 terrorist attacks, Fukuyama reluctantly agrees: 'there does seem to be something about Islam, or at least the fundamentalist versions of Islam that have been dominant in recent years, that makes Muslim societies particularly resistant to modernity. Of all contemporary cultural systems, the Islamic world has the fewest democracies (Turkey alone qualifies), and contains no countries that have made the transition to developed nation status in the manner of South Korea or Singapore'. Francis Fukuyama, 'The West Has Won', *The Guardian*, 11 October 2001, https://www.theguardian.com/world/2001/oct/11/afghanistan.terrorism30 (accessed 28 September 2017).
48. See, e.g., the books covered in Frederick C. Tiewes's review essay, 'Carter's Foreign Policy: The Perception of Failure', *Australian Outlook* 41, no. 1 (1987): 53–55.

49. Plutarch, *Peri dysōpias*, also known as *De vitioso pudore*, in Plutarch, *Moralia*, 7.41.
50. Fukuyama, *End of History*, 188.
51. For detailed background, see Paul Williams, 'President Obama's Approach to the Middle East and North Africa: Strategic Absence', *Case Western Reserve Journal of International Law* 48, no. 1 (2016): 83–101, available at: http://scholarlycommons.law.case.edu/jil/vol48/iss1/5 (accessed 28 September 2017).
52. George Stephanopoulos, ABC News, 'Romney on "Skeptical" Obama: "This Is Not the Time for Hamlet"', http://www.foreignpolicyi.org/content/abc-news-romney-skeptical-obama-not-time-hamlet (accessed 6 January 2018).
53. Jonathan Freedland, 'Enough of Playing Hamlet: Obama Needs to Act Now', *The Guardian*, 3 September 2013, https://www.theguardian.com/commentisfree/2013/sep/03/enough-hamlet-obama-act-now-syria (accessed 28 September 2017).
54. Robert David Jaffee, 'Hamlet and Obama: Strange Bedfellows', Huffington Post, 8 September 2013, http://www.huffingtonpost.com/robert-david-jaffee/hamlet-and-president-obam_b_3884171.html (accessed 28 September 2017).
55. Victor Davis Hanson, 'Obama as Hamlet', *National Review*, 11 March 2011, http://www.nationalreview.com/corner/261940/obama-hamlet-victor-davis-hanson (accessed 28 September 2017).
56. Sam Schulman, 'President Hamlet', *The Weekly Standard*, 9 March 2009, www.weeklystandard.com/president-hamlet/article/17292 (accessed 28 September 2017).
57. Peter Wehner, 'Barack Obama's Staggering Incompetence', *Commentary*, 2 September 2013, https://www.commentarymagazine.com/foreign-policy/middle-east/barack-obamas-staggering-incompetence/ (accessed 28 September 2017).
58. Tim Wall, 'To Bomb Or Not to Bomb? Obama's Hamlet Omnishambles', *Russia Today*, 14 September 2013, https://www.rt.com/op-edge/obama-hamlet-performance-syria-839/ (accessed 28 September 2017).
59. Howard Feldman, 'Obama, Hamlet, and the Tragedy of Procrastination', *The Times of Israel*, 3 March 2015, http://blogs.timesofisrael.com/obama-hamlet-and-the-tragedy-of-procrastination/ (accessed 28 September 2017).
60. Hisham Melhem, 'Obama as the Hamlet of Syria', *Al Arabiya*, 15 February 2014, http://english.alarabiya.net/en/views/news/middle-east/2014/02/15/Obama-as-the-Hamlet-of-Syria.html (accessed 28 September 2017).
61. Harry Berger, Jr., and Scott L. Newstok, 'Harrying after VV,' in Biberman, *Shakespeare Yearbook*, 'Shakespeare after 9/11,' 141–52; cp. Scott Newstrom, 'Right Pitches Dubya as Henry V', Alternet, 28 May 2003, http://www.alternet.org/story/16025/right_pitches_dubya_as_henry_v (accessed 28 September 2017).
62. 'The attempt of liberal politics in the Hobbes-Locke tradition to banish the desire for recognition from politics or to leave it constrained and impotent left many thinkers feeling quite uneasy' (Fukuyama, *End of History*, 188).
63. For further discussion of Shakespeare's engagement with Aristotelian ethics, especially the concept of equity, as well as a review of key primary and secondary sources, see Patrick Gray and Helen Clifford, 'Shakespeare, William', in *The Encyclopedia of Renaissance Philosophy*, ed. Marco Sgarbi (London: Springer, in press). See also, e.g., M. Decoursey, 'Three Interpretations of the Lesbian Rule in Early Modern Europe', *Notes and Queries* 58 (2011): 293–95.
64. Peter G. Phialas, 'Shakespeare's Henry V and the Second Tetralogy', *Studies in Philology* 62, no. 2 (1965): 155–75, here 167–68.

Chapter 1

Shakespeare in Sarajevo
Theatrical and Cinematic Encounters
with the Balkans War

Sara Soncini

Commenting on his widely praised production of *1 Henry VI* for the 2012 Globe-to-Globe project, Serbian director Nikita Milivojević claimed that Shakespeare's history play felt like 'our modern history'.[1] This perception was equally shared by the Albanian and the Macedonian theatre companies that were appointed to perform, respectively, the second and the third part of *Henry VI* but also, earlier in the process, by the Globe management when commissioning what instantly became branded as the 'Balkan trilogy' for the multinational Shakespeare marathon they contributed to the Cultural Olympiad.[2] Though the three productions were developed separately and performed, albeit over the same weekend, as stand-alone plays, the trilogy could be seen as aiming to reconstruct a shared narrative about the bloody ethnic conflicts that had ravaged the Balkan region during the 1990s. This aspect became even more prominent when

Notes for this section begin on page 43.

the National Theatres of Serbia and Albania were invited to join the National Theatre of Macedonia and perform all three parts of *Henry VI* at the 2013 Shakespeare Festival in Bitola. Although the absence of a Bosnian voice arguably prevented the trilogy from fully qualifying as a theatrical form of reconciliation,[3] the Olympic flame that ignited these Balkan collaborations has kept on burning, as shown by the very recent joint production of *Romeo and Juliet* by a Serbian and a Kosovan Albanian theatre company. A bilingual performance deliberately lacking subtitles, this new Balkan take on Shakespeare opened in April 2015 at the National Theatre in Belgrade before transferring to the National Theatre in Pristina, and was expressly envisaged as a way to promote dialogue and defuse the animosity that still governs Serbian-Kosovan relations after years of bloodshed and political tension.[4]

This chapter, however, centres on a different brand of Shakespeare-inflected responses to the war in the former Yugoslavia. Unlike the more recent performances mentioned above, the Balkan Shakespeares examined here are chronologically closer to the conflict, but geographically more distant from the actual theatre of operations; they articulate an outsider's viewpoint and show a clear awareness of the problematic implications of this discursive positioning. My choice of corpus is guided by a desire to broaden the range of Shakespearean (re-)productions to consider dramatic rewrites and cinematic adaptations as well, selecting one representative example for each mode of production. Alongside Katie Mitchell's staging of *3 Henry VI* at the Royal Shakespeare Company in 1994, my own 'Balkan trilogy' includes Sarah Kane's reworking of *King Lear* in her by now legendary play *Blasted* (1995), as well as Mario Martone's 1998 documentary-style film, *Teatro di guerra* (*Rehearsal for War*), which centres on the preparations for a performance of Aeschylus's *The Seven Against Thebes* by an experimental theatre company in Naples, but also features scenes from a concomitant production of *The Taming of the Shrew*. Although they each illustrate distinctive creative possibilities and modes of intervention, these Balkan Shakespeares all share an explicit focus on the war in Bosnia, the material and symbolical epicentre of the Yugoslav tragedy. They also reveal a strikingly consistent set of attitudes, concerns and strategies in their approach to the troubling reality of ethnic-driven violence in the region and their attempts to refigure it through a Shakespearean lens.

Mitchell's production, Kane's play and Martone's film originated from a deep-felt need, even a moral obligation, to bear witness to the Bosnian crisis, a bloody conflict that was raging on the very doorstep of Western Europe but became invariably othered in public and media discourse. Bent as they are on turning the spotlight on this European heart of darkness, these artists share, however, an extreme wariness about the representational resources afforded by their medium of choice. Their work is declaredly 'about' Bosnia, but in all three productions the Balkan war zone is resolutely kept off the picture, turned into a ghost-like elsewhere that is mentioned, evoked, alluded to, but never shown on stage or screen. The invisibility of the Bosnian war remains constant; meanwhile, the Shakespearean presence becomes progressively unstable and fragmented, directly mired in the violence of war or turned into a site of conflict in its own right. The artists put to the question their own premise that Shakespeare's plays can serve as a hermeneutic tool for bridging the gap between the audience's here and the Balkan elsewhere, leading to probing scrutiny of their own discursive limitations and ethical dilemmas.

'On our own turf': Katie Mitchell's *3 Henry VI*

When she settled on the final part of the *Henry VI* trilogy for her first Shakespeare project at the RSC in 1994, Katie Mitchell was drawn to this somewhat odd choice in part by the freedom afforded to a play that had never been performed on its own in Stratford and was therefore not encumbered by the 'production luggage' attached to house favourites.[5] As an emerging woman director within a traditionally male-dominated institution, Mitchell was bent on 'making it new'; by rendering the third part in the Shakespearean trilogy autonomous, a decision further underscored by the added subtitle of 'The Battle for the Throne', she flaunted her project's discontinuity with the long-ingrained custom of staging the histories as grand epic cycles pivoted on the memorialization of national history.[6] This critical stance towards the nationalist agenda underpinning established RSC tradition underscored Mitchell's main reason for turning to this difficult play, namely a deep-felt urge to engage with what she described as 'the civil wars that torment our planet today', more specifically her perception that *3 Henry VI* might provide some means to 'think more rationally' about the appalling reality of the genocidal outbreak in Bosnia.[7] Mitchell did not attempt this appropriation of Shakespeare's cognitive firepower, however, through the well-oiled directorial practice of updating the narrative by transposing it to a present-day context.[8] Rather than offering a Balkan-like version of the War of the Roses, Mitchell's particular method for bringing the horrors of Bosnia closer to a UK audience was to present 'a civil war ... which occurred on our own turf',[9] a staging of *3 Henry VI* that remained firmly anchored in England's own internecine carnage during the fifteenth century.

Enacting a move common to the other Balkan Shakespeares I consider here, Mitchell resolutely hid from the audience's view the present-day context that triggered and animated her take on *3 Henry VI*; the reviews of the Stratford performances register the critics' surprise over a production that was declaredly tackling the conflict in Bosnia, but rejected 'contemporary war-torn parallels' in favour of a 'strikingly medieval' mise-en-scène.[10] As the director herself explained, this embargo on visual representation stemmed from a need to counter the cognitive muddle and affective numbness induced by media images of contemporary wars:

> We need to re-observe the world through a new pair of glasses. That is why I did not want to update the play, or stuff it with graphic images from the television or newspapers. We are completely immune to modern reports of human horror anyway.[11]

The medievalism of Mitchell's production reflects the director's wholehearted embrace of the allegorical mode of Shakespeare's history play, here deployed as a Brechtian distancing device to counter the impairing effects of spectacular realism on our ability to understand the patterns and mechanisms of the wars that continue to ravage our world. Hence, it was not only the war in the former Yugoslavia that was banned from the visual field of representation in the RSC performance. The medieval battle scenes that punctuate Shakespeare's play were fought offstage, overheard by the audience as a sometimes deafening soundscape of rushing winds, heavy rain, howling wolves, bird cries and battle-maddened horses. Mitchell's signature anti-mimetic approach was nowhere so evident as in the famous scene in Act Two where King Henry witnesses first a son dragging in the father he has killed, then a father with his similarly murdered son. In the RSC performance, the soldiers' corpses were replaced by a red and a white rose, like the ones placed on the makeshift crosses that gradually multiplied around the perimeter of the stage.

By stripping her production of the pomp and pageantry traditionally associated with modern-day performances of Shakespeare's histories, Mitchell enabled a more focused, clear-eyed perception of the sectarian violence the play depicts. Her reductionist approach also brought out the trans-historical topicality of *3 Henry VI*. Without ever forcing or even stating the parallels, Mitchell's distilled rendition laid bare the deep structures of civil wars past and present, giving weight to the Biblical maxim, quoted in the RSC programme, that 'the thing that hath been, is that which shall be; and that which is done is that which shall be done: and there is nothing new under the sun'. Mitchell came to her first professional venture into Shakespeare with an established reputation for sharp, minutely wrought recreations of bourgeois interiors and familial strife. As reviewers noted, the most striking stylistic feature of Mitchell's *3 Henry VI* was its conversational tone, the vein of domesticity that the actors' contained, low-key, almost stylized performances were able to draw from a text designed for searing rhetorical intensity. Rae Smith's minimalist set design and the intimate quality of The Other Place, the RSC's small studio space, added to the effect of 'a symphony played by a small ensemble'.[12] This pocket-sizing of Shakespeare's vast historical canvas takes its cue from Mitchell's decision to present *3 Henry VI* as a stand-alone play, detaching the political and moral breakdown of English society depicted in the trilogy's blood-drenched finale from its teleological epic frame. The mighty adversarial struggle between Yorkists and Lancastrians thus loses any sense of an epic progression. Reduced to an unheroic turf war, the War of the Roses reappears as a matter of personal vendettas, of power shifting to and fro between a small, close-knit group of ambitious warlords: a 'low-intensity conflict' like those associated with present-day ethnic violence.

In addressing the war in Bosnia through the lens of a national trauma, Mitchell's production foregrounded the palimpsestic nature of the so-called 'new wars',[13] synchronized different historical times and spaces, and provocatively broke down the barriers between the audience's 'here' and the Balkan 'elsewhere', the civilized Self and the barbaric Other. Giving a markedly political and progressive slant to the notion of Shakespeare's universality, her staging of *3 Henry VI* used it to implicate the audience and counter a widespread tendency to confine the horrors of ethnic violence to a supposedly non-European region mired in atavistic hatreds and endemic nationalism. Mitchell mobilized Shakespeare as authoritative evidence that history repeats itself, and that Britain was no more immune to genocidal bloodshed in the present than it was in the past. From this perspective, the heightened medievalism of the RSC performance reads as a pointed reminder of the 'Balkanism' that was prevalent in the Western European public sphere, namely the systematic process of othering whereby, following the end of the Cold War, the Balkan region was constructed as an antitype of civilization not only in mainstream political and media discourse, but also, more surreptitiously, in apparently liberal thinking.[14] A pervasive notion within the international community that the Yugoslav conflict was a throwback to the past, a resurgence of primordial hatreds peculiar to the Balkan area, and which the Cold War had only temporarily held in check, contributed to depoliticize the aggressive nationalist policies in the region, to promote a fatalistic view of Balkan 'tribalism' as an inevitable and intractable phenomenon, and ultimately to legitimize the same inflammatory perception of the conflict that the nationalists involved wished to propagate.

Mitchell's RSC production skilfully subverted this determinist reading of the Balkan conflict. Catholic rituals and symbols occupied a major space in Mitchell's ethnography of genocidal violence, throwing into further relief the opposing factions' steady recourse to religious sanction to justify the vengeful blood baths that pattern the action. Costume design emphasized the arbitrary and artificial nature of sectarianism: Yorkists and Lancastrians wore the same grey-cloth tunic and rusty armour and were impossible to tell apart, but for the white or red rose that marked them off as enemies. At the same time, then, as it defamiliarized the Yugoslav conflict, reapplying it to England, Mitchell's *3 Henry VI* also drew attention to the role of religion in the polarization of political identities in the Balkan theatre of war, and of the factitious, specious nature of this kind of sectarian allegiance – then as well as now.

A Bosnian *King Lear:* Sarah Kane's 'blasted heath'

As Katie Mitchell's *3 Henry VI* was running in Stratford, Sarah Kane's first full-length play had already been programmed as part of the new writing season with which Stephen Daldry would inaugurate his tenure as the new artistic director of the Royal Court Theatre in London. On 12 January 1995, *Blasted* opened at the Theatre Upstairs and achieved infamy overnight, not least on account of its author's manifest intention to confront the war in Bosnia, a topic that the critical establishment saw as beyond the scope appropriate to a young woman playwright at her debut. As has been endlessly rehashed, after this stormy start the tide quickly turned, and in less than a decade Kane's work went from notoriety to the canonical status it enjoys today. Although *Blasted* has gone down in theatre history as Kane's 'Bosnian play', she did not originally conceive it as a response to the war in the former Yugoslavia. Likewise, even though it constitutes her most extensive engagement with Shakespeare, Kane did not initially envisage her debut play as a reworking of *King Lear*, the main thread in a thick intertextual web. According to her own testimony, the Balkans and Shakespeare broke, instead, unexpectedly and almost simultaneously into the process of writing what started as 'a play about a man and a woman in a hotel room',[15] transforming socially realistic domesticity into a nightmarish theatre of war.

In its final version, *Blasted* still bears traces of Kane's turnabout in the mortar bomb that detonates midway into the play and marks a radical split between the realistic first half – a highly eccentric but still recognizable variation on the 'chamber piece about relationships'[16] – and the brutal effacement of this genre's familiar signposts in the 'Bosnian' second half. From the explosion onwards, the naturalistically described hotel room in Leeds that provides the setting for the fraught relationship between Ian, a middle-aged tabloid journalist, and Cate, a naïve twenty-one-year-old whom he appears to have been sexually exploiting since she was practically still a child, becomes refigured as a surreal landscape filled with unspeakable and escalating horrors. While the time and action are disrupted, however, the unity of place is strategically retained, with the 'large hole in one of the walls' (39) left by the bomb blast acting as a powerful reminder of Cate's violated body, and marking out Ian's individual violence as the seed of the full-scale destruction of war. As Kane herself explained, this signature formal gesture encapsulates the politics of her play. Through its violent slippage of place, *Blasted* asks the audience to connect the rape of a young woman in a hotel room in Leeds to the mass-scale atrocities in Bosnia, to realize that there is only 'a paper-thin wall between the safety of peacetime Britain and the chaotic violence of civil war' and that this wall 'can be torn down at any time, without warning'.[17]

As in Mitchell's anti-Balkanist production of *3 Henry VI*, so too in *Blasted* Shakespeare helps Kane shatter British political complacency, the belief that the 'tribal' bloodshed of ethnic conflict could never happen in a civilized European country. Although the *King Lear* subtext is key to the play's universalizing impulse, however, Kane's reliance on Shakespeare is more oblique and complex than Mitchell's. The references to *King Lear* initially made their way into *Blasted* as unconscious or maybe subconscious suggestions and were therefore subjected to radical dramaturgical reinvention.[18] The Shakespearean elements in Kane's play often appear, moreover, in connection with references to *Waiting for Godot*, and are sometimes actually mediated by Beckett's own engagement with *Lear* in his play. The influence of Beckett on Kane's response to Shakespeare's tragedy can be seen, most notably, in Ian's attempted suicide after he has been raped and blinded by the Soldier, a moment Kane has retrospectively described as 'Ian's Dover scene' and a 'blatant rewrite of Shakespeare', but which in actual fact bears a closer resemblance to Beckett's own adaptation of Gloucester's mock suicide than it does to Shakespeare's original version.[19]

Kane herself was aware of the conflation of Shakespearean and Beckettian elements in her play. For example, to clarify that underneath Cate's simple-minded naivety is a complex, intelligent woman, she described her character as an amalgam of the Fool in *Lear* and of Beckett's two *idiots savants*, who show a similar capability for 'massive insight' underneath their clownish garb.[20] Kane, she explained, was reading *Godot* alongside *King Lear* during the writing of *Blasted*, hence the frequent overlaps. In light of her commitment to tackle the Yugoslav war, however, Kane's joint mobilization of these two European classics acquires a distinctly political edge, especially when one considers the important precedent set by the production of *Waiting for Godot* directed by Susan Sontag at Sarajevo's Youth Theatre, with a local cast, during the summer of 1993. Sontag's project could hardly have escaped Kane's attention, given the extensive media coverage it received; in 1993, *Blasted* was in the early stages of its development, and the alliance between Shakespeare and Beckett that emerges from the final version of Kane's play reads as a powerful reassertion of the anti-Balkanist spirit that animated Sontag's earlier theatrical intervention in the Bosnian situation. In *Waiting for Godot* Sontag saw a play that seemed 'written for, and about, Sarajevo', but also an opportunity to express solidarity with the war-ravaged city by re-inscribing Sarajevo and its multi-ethnic population within European high culture: 'What my production signifies', she recorded in her diary, '... is that this is a great European play and that [the people of Sarajevo] are members of European culture'.[21]

A kindred spirit of committed cosmopolitanism seems to have guided Kane throughout the development of her 'Bosnian play'. During the writing process, as the Shakespearean framework came into focus, Kane excised eventually all direct reference to the Balkan context. In the 1993 drafts of the play, the Soldier who broke into the hotel room was called Vladek and informed Ian that Leeds had been taken over by Serbian forces;[22] in the final version, the Soldier has no name and no nationality, and all geographical and ethnic associations have been strategically muted. While reproducing the familiar imagery conveyed by the media coverage of the Yugoslav wars, the atrocities reported or performed in *Blasted* are divested of their geopolitical specificity in order to take on a more disturbing archetypal quality. The ultimate act of brutality the Soldier perpetrates against Ian, a bloodcurdling blinding ritual, was inspired, for instance, by a journalistic account of football hooliganism in the UK.[23] Many elements in the scene hark back to the equally graphic horror of Gloucester's eye-gouging in *King Lear*. Conflating Gloucester and Lear, Kane subjects Ian to both the former's literal blindness and the latter's mental torment, then reproduces this duality in the insane retributive logic that governs his journey of re-education. Ian's physical brutalization is presented by the Soldier as a repetition of atrocities perpetrated on his girlfriend by another soldier. Since Ian is a tabloid journalist, therefore someone who by profession uses his eyes, his blinding amounts to a form of metaphorical castration, and in this sense retribution for the appalling violence he inflicted on Cate. Ian's blinding serves as a symbolically appropriate punishment, as well, for his failure to live up to his testimonial duty as a journalist; earlier in the scene, Ian rejects the Soldier's request to report his horrifying account of the war crimes he has witnessed or even committed, explaining that as 'a home journalist, from Yorkshire' he does not 'cover foreign affairs' (48).

In the 'Bosnian' section of the play, Kane calls on Shakespeare as a catalyst to strengthen her blending of foreign and domestic, particular and universal, real and oneiric; Shakespeare assists in a process whereby a force that is no longer definable in national or ethnic terms bursts into the room and turns the setting into a protean 'third space', both Leeds and Bosnia, while crucially neither. Through its forged unity of space, *Blasted* points out structural similarities between Ian and Cate's chamber-sized battlefield and the singularly 'domestic' quality of armed conflict in Sarajevo, a theatre of operations where 'front lines cut through neighbourhoods and streets, ran through the stairwells of apartment buildings, through bedrooms and kitchens, only to sink down into cellars, sewers, and underground tunnels'.[24] From the point of view of the action, however, these two overlapping scenarios are subsumed into Ian's Lear-like ordeal. Like Cate's rape, the violence of the war that is reportedly raging outside remains hidden from our view, but is re-inscribed onto the body of the only character who stays in the room for the entire duration of the performance. Like the cruel old king in Shakespeare, Ian must 'get as low as humanly possible'[25] before he can begin to rediscover his lost humanity.

Once he is left alone in the room after the Soldier has killed himself and Cate has gone out hunting for food, Ian's brutal punishment culminates in what Kane consciously sets up as an equivalent of the storm scene in *King Lear*. Like the Shakespearean king on the blasted heath, Ian is reduced to a 'poor, bare, forked animal' (*King Lear*, 3.4.105–6) in a prolonged sequence of mostly mute vignettes where he is shown masturbating, defecating, strangling himself, crying '*huge bloody tears*' (*Blasted*, 60) – shown 'getting as low as humanly possible', to return to Kane's words, while at the same time repeating in distilled form some of the actions performed or mentioned in the realistic first half of the play. Rather than being the work of an external force, Ian's disintegration is brought about by his own personal storm. The final stage in the havoc wrought by the cataclysmic violence of war on Ian's body and soul is Shakespeare's 'all-shaking thunder' becoming fully embodied in Ian himself.

Such interiorization of the storm is by no means novel in the performance history of *King Lear*. *Blasted* goes one step further, however, in that here the disappearance of the raging elements is reflected in a parallel dislocation and dissolution of the Shakespearean source itself. Ian's scene on the blasted heath involves a 'complete breakdown of language', a purely imagistic rendition of the shattering experience of extreme trauma.[26] Kane dissociates Shakespearean images from the verbal text wherein they were originally nested and reconfigures them as Ian's nightmarish phantasms. The moment in the play when intertextual intention is most conscious and manifest is also, therefore, the one in which Shakespearean elements are radically and deliberately effaced.

Like a palimpsest, *Blasted* writes over its origins, yet retains traces of their influence. This displacement of the war in Bosnia, as well as of Shakespeare's *King Lear*, recurs in the reception of the play. Kane was deeply distressed by the hysterical outcry that followed the premiere of *Blasted*, a disproportionate commotion which she saw as the manifestation of a widespread mechanism of denial:

> While the corpse of Yugoslavia was rotting on our doorstep, the press chose to get angry, not about the corpse, but about the cultural event that drew attention to it. That doesn't surprise me. Of course the press wish to deny that what happened in Central Europe has anything to do with us, of course they don't want us to be aware of the extent of the social sickness we're suffering from – the moment they acknowledge it, the ground opens up to swallow them.[27]

In the reviews of the 1995 performances, Shakespeare's sustained presence throughout the play was likewise ignored, in favour of disparaging contrasts between the 'adolescent desire to shock' and 'abject puerility' attributed to Kane's depiction of stage violence and the Bard's exemplary control over his subject matter.[28] Critics' targeting of Kane's deplorably un-Shakespearean rawness went hand in hand with their dismissal of her pretension to offer a serious theatrical response to the war in Bosnia:

> Who are the soldiers who appear to have taken over Leeds? Is the play meant to be drawing parallels between Britain and Bosnia? Kane hardly seems to care, she's too busy thinking up her next atrocity. ... Extreme violence in the theatre can be justified, as Shakespeare showed. But *Blasted* is a work entirely devoid of intellectual or artistic merit.[29]

By 2001, when it was revived as the highlight of a Sarah Kane season at the Royal Court, *Blasted* was in contrast already largely considered a modern classic. The new production by James Macdonald on the Court's main stage met with general public acclaim, and saw many of the critics who had slated *Blasted* on its debut make amends for their initial inability to understand the clearheaded timeliness of Kane's vision of apocalyptic violence. In particular, reviews of the 2001 revival tend to vindicate the 'dramatic purpose' of the play's excesses in coordination with a belated acknowledgement of 'the density of its references' to *King Lear*.[30] Recognition of a Shakespearean lineage paved the way for seeing Kane's work as part of a time-honoured, heretofore male tradition of contemporary meditations on human cruelty and war's insanity, ranging from Beckett to Pinter, Bond, Brenton and Barker. This sense of *Blasted* as taking its place in an established literary history greatly contributed to its critical revaluation. As the once dismissive Michael Billington was now ready to admit, Kane manages to 'shock us into an awareness of the emotional continuum between domestic brutality and the rape camps of Bosnia and to dispel the notion of the remote otherness of civil war'.[31] Regrettably, however, by 2001 the situation on the ground had changed; there was no longer the same urgent need, at least in relation to Bosnia, to shake audiences awake, dispel their myopic Balkanism, and indict their culpable lack of a due sense of responsibility.

Missed encounters: *Rehearsal for War*

Ambivalence about using Shakespeare to help represent the Balkan conflict, as in *Blasted*, becomes an overt thematic focus in Mario Martone's *Rehearsal for War*. Screened at the 1998 Cannes Film Festival, this documentary-style film, originally conceived as a theatre project, was several years in the making. Martone, a key figure in the Italian experimental scene and a prominent exponent of the New Neapolitan Cinema, began to formulate his response to the war in Bosnia in July 1995, during the Avignon Theatre Festival. Confronted with the activism of his French colleagues, Martone came to see the absurdity of his own detachment from a conflict that was in fact very close to him, if only on account of Italy's geographical and cultural proximity to the former Yugoslavia. Marco Baliani, one of Martone's closest collaborators on the project, has spoken in like vein of the 'culpable ignorance' resulting from his televisual apprehension of the Balkans war; like the vast majority of Italian viewers, he saw the horror of ethnic slaughter but failed to grasp its essence.[32] Martone's first instinct, in reacting to this media-induced numbness, was to turn to the stage. Given its long-standing record for fathoming the depths of tragic events in Western culture, he hoped that theatre might provide a viable means to approach the Bosnian crisis. He soon concluded, however, that any attempt to give dramatic shape to war atrocities would be overwhelmed by the barrage of images generated by day-to-day news coverage. As he was still struggling to find a suitable angle to approach his subject, the war in Bosnia came to an end.

Not only a powerless but also a belated witness, Martone finally envisaged a way to 'penetrate the void':[33] he would shift the focus from wartime Bosnia to peacetime Italy and dramatize his own missed encounter. Set in 1994, *Rehearsal for War* charts the vicissitudes of Leo (Andrea Renzi) and his underground theatre ensemble as they work on a stage production of Aeschylus's *Seven Against Thebes* that is meant to be taken to Sarajevo as an act of solidarity with the besieged city, but in the end never leaves the rehearsal room in Naples. Martone's indebtedness to Sontag's historic production of *Waiting for Godot* is even more direct than Kane's; Sontag's project is mentioned in the film only briefly, but surfaces time and again in the production diary, as a case study in discursive entitlement. During their journey to post-war Sarajevo in search of a local actor for the role of Jasmin, the theatre director who, in the film, invites Leo's company to perform in the Bosnian city, Martone and Renzi met Haris Pašović, the real-life director of the Youth Theatre where Sontag staged her Bosnian Beckett. As reported in the production diary, Pašović was unconvinced by Martone's project, which he saw as a purely narcissistic engagement with the Bosnian tragedy, and quite put out by the Italian filmmaker's idea of having an actor from Sarajevo perform in fictional scenes. There was widespread mistrust, Martone adds by way of explanation, of foreigners who presumed they could capture the reality of the siege through 'a story'; only those who had come to Sarajevo during the war, like Susan Sontag, were exempt from suspicion.[34]

Ineligible to document the Bosnian war on account of his shaky credentials as a second-hand witness, Martone opted for an alternative form of documentary authenticity: the film would evolve from a real staging of Aeschylus's tragedy, and the screenplay would be written around the filmed rehearsals. On screen, these two narrative levels blend seamlessly, thanks to Pasquale Mari's cinematography, and function as twin metonyms for the invisible, inaccessible Balkan war zone. In the rehearsal scenes, Sarajevo is recalled both through the setting of *The Seven Against Thebes* – a besieged city in the grips of civil war – and through the framing reality of the makeshift rehearsal space. The run-down basement room where the company works is surrounded by the violent reality of Naples' infamous Spanish Quarter. Outside the sheltered area of the Teatro Nuovo wherein the actors, towards the end of the film, are advised to barricade themselves, is a city mired in internecine Camorra warfare, incessant drug peddling and endemic social malaise. Martone emphasizes how this offstage 'theatre of war' continually interferes with their work; the high-pitched roar of stolen mopeds, the thump of a soccer ball against the stage door, the screams of housewives all affect the anguished rehearsals, just as the war in Sarajevo, one assumes, affects the theatre there.[35] On a more metaphorical level, Leo's company must withstand the besieging force of a prevailing commercial logic which stifles experimental work in favour of the hollow entertainment dished up by mainstream theatre, represented in the film by the lavish production of *The Taming of the Shrew* being staged by Franco Turco, the all-powerful and arrogant director of Naples' city theatre.

Unmistakably enlisted in the ranks of the enemy forces, Shakespeare is cast by Martone as the antithesis of Leo's unwavering commitment to experimentation and topicality. Turco's Neapolitan version of *The Shrew* is a tame, frivolous, escapist product designed for unthinking consumption by an audience of season-ticket holders. There seems to be no meaningful space left for Shakespeare in a project that was hailed by Italy's eminent film critic, Morando Morandini, as 'the best picture about theatre ever' and 'the most original filmic meditation on the Yugoslav tragedy'.[36] Adding yet another sadly missed encounter, in *Rehearsal for War* Shakespeare is the proverbial odd man out, an embarrassing presence akin to Turco's lead actress, Sara Cataldi, when she is ditched from *The Shrew* and ends up in Leo's underground production.

This presentation of Shakespeare as a putative foil to Martone's own endeavour works to conceal the considerable relevance of the Shakespearean subplot to the film as a whole. The presence of *The Taming of the Shrew* has gone virtually unnoticed in reviews, and *Rehearsal for War* has received close to no attention in critical literature about Shakespearean offshoots.[37] Rather than simply denying Shakespeare's suitability as a vehicle for addressing contemporary armed conflict, however, Martone's project seems intent on addressing its own ambivalence about this possibility. It is worth remembering, for instance, that although the film ostensibly denounces the definitive taming of Shakespeare in Italian theatre culture, both Martone and his collaborator on the project, Marco Baliani, came to *Rehearsal for War* with two 'militant' Shakespeare productions fresh behind them. In February 1993, Martone had directed *Richard II* at the Galleria Toledo, a tiny fringe theatre in the Spanish Quarter, offering a reading of the Shakespearean tragedy in light of the political upheavals of post-Wall Europe. Baliani's adaptation of *King Lear* into a one-man monologue, presented at the Santarcangelo Festival in July 1994, explicitly linked the horrors of civil war in the Shakespearean play to the ongoing ethnic bloodshed in the very heart of Europe.

Similarly, the emphasis in *Rehearsal for War* on the jarring contrast between the Balkan war zone and the rich city theatre where *The Shrew* is being staged is at odds with the evidence gathered by Martone and Renzi, during their post-war trip to Sarajevo, testifying to Shakespeare's significant presence in the Bosnian city during the siege.[38] Crucially, moreover, the film itself grants visual primacy to Shakespeare's text, albeit to ironic effect. In one of the opening sequences, before *The Seven Against Thebes* has even been mentioned, the camera lingers on a paperback edition of *The Taming of the Shrew* which Leo irreverently uses as a tray to roll himself a joint after a long day in the rehearsal room. A little later, when we learn that Leo's flatmate, Diego, is playing in Turco's *Shrew*, we are invited in retrospect to connect Leo's debunking gesture to the kind of escapist relief that this Shakespeare production is designed to provide. That short but revealing juxtaposition anticipates the film's subtle deconstruction of the surface opposition between mainstream and underground, Shakespeare and Aeschylus, *Shrew* and Sarajevo. While Leo mishandles *The Shrew*, Diego watches on TV *The Seven Samurai*, a film inspired by *The Seven Against Thebes*. This cinematic allusion ironically prefigures not only Diego's angry defection from Turco's production, but also the more general and constant flow of actors, technicians and even money between the two theatres. Leo's Antigone, Luisella, switches to Turco's cast, and Sara, who replaces her, continues to be on Turco's payroll, just as Leo's independent production receives financial support from the moneyed Teatro Stabile.

Such continuities call into doubt the ethical underpinnings of Leo's project. When we actually witness Turco at work on Shakespeare's play, the disparaging comments about his pointless, 'crappy' *Shrew* voiced by Diego, the mutinous actor, and Riccardo, the set designer who works on both productions, are apparently confirmed. We see the bombastic actor-manager play Petruchio opposite Sara Cataldi's Katherine in the fourth-act dinner scene, where the despotic shrew-tamer claims that the meat is burnt and, to the dismay of his famished wife, throws away all the food. The atmosphere is tense; Turco is irritated by the repeated pauses Sara introduces, as a sign that Katherine is bewildered by her husband's inconsiderate actions. It becomes clear that for this shrewd impresario theatre is a dish that must be served and consumed quickly, leaving the audience with no time to ponder over meaning. The food Petruchio squanders in order to break Katherine's will hints at the redundant opulence of Turco's production and the 'tame' Shakespeare it aims to produce. Even as it strengthens the opposition, however, between Turco's *Shrew* and Leo's minimalist production, this rehearsal scene also sheds light more indirectly on the exploitative underside of the company's act of solidarity with Sarajevo. Leo's overriding concern is with how to direct the play effectively, rather than with how to connect to a Bosnian audience. His exacting laboratory approach to theatre-making leaves him open to charges of self-indulgent intellectualism. In a heated discussion, Leo's spirited Antigone argues that a Greek tragedy performed uncut in Italian might well prove completely useless to the people in Sarajevo, who have far more pressing material needs. Luisella's allegations that this project may ultimately be a way to alleviate their bad conscience, rather than a means of bringing relief to their Bosnian friends, are hard to rebut.

Ironically, Luisella's arguments are eventually picked up by Turco at the dinner party following the successful premiere of *The Shrew*. Queried by a member of the cast about 'those lads who wanted to go to Sarajevo', the director of the Stabile patronizingly mocks their Godot-like failure to leave the Spanish Quarter by explaining that the people of Bosnia have no use for theatre: 'It's weapons they need, not a play! Weapons! Get it?'. Even before that, the credibility of Luisella's call to integrity has been undercut by her opportunistic readiness to leave Leo's production the moment money and fame come knocking at the door. And just as Luisella deserts the underground theatre of war in the Spanish Quarter, so too many intellectuals are fleeing the hell of Sarajevo, as Leo is pointedly reminded by Mrs Hamulić, the friendly Bosnian librarian at Naples' National Library. At all levels, the film shows, escapism is a truly ubiquitous phenomenon; many of the actors on both productions, for example, take refuge in various drugs. In the end, one begins to wonder whether the light entertainment provided by Turco's *Shrew* might not be a better remedy for the hardship of Sarajevo life than Leo's daunting Aeschylus. This doubt is actually spelt out in Martone's original storyline. In the film, the Bosnian theatre director is named Jasmin and never allowed to leave Sarajevo. In the original screenplay, however, Samir, the Bosnian theatre director, is brought over to Naples to supervise the production, and by extension lend it legitimacy by his approval. To Leo's dismay, war-weary Samir is far more attracted by the crass comedy of Turco's Neapolitan-style *Shrew*; dragged to attend a rehearsal at the Teatro Stabile, 'he understands nothing of the dialect, but laughs and responds nonetheless'.[39]

Martone illustrates this instability of roles and prerogatives emblematically in two scenes, both of which feature a surprising overlap between 'Neapolitan' Shakespeare and 'Bosnian' Aeschylus. These two uncanny encounters are all the more remarkable given that the film lays so much stress on missed opportunities. In the first scene, Luisella/Katherine, in Elizabethan dress, leaves the stage from a side door and bumps into Sara Cataldi, who has come to collect her paycheck at Turco's theatre. For a moment, the two shrews are dumbstruck; even though Sara, in the embarrassed conversation that follows, is civil enough to admit that they are both trespassers in the other's territory, we cannot but share the diva's bewilderment at the apparent ease and obvious relish with which Luisella, the former female lead of the underground theatre collective, has slipped into her costume and her role. The second encounter takes place during the dress rehearsal of *The Seven Against Thebes*. Sara has finally got into the part: no longer awkwardly out of tune with Leo's 'poor theatre' methods, she gives a powerful performance as the defiant Antigone, culminating in the iconic rebellious gesture when she gets hold of the carpet that doubles as a table set for a feast and, scattering food all over the floor, turns it into a burial cloth for her dead brother's body. Sara's rendition of Antigone's rebellion, we realize, is a modified version of her belligerent departure, in protest over Turco's philistine directorial tyranny, earlier in the film. During a pause in rehearsal, Turco/Petruchio was served coffee on the prop table on stage; as he was talking to another actor, Sara/Katherine re-entered unseen, overheard Turco's taunt, grabbed hold of the tablecloth and unceremoniously cleared the table.

With this unscripted coda to the *Shrew*'s dinner scene, Sara unequivocally signalled her refusal to be tamed. When her subversive bending of the Shakespearean script becomes newly incarnated as Antigone's brave show of defiance, an unsettling vertigo effect is created. For a moment, Aeschylus and Shakespeare, Thebes and Padua, Leo's besieged production and its subsidized assailant are brought together in the same space. This sudden convergence forcefully offsets the utter invisibility of the third stage that haunts the picture with its impossible presence: a theatre of war, in a not-so-distant corner of Europe, where the citizens of Sarajevo were left alone to perform their harrowing act of resistance.

Sara Soncini is Associate Professor of English Literature at the University of Pisa. Her areas of interest include contemporary British drama, with specific emphasis on the representation of war and conflict, modern-day appropriations of Shakespeare, and Restoration and early 18th-century theatre culture. She has recently published *Forms of Conflict: Contemporary Wars on the British Stage* (University of Exeter Press, 2015).

Notes

1. Quoted in Randall Martin, '"This Is Our Modern History": The Balkans *Henry VI*', in *Shakespeare beyond English: A Global Experiment*, ed. Susan Bennett and Christie Carson (Cambridge: Cambridge University Press, 2013), 170.
2. Stuart Hampton-Reeves, 'States of the Nations: Henry VI, the London Olympics and the Spectacular City', in *Shakespeare on the Global Stage: Performance and Festivity in the Olympic Year*, ed. Paul Prescott and Erin Sullivan (London: Bloomsbury, 2015), 84–85.
3. Ibid., 85.
4. Kit Gillet, 'Borrowing Cupid's Wings: Romeo and Juliet Helps Heal the Scars of Kosovo War', *The Guardian*, 5 April 2015, https://www.theguardian.com/stage/2015/apr/05/romeo-and-juliet-kosovo-war-shakespeare-serbia (accessed 10 March 2016).
5. Mitchell in Barbara Hodgdon, 'Making it New: Katie Mitchell Refashions Shakespeare-History', in *Transforming Shakespeare: Contemporary Women's Re-Visions in Literature and Performance*, ed. Marianne Novy (London: Palgrave, 1999), 14.
6. The more notable examples of the RSC's tendency to produce Shakespeare's historical dramas as monumental theatrical marathons are Peter Hall and John Barton's adaptation of the first tetralogy as *The Wars of the Roses* (1963) and Adrian Noble's as *The Plantagenets* (1988), as well as the celebrated stagings of the complete *Henry VI* trilogy by Terry Hands (1977) and, closer in time, Michael Boyd (2000). This epic style of presentation has by no means been confined to the RSC or the first tetralogy, as shown by Michael Bogdanov's seven-play cycle for the English Stage Company, *The Wars of the Roses* (1986–89) and, more recently, by the BBC TV series *The Hollow Crown*, likewise encompassing both tetralogies.
7. Mitchell in Paul Taylor, 'An Eye for the Small Print', *Independent*, 9 August 1994, http://www.independent.co.uk/arts-entertainment/theatre-an-eye-for-the-small-print-katie-mitchell-has-chosen-to-cut-her-shakespearian-teeth-on-henry-1382536.html (accessed 8 March 2016).
8. I have discussed some examples of this form of relocation in 'War Images / War of Images: Looking at Contemporary Conflict through Shakespeare', *Stratagemmi* 24/25 (2013): 85–113.
9. Alfred Hickling, 'Choice Part for Katie', *Yorkshire Post*, 12 October 1994, quoted in Hodgdon, 'Making it New', 16.
10. Robert Lore-Langton, review of *Henry VI: The Battle for the Throne*, *Daily Telegraph*, 15 August 1994, in *Theatre Record* 14 (1994): 1020.

11. Hickling, 'Choice Part for Katie'.
12. John Peter, review of *Henry VI: The Battle for the Throne*, *Sunday Times*, 14 August 1994, in *Theatre Record* 14 (1994): 1018.
13. Mary Kaldor, *New and Old Wars: Organized Violence in a Global Era* (Cambridge: Polity Press, 2002), 3.
14. Andrew Hammond, 'The Danger Zone of Europe: Balkanism between the Cold War and 9/11', *European Journal of Cultural Studies* 8 (2005): 135. Modelled on Edward Said's notion of Orientalism, the term 'Balkanism' was originally coined by Milica Bakić-Hayden and subsequently picked by Maria Todorova in her influential study, *Imagining the Balkans* (New York: Oxford University Press, 1997). For these references I am indebted to Duška Radosavljević's insightful article, 'Sarah Kane's Illyria as the Land of Violent Love: A Balkan Reading of *Blasted*', *Contemporary Theatre Review* 22, no. 4 (2012): 499–511.
15. Kane in Graham Saunders, *'Love Me Or Kill Me': Sarah Kane and the Theatre of Extremes* (Manchester: Manchester University Press, 2002), 38.
16. David Greig, 'Introduction', in Sarah Kane, *Complete Plays* (London: Methuen, 2001), ix. Further references to this edition are given after quotations in the text.
17. Kane in *Rage and Reason: Women Playwrights on Playwriting*, ed. Natasha Langridge and Heidi Stephenson (London: Methuen, 1997), 131.
18. 'The first two drafts of *Blasted* were written emotionally rather than technically. And although parts of it are very deliberate reworkings of *King Lear*, I didn't make that decision until some time in the process. Many of the thematic similarities were there, but I didn't become consciously aware of them until the third draft, after someone suggested I should re-read *King Lear*'. Kane in Saunders, *'Love Me Or Kill Me'*, 58–59.
19. See on this Saunders, *'Love Me Or Kill Me'*, 59, as well as my article '"A Horror So Deep Only Ritual Can Contain It": The Art of Dying in the Theatre of Sarah Kane', *Altre Modernità* 4 (2010): 116–31.
20. Saunders, *'Love Me Or Kill Me'*, 68.
21. Susan Sontag, 'Waiting for Godot in Sarajevo', *Performing Arts Journal* 16, no. 2 (1994): 88, 90.
22. 'This is a Serbian town now. Where is your passport? ... You are an Englishman, a journalist, staying in a foreign hotel and you do not have a passport?' Quoted in Ken Urban, 'The Body's Cruel Joke: The Comic Theatre of Sarah Kane', in *A Concise Companion to Contemporary British and Irish Drama*, ed. Nadine Holdsworth and Mary Luckhurst (Oxford: Blackwell, 2008), 157.
23. This is Bill Bruford's *Among the Thugs*, first published in 1990. Kane is quoted acknowledging this source in Aleks Sierz, *In-Yer-Face Theatre: British Theatre Today* (London: Faber, 2001), 102–3.
24. Branislav Jakovljevic, 'Theater of Atrocities: Toward a Disreality Principle', *PMLA* 124, no. 5 (2009): 1813–19 (special issue on 'War'), here 1816.
25. Kane in Saunders, *'Love Me Or Kill Me'*, 63.
26. Ibid.
27. Kane in Langridge and Stephenson, *Rage and Reason*, 131.
28. Respectively in Charles Spencer's review in the *Daily Telegraph* (20 January 1995) and Paul Taylor's in the *Independent* (20 January 1995); both in *Theatre Record* 15 (1995): 40, 38.
29. Charles Spencer, review of *Blasted*, 40.

30. Michael Billington, review of *Blasted*, *The Guardian*, 4 January 2001, in *Theatre Record* 21 (2001): 421. In Billington's review of the original production, *Blasted* was famously written off as 'naïve tosh'.
31. Ibid.
32. Martone explained this in *Teatro di guerra: un diario* (Milan: Bompiani, 1998), his account of the creative process. Baliani's remarks are reproduced in 'Napoli-Sarajevo-Napoli: un viaggio alla fine del '900', a documentary making-of included in the 2015 restored DVD edition of the film. All translations from Italian sources are mine.
33. Martone, *Teatro di guerra*, 18.
34. Ibid., 47.
35. This, too, finds a parallel in Sontag's description of the daunting working conditions at the Youth Theatre during the summer of 1993: see Sontag, 'Waiting for Godot in Sarajevo', 94–96.
36. Morando Morandini, review of *Rehearsal for War*, *Il Giorno*, 5 May 1998, in *Il Patalogo* 21 (1998): 239.
37. To the best of my knowledge, the only brief mention in this context is to be found in Richard Burt's essay 'Mobilizing Foreign Shakespeares in Media', in *Shakespeare in Hollywood, Asia, and Cyberspace*, ed. Alexander C. Y. Huang and Charles S. Ross (West Lafayette, IN: Purdue University Press, 2009), 231–38, where *Rehearsal for War* is briefly and incorrectly described as being 'about an Italian stage production of *The Taming of the Shrew* performed in Sarajevo where theaters have remained open' (232).
38. See Martone, *Teatro di guerra*, 48 and 'Napoli-Sarajevo-Napoli'.
39. Martone, *Teatro di guerra*, 32.

Chapter 2

John of Lancaster's Negotiation with the Rebels in *2 Henry IV*

Fifteenth-Century Northern England as Sixteenth-Century Ireland

Jane Yeang Chui Wong

> After this bataille [in Shrewsbury] was ydo, the knyghtis and squiers of the north cuntre that had be with ser Henri Percy, wente hoom ayen in to Northumbirlond, and kepte thaymself in strong holdis and castellis and wolde not truste in the kyngis grace.
> —From an early version of the *Brut*, translated from the Latin

Given long-standing interest in resolving the ethical problems in the *Henriad*, it is surprising that one of its most glaring instances of ethical violation has not yet received more attention: the negotiation in *2 Henry IV* between the Northern rebels and the king's representatives, Westmoreland and Prince John of Lancaster. At the meeting between the two parties, Westmoreland assures the Archbishop of York that the king has attended to the rebels' grievances and will reconcile with them, an assurance which the rebel leaders welcome.

Notes for this section begin on page 63.

But even after Lancaster promises their safe passage, Westmoreland arrests them:

> WESTMORELAND. Good tidings, My Lord Hastings, for the which
> I do arrest thee, traitor, of high treason.
> And you, Lord Archbishop, and you, Lord Mowbray,
> Of capital treason I arrest you both.[1]

This scene is arguably even more troubling than Henry V's slaughter of the French prisoners in Harfleur.[2] In *2 Henry IV*, Lancaster and Westmoreland expressly violate their promises to the Northern rebels, vows which their fellow countrymen accept in good faith, in order to seize them abruptly and put them to death.

Lancaster's treatment of the rebels is not as simple as the familiar model of subversion contained but instead can be better understood as part of Shakespeare's exploration of an immensely delicate system of exchanges between ruler and ruled, akin to Williams' later debate with King Henry V. Not only do subjects have a duty to their sovereign; the sovereign also has a duty to his subjects. In times of war, however, the loyalty that underpins this sense of mutual obligation is dangerously strained, all the more so given that it tends to be mediated by third parties, rather than direct. Lancaster's double-dealing with the Northern rebels reveals the distrust between king and subjects when they are forged at a distance by representatives of the crown. To understand Lancaster's justification of his own treachery, it is helpful to consider a historical parallel which can be found in a document written during the Nine Years War (1594–1603), when Shakespeare seems likeliest to have been writing *2 Henry IV*.[3] Its contents provide a rare glimpse into contemporary negotiations between rebels and crown representatives. Moreover, the unique administrative features of fifteenth-century Northern England correspond closely to the sixteenth-century adaptation of those structures in Ireland.

In the fifteenth century, the English government's administrative reach into areas more than 300 miles from London was limited. Even in the early Tudor era, the king's writ did not run in half the English counties; governance in the North was largely reliant on the marcher lords.[4] This long-distance mode of governance, dependent on feudal loyalties and obligations, was the most economical and efficient way of extending royal authority into the Northern counties. The provincial lords maintained private armies, which allowed them to respond quickly to threats from the Scottish border, as well as regional attempts at rebellion. As Steven Ellis explains, 'In this highly regional land, with its turbulent marcher society, ties of kinship remained strong, and real power rested with a powerful territorial nobility who organized the rule and defense of their compact lordships through a numerous and warlike tenantry'.[5] Tight kinship ties among the marcher lords also meant that if they collectively decided to rise in rebellion, they could form a truly formidable threat.

The possibility of such a revolt was one of the main problems with proxy rule. In order to maintain peace, a great lord had to win the trust of his tenants, both in his own right and as a representative of the king. With that trust, however, came competing loyalties. The Northern English chronicler John Hardyng, who fought alongside the Percies in Shrewsbury, remarked: 'for trust it true there is no lorde in Englande that may defende you agayn Scotlande so well as he [Hotspur], for they haue the hertes of the people by the North, and euer had: and doute it not, the North parte bee your trewe liegemen'.[6] Even as Hardyng declares the Northerners unwavering loyalty to the Percy family, he complicates this claim by asserting their loyalty to the king. Parallel loyalties such as these can also be divisive. As Alastair MacDonald has observed, 'Those who are said to have shouted "Henry Percy Kyng" at Shrewsbury (John Hardyng among them?) were unable to resolve their problem by making the royal line and the Percies one and the same'.[7] In the following decades, the crown attempted to prevent the possible rise of over ambitious subjects through a series of reforms aimed at decentralizing the powers of traditional magnates and consolidating the authority of the monarch. The establishment of the Council of the North in 1472 set a precedent for the extension of royal jurisdiction into outlying areas of the English kingdom but more direct interference in Northern affairs also introduced a climate of suspicion.

As in the North of England in the fifteenth century, so also in Ireland in the sixteenth century, proxy governorship often underscored the power struggle between English monarchs and regional magnates. Early Tudor Ireland was traditionally governed by Anglo-Irish families, most notably the immensely powerful Geraldine earls of Kildare. In the first edition of *Holinshed's Chronicles* (1577), Richard Stanihurst insists that English subjects from the Pale have always been loyal to the English monarch, but they are also fiercely loyal to the Kildares. 'If the north of England "knew no prince but a Percy"', Ellis notes, 'the Palesman "covet[ed] more to see a Geraldine to reign and triumph than to see God come amongst them"'.[8] Henry VII's oft-quoted comment – '[If no gentleman can rule Kildare] then in good faith shall this earle rule all Ireland' – became problematic for his heirs after the collapse of the Kildare ascendancy and the practice of appointing only English-born lord deputies put an end to the governorship of the Anglo-Irish lords.[9] The so-called 'final conquest' of Ireland was an attempt to extend royal authority and English common law to regions beyond those already under English jurisdiction. To do so, bastard feudalism had to be replaced, undercutting the power of local magnates. The 'surrender and regrant' policy proposed by Antony St. Leger during Henry VIII's reign was the first of many reform policies aimed at dissolving traditional loyalties to Irish magnates in favour of loyalty to the crown.[10] The programme granted English titles to native chieftains and provided them protection and support from the crown. They surrendered land holdings to the king, which were then returned to them, on condition that they pay rent, support crown initiatives, abandon Irish customs and habits, and swear allegiance to the English king. This transfer of loyalty was in part designed to undermine kinship ties among the predominantly Irish ruling lordships.

The success of St. Leger's programme was limited and did little to curb some of the most turbulent revolts in Ireland later in the sixteenth century, many of which were led or instigated by Irish chieftains who had ostensibly submitted to the surrender and regrant programme. For John Hooker, editor of the second edition of *Holinshed's Chronicles* (1587), this recidivism came as no surprise. He believes that the Irish are 'a people constant onlie in inconstancie, firme in wauering and faithful in untruths'.[11] Crown representatives in Ireland complained of the queen's leniency towards such rebels and repeatedly warned her that Ireland could not be subdued if she so liberally accepted their coerced protestations of submission. 'Without accepting the English assumption that the Irish were inveterate liars', K. J. Kesselring observes, 'it is clear that their humble submissions more often derived from pragmatism and fear of coercion than from sincere sorrow'.[12] Other reform programmes included the establishment of presidential councils in the 1560s. The characteristics of the Irish presidential councils were not unlike the councils in the marches of Wales and Northern England.[13] They were accompanied by efforts to colonize and garrison strategic areas of Ireland which had theretofore been neglected. The council's imposition of a crown-appointed president to govern areas once under the control of the native aristocracy meant that royal authority encroached ever more closely on those who resisted

English jurisdiction. This tension culminated in Hugh O'Neill's great revolt, which then led to the outbreak of the Nine Years War.

It makes sense to examine Lancaster's dealings with the Northern rebels in *2 Henry IV* in light of the historical context of early modern Ireland. As an indication of contemporary norms in such negotiations, Hugh O'Neill's list of grievances is of particular importance.[14] The documents were composed during a ceasefire negotiation at the end of 1597, when Blackwater fort, an important English garrison, fell into the hands of rebel forces. The significance of this loss was reflected in the English government's agreement to consider O'Neill's submission and demands. On the side of the Irish, O'Neill represented and negotiated on behalf of all his allies. On the side of the English, crown representatives included the Lord Justices Adam Loftus and Robert Gardiner, as well as Thomas Butler, Earl of Ormond, the queen's acting lieutenant-general of Ireland. The ceasefire documents consist of three main parts: the first, O'Neill's submission and his promise to be loyal to the queen; the second, his response to the conditions of the ceasefire set by Ormond; and the third, his demand for the restoration of his ancient rights, including a 'book of grevances' explaining his recent 'disloyalty' to the crown.[15] Hiram Morgan's description of the negotiation between O'Neill and crown representatives gives a sense of the immediate context of the documents in question:

> The preliminary meeting on 8 December was only agreed after Black Tom [Thomas Butler] had given his word assuring the safety of O'Neill and his party. Even then O'Neill at first stood off from Ormond and only after further encouragement did he dismount and come forward in person to speak to Ormond across a small river. O'Neill immediately complained about Marshal Sir Henry Bagenal and other enemies who had sought his life ... The negotiators tried their best to assuage these fears but O'Neill refused to be convinced.[16]

Crown negotiators dismiss O'Neill's fears as unfounded and maintain that his purported knowledge of murder plots against him were rumours 'conjured up by the priests to make him and others distrust the Queen's government'.[17] Negotiation thus hinges on establishing acceptable truth-claims, and early modern writers are well aware of the difficulty of balancing the need to preserve the monarch's honour and the practical exigencies of governance.

Humanist treatises that discuss ideas of good faith and its use (or abuse) as a political instrument in Renaissance Europe are largely consistent in their sense that trust between sovereign and subject is important in achieving social and political order. Machiavelli's chapter on 'How Rulers Should Keep Their Promises', or rather, how they are not obligated to do so, is the proverbial exception that proves the rule, breaking with a long line of writers who condemn such bad faith. In the classical tradition, Cicero shares Ennius's observation that 'there is no fellowship inviolate / No faith is kept, when kingship is concerned'.[18] Early modern writers like Thomas Elyot and Lodowick Bryskett believe that kings and governors, above others, are bound to their promises: 'there is nothing more fitting for a King then truth and veritie', Bryskett writes, 'as he should neuer haue one thing in his mouth and another in his heart'.[19]

O'Neill's list of grievances shows a breakdown of this kind of trust between crown representatives and the Irish confederacy as a result of a long history of broken promises, dissimulation and outright deception. In his letter of submission, O'Neill admits that he has repeatedly broken oaths of loyalty to the crown. Nonetheless, he hopes that the queen will prove a fair judge in reconsidering the charges made against him.[20] Crown authorities agree to convey his grievances to the queen and assure him that the contents of the document will be 'faithfully transcripted to her maiesty' on the condition that it should not contain 'frivolous or unnecessary' matters. The crown commissioners' agreement to transcribe O'Neill's complaints 'faithfully' suggests that his previous petitions to the queen may have indeed been intercepted or tampered with on different occasions, and that she is entirely unaware, as he sees it, of the doings of her 'badd officers' in Ireland, whose 'wrongs and hard dealings that many waies were used to me'.[21] O'Neill justifies his refusal to present himself when summoned by English authorities by explaining that he is afraid of being assassinated, a danger whose possibility he corroborates with examples of English treachery. He points out multiple incidents in which the English promised the Irish safe passage, then reneged on their assurances once the Irish had honoured their end of the bargain.[22] What emerges as a result of the unreliability and treachery of the crown representatives, then, is the dissolution of trust between English monarch and Irish subject; O'Neill's grievances in the ceasefire documents bear a striking resemblance to the Northern rebels' complaints and Lancaster's treatment of the rebels in *2 Henry IV*.

It is difficult to make sense of the fraying bonds of trust between monarch and subjects in *2 Henry IV* without first considering their antecedents in *1 Henry IV*. The link between them is the induction to *2 Henry IV*, featuring Rumour personified.[23] The fluid and unstable nature of Rumour underscores the deep distrust between the king and the English nobility. It also presents the legitimacy of the rebellion as a question. Who has betrayed whose loyalty? The rebels' quarrel with the king in *1 Henry IV* stems from their assumption that the king is honourable and that he will keep his promises to them. But as Hotspur complains, the king's memory is 'poor': having helped Henry IV usurp the throne, the Percies have 'for his sake [worn] the destested blot / Of murderous subornation' and are now abused.[24] Unwilling to accept this treatment, Hotspur declares it is time for the Percies and their allies to redeem their 'banished honors' and to restore themselves 'into the good thoughts of the world again'.[25] From his perspective, Henry's refusal to honour promises made both before and after becoming king is unambiguous evidence that the king cannot be trusted.

Opening the play with Rumour personified contributes to this sense of King Henry IV's reputation as dubious. Rumour speaks of 'King Harry's victory', of Prince Hal defeating Hotspur's 'bold rebellion', but also sends 'noise abroad that Harry Monmouth fell / Under the wrath of noble Hotspur's sword'.[26] The king is victorious, yet so is the rebel. Rumor in this light recalls the emblem, Fama, an androgynous figure with a trumpet in his hands and ears painted on his body.[27] In keeping with the induction, Northumberland is sceptical in the opening scene of the play proper; a truth-claim is immediately called into question when Lord Bardolph arrives with news of Hotspur's victory at Shrewsbury: 'Saw you [Hotspur] in the field?' 'Came you from Shrewsbury?'[28] For Northumberland, seeing is more reliable than hearing.[29] But for Bardolph, hearing is as good as seeing, because, he explains, the news is derived from 'a gentleman well bred and of good name'.[30] As he sees it, the anonymous gentleman's social status and reputation secure the validity of his truth-claim. As Keith Botelho observes, men's 'fame or reputation' in early modern England is 'derived from other men'.[31] Bardolph's assumptions about the reliability of 'well bred' gentlemen suggests that men's reputations, even kings', are no more reliable than rumours. To separate truth from falsehood, one must be what Botelho describes as a good 'earwitness'.[32]

As Botelho explains, Renaissance commentaries influenced by religious admonitions emphasized the importance of the ear as a locale of discernment. Thomas Vicary observes that the ear is the entryway into the head: 'it should keepe the hole that it standeth over, from thinges falling in, that might hinder the hearing'.[33] For the good Christian, 'the training of the ears to listen for the truth of God's Word became an outline for redemption'.[34] On the political front, monarchs from antiquity were expected to seek counsel from their advisors; Francis Bacon compares sovereignty and counsel to a married couple.[35] Harder to find, however, is any mention of the monarch giving ear to his subjects should they wish to air their grievances. It is this 'deafness' of the king that drives the Northern noblemen in *2 Henry IV* to threaten rebellion:

> ARCHBISHOP. I have equal balance justly weighed
> What wrongs our arms may do, what wrongs we suffer,
> And find our griefs heavier than our offenses.
> We see which way the stream of time doth run,
> And are enforced from our most quiet there
> By the rough torrent of occasion,
> And have the summary of all our griefs,
> When time shall serve, to show in articles;
> Which long ere this we offered to the King,
> And might by no suit gain our audience
> When we are wronged and would unfold our griefs,
> We are denied access unto his person
> Even by those men that most have done us wrong.[36]

The Archbishop's main complaint is that the rebels are denied access to the king. Westmoreland refuses to give the complaint credence: 'When ever yet was your appeal denied? / Wherein have you been gallèd by the King?'[37] The response is subtly ambiguous. It could be that the king is indeed aware of the rebels' grievances and that he has decided to turn a deaf ear to them. It could also be the case that Westmoreland is guilty of blocking the rebels' access to the king. The difficulty of trying to reach the monarch's ear was a real concern in Northern England in the fifteenth century, when communication between king and subjects relied on the discretion of crown representatives.

In sixteenth-century Ireland, it was physically impossible for the Irish rebel to reach the queen's ear without crossing the Irish Sea. Her officers were her eyes and ears, and her knowledge of the political problems in Ireland was entirely derived from their reports. In the ceasefire documents, O'Neill describes these officers as egregiously corrupt and maintains that their treachery towards him 'could not have byne knowne by her highness'.[38] He maintains that his attempts to communicate with the queen before he was proclaimed traitor were futile because the Earl Marshall 'did intercept the messenger, by the way and stayed his letters'.[39]

Morgan's commentary on the papers highlights an important detail. O'Neill refuses the crown representatives' demand that he surrender *ab initio* and insists that they revise the document they will convey to the queen to include details explaining how he was provoked into rebellion. By doing so, Morgan explains, O'Neill calls attention to 'the weakness of the state's position'.[40] In the absence of the queen, her representatives run the risk of reaching agreements that may tarnish the monarch's honour.

The 1597 ceasefire negotiation suggests the importance given to protecting the royal reputation in *2 Henry IV* as well. Westmoreland's rejection of the Archbishop's claim – that his (the Archbishop's) quarrel is with the 'commonwealth' – resembles the response of Geoffrey Fenton (Principal Secretary of State in Ireland) to O'Neill's request to present his and his confederates' demands to the queen more directly. Such a petition, as Fenton sees it, is 'neither meet for a rebel to prefer to his Prince nor fit for any good servitor to receive'.[41] In Shakespeare's play, Westmoreland also believes that the Archbishop has no right to seek redress for those who are dissatisfied with the king. Mowbray tells Westmoreland that the Archbishop has every right to address the king's injustice on their behalf; Westmoreland's response, then, to the more outspoken Mowbray is even more troubling:

> O, my good Lord Mowbray,
> Construe the times to their necessities,
> And you shall say indeed, it is the time,
> And not the King, that doth you injuries.[42]

Here, Westmoreland excuses the king by arguing that political expediency outweighs moral accountability. Moreover, he claims that Mowbray has no right to complain, since Mowbray has already been restored of his signories. Mowbray quickly reminds Westmoreland that the matter of contention is not the restoration of his ancient rights, but the restoration of his late father's, the Duke of Norfolk's, honour. Westmoreland's response to this objection shows how history and memory are framed by the king and the king only. Insisting that 'The Earl of Hereford was reputed then / In England the most valiant gentleman', and that the people 'cried hate upon [the Duke of Norfolk]', Westmoreland displaces Mowbray's accusation of the king's unjust behaviour onto 'Fortune', rather than the king: 'Who knows on whom Fortune would then have smiled?'[43]

Even though his casuistry is off-putting, Westmoreland proves an exemplary crown negotiator, fulfilling his charge to protect the king's honour. Throughout her reign, Elizabeth insisted that all crown negotiations with Irish rebels had to be conducted from a superior position. In his negotiation with O'Neill in 1597, Ormond was given explicit instructions that the form of the negotiation was no less important than its content, lest 'it shall appear to the World that in such sorte we will give way to any of their [the rebels'] pride'.[44] As Morgan explains, the state negotiators in 1597 'had to maintain the Queen's honour and their official dignity. They did get a submission of sorts and they did avoid, or at least their communications did not mention, the type of civilities towards the rebel which landed Commissioners Wallop and Gardiner in the Queen's bad books in early 1596'.[45] Taking into consideration the priorities and expectations of such truce negotiations, it is necessary to rethink Westmoreland's exchanges with the rebels; he communicates with them with a rhetorical flourish that focuses on negating the rebels' claims, effectively falsifying them and 'factualizing' rather than justifying the king's actions against the rebels. The competing versions of truths that arise from the negotiation inform equally contentious ideas of trust between rebel-subject and king.

At one point in the *2 Henry IV*, Mowbray expresses reluctance to continue the truce negotiation with Westmoreland because he is convinced that the king's offer of giving audience to the rebels' demands 'proceeds from policy, not love'.[46] As Mowbray sees it, such 'policy' cannot be trusted, and his fears are well-placed. Westmoreland uses so-called 'policy' to absolve wrongdoings, renege on promises and invalidate truth-claims, but Mowbray's fellow rebels are less suspicious and are content to know simply that Lancaster has 'full commission' to represent his father.[47] Hastings asks the prince directly if 'in ample virtue of his father', he has the authority 'to hear and absolutely to determine / Of what conditions we shall stand upon'.[48] Westmoreland mocks Hastings for asking what he thinks is an absurd question; since the king has delegated his authority to Lancaster, then he has full authority to negotiate conditions. Hastings' satisfaction with this assurance reveals his trust in Lancaster; negotiating with the prince is in effect the same as negotiating with the king himself. The Archbishop also assumes that Lancaster and Henry IV are one in this matter, and he dismisses Mowbray's wariness as unduly suspicious:

> No, no, my lord. Note this. The King is weary
> Of dainty and such picking grievances.

> For he hath found to end one doubt by death
> Revives two greater in the heirs of life,
> And therefore will he wipe his tables clean
> And keep no telltale to his memory
> That may repeat and history his loss
> To new remembrance.[49]

The Archbishop is in fact the one making a misjudgement as a result of three flawed assumptions: (1) Lancaster will review the rebels' conditions as if he himself were guilty of his father's misdeeds; (2) if the king does not agree to the rebels' conditions, the revolt will intensify, and the king will not be able to contain civil war; and (3) the king's reconciliation with the rebels will improve his reputation. Both Hastings and the Archbishop take Lancaster's commission and his representation of royal authority more literally than Lancaster himself interprets it. Although Lancaster acts in the king's name, he is *not* the king. The authority delegated to him allows him to make decisions that *he* perceives to be in the best interest of the crown, which is not quite the same as carrying out the wishes of the king. At best, the rebels can only hope that the king's general is trustworthy and that he will convey their grievances as promised.[50] Promises may be made and assurances provided; nevertheless, there is no way of knowing if and when messages may be intercepted or misrepresented. The rebel has no choice but to trust the crown negotiators, exposing themselves to the risk of unreliable mediation.

Rumour's destabilizing representation of competing truth-claims at the opening of *2 Henry IV* takes on a more sinister implication in the wake of the rebel leaders' meeting with crown representatives. Westmoreland assures the rebels that he will 'show the General' their articles of grievances and communicate their desire to reconcile with the king; Shakespeare gives no sign that he passes on any message(s).[51] If Westmoreland does in fact convey the rebels' wishes to Lancaster, that conversation occurs off-stage, unseen, unheard; Shakespeare leaves the audience to decide if it takes place at all. In his opening speech to the rebels, Lancaster, endowed with royal authority, condemns the Archbishop's cause:

> O, who shall believe
> But you misuse the reverence of your place,
> Employ the countenance and grace of heaven,
> As a false favorite doth his prince's name,
> In deeds dishonorable? You have ta'en up,
> Under the counterfeited zeal of God,

> The subjects of His substitute, my father,
> And both against the peace of heaven and him
> Have here upswarmed them.[52]

Lancaster's foremost concern here is to distinguish between truth and counterfeit. The Archbishop, in revolting against the king, has broken his oaths of loyalty to God, to the king, and he has become a 'false favorite'.[53] The king, in contrast, is God's true and rightful 'substitute', just as Lancaster is the 'substitute' here for the king. The Archbishop in response demands to know if the king's representatives are the champions of justice and truth that they claim to be:

> I sent your Grace
> The parcels and particulars of our grief,
> The which hath been with scorn shoved from the court,
> Whereon this Hydra son of war is born,
> Whose dangerous eyes may well be charmed asleep
> With grant of our most just and right desires,
> And true obedience, of this madness cured,
> Stoop tamely to the foot of majesty.[54]

In order for Lancaster's speech to be honourable, his promise to convey the rebels' grievances to the king must first be fulfilled. Mowbray, too, is keen to know if the king has heard their grievances; if he has not, he warns, the rebels will fight to the 'last man'. The rebels' quarrel with the negotiators is not grounded in the king's refusal to consider their demands, but instead in their concern that he may not even be aware of their grievances. They are afraid that their petitions have not been passed on.

Shakespeare presents the scene from the perspective of the rebels; the audience has a full view of their debates among themselves. In sharp contrast, the king's negotiators remain largely offstage, inscrutable. When pressed about the king's response to the rebels' grievances, Lancaster declares:

> I like them all, and do allow them well,
> And swear here, by the honor of my blood,
> My father's purposes have been mistook,
> And some about him have too lavishly
> Wrested his meaning and authority ...
> I give [my princely word] to you, and will maintain my word.[55]

The Archbishop welcomes Lancaster's promise cheerfully, but Mowbray, still suspicious, says that he feels ill, and rightly so; the speeches of the crown representatives are soon laced with dramatic irony:

> ARCHBISHOP. Against ill chances men are ever merry,
> But heaviness foeruns the good event.
> WESTMORELAND. Therefore be merry, coz, since sudden sorrow
> Serves to say thus, 'Some good thing comes
> tomorrow'.[56]

Lancaster gives orders for the Archbishop to dismiss the rebel armies, while he secretly retains the king's troops and utters the line that foreshadows their doom: 'I trust, lords, we shall lie together tonight'.[57] The equivocal verb 'lie' is the crux of the line: for the rebels, lying here means resting; for Lancaster, however, it means deceiving. Lancaster is playing a game of dissimulation. As Jon Snyder argues, 'dissimulation was the most radically subversive and most feared of all dialogue games ... for it was often difficult, if not impossible, for those taking part in the dialogue to tell who was playing and who was not'.[58]

Elizabethan audiences familiar with Shakespeare's plays must, like Mowbray, have been suspicious of Lancaster's promise. In Shakespeare's plays, kings and princes are as likely to deceive, lie and break promises as merchants and paupers. As Craig Muldrew has shown, the notion of creditworthiness in early modern England was deteriorating at an unprecedented rate, due to the transformation of the market economy.[59] Others have also noted that Shakespeare's references to bonds and promises double as commentaries on less-quantifiable social and political bonds of trust: 'In terms of total numbers, suits over bonds and other legal instruments increased by over 500 per cent between 1560 and 1606 ... At the time Shakespeare penned *The Merchant*, the country was awash with lawsuits, the vast majority of which centred on allegations of broken promises or hard dealings'.[60] These problems were not confined to England. In keeping with contemporary interest in Machiavelli, critics such as Andrew Hadfield and Perez Zagorin, as well as Snyder, see this period in Europe as an age of dissimulation.[61]

Lancaster's 'princely word' to the rebels does not seem like this kind of equivocation; if anything, the oath he swears must be all the more binding because it is sworn on the honour of his father, the king and on his royal blood.[62] Mowbray is suspicious of Lancaster's intentions, but a promise of such gravity offers some reassurance. Oaths are a form of 'mortgaged honor', in John Kerrigan's words. As he goes on to explain, their binding nature has limitations: 'honour is not the same as honesty. You swear to something because it might be doubted, though this frequently heightens doubt. You make your honor, your status, the stake of your word, yet honor can be held in the breaking of a word if it brings honor by other means'.[63] Citing an example from the Nine Years War in Ireland, Kerrigan adds: 'military treatises of the time, many of them dedicated to Essex, are clear that soldiers should keep their word, but that such undertakings could, "vpon iust cause", be broken'.[64] In the ceasefire documents, O'Neill calls 'to mynde a collecion of the particularities of my greffes, aswell againste the marshall, as also declaring the not performance of promyses, made unto me, in the late lord general Norreys his time'.[65] Here again, time erodes words; promises made one day are not honoured the next. Characters like Westmoreland and Lancaster play the game of dissimulation; they operate under the cloak of time, and time, like the ambiguity of language, is used to absolve their treachery. As Lancaster sees it, his role as the king's chief negotiator requires him to treat the rebels dishonourably; his first duty is not to them, or his honour, but to protect the king's honour, even if it can only be achieved with dishonourable actions. His success at betraying his countrymen invites a moral question: if the king's honour is, as Kerrigan suggests, 'mortgaged' in his promise to the rebel, will that honour not be tainted when his promise is broken?[66]

In the early stages of the negotiation, Lancaster gives the rebel leaders the impression that he has conveyed their grievances to the king, that the king has accepted their conditions and that the king is willing to make peace with them. But as soon as the rebel armies are disbanded, Westmoreland arrests the Archbishop, Hastings and Mowbray:

MOWBRAY.	Is this proceeding just and honorable?
WESTMORELAND.	Is your assembly so?
ARCHBISHOP.	Will you thus break your faith?
LANCASTER.	I pawned thee none.
	I promised you redress of these same grievances
	Whereof you did complain, which, by mine honor,
	I will perform with a most Christian care.[67]

The exchange reveals that two systems of honour, one relatively simple, one much more complex, have been operating simultaneously for some time. To denounce Westmoreland and Lancaster as liars would be to overlook the nuances of their own interpretations of their deception of the rebels. Westmoreland's response to Mowbray's question, 'Is this proceeding just and honorable?' is of the utmost importance; it subverts the ethical implications of the scene. 'Is your assembly so?' With this rhetorical question, Westmoreland justifies

Lancaster's reneging on his promise. The rebels have broken their oath of allegiance to the king, therefore his representatives are not obligated to deal with them in good faith.

Nearly a decade before this scene appeared on stage, a similar historical episode took place at the Siege of Smerwick in 1580, during the Second Desmond Rebellion, when Lord Arthur Grey de Wilton, the queen's lord deputy in Ireland, led a force against Irish rebels. The outcome of the incident was controversial. Grey purportedly assured safe passage to those who surrendered but later broke his promise and slaughtered all those who were present, including women and children, once the rebels had laid down their weapons. His actions remained unforgotten long after the massacre, most famously in Spenser's *A View of the Present State of Ireland* (1596–98), where he was, according to Spenser (who was Grey's secretary), unjustly labelled a 'bloodie man'.[68] After the incident, 'Grey's faith' became a by-word for bad faith. O'Neill cites Grey's brutality in the Pale in his list of grievances, for example in the executions and attainders of the Palesmen 'upon the witness of a raskall horseboy'.[69] In his report to the queen, the lord deputy defended his actions with an argument that resonates with Lancaster's treatment of the rebels in *2 Henry IV*. According to Grey's account, he was not obligated to keep faith with rebels; their war was not a just war, because they were not fighting under the banner of a king.[70] The queen's praise of Grey's actions reveals that his explanation was acceptable.[71] Royal representatives had to honour their duties to the crown even if doing so entailed breaking promises to others.

Westmoreland and Lancaster may appear amoral. They take pains to justify their actions by the standards of contemporary practices of negotiation. Westmoreland focuses on the injustice and dishonour of the rebels' assembly. Lancaster questions the standing of the rebels in the eyes of God, as well as the king. He insists that he has not broken his faith ('I pawned thee none') and that he has, as he says, attended to them 'with a most Christian care'. From his own perspective, he is a good and faithful Christian; the rebels are not. As Westmoreland implies that the rebels' disobedience to the king, God's 'substitute' is tantamount to their disobedience to God. 'God, not we, hath safely fought today', Lancaster claims, in his closing commentary, 'Some guard these traitors to the block of death, / Treason's true bed and yielder up of breath'.[72]

Put another way, Lancaster treats the rebels in *2 Henry IV*, whom he sees as failed, disobedient Christians, as infidels. His promises to them can be broken, because promises to rebels, like those to infidels, are not morally binding. As Andrew Hadfield has observed, lying in the early modern period was considered more acceptable if it was used to deceive infidels. He notes a passage from Christopher Marlowe's *Tamburlaine, Part Two*, in which the Hungarian Sigismund reminds Baldwin that they swore 'oaths and articles of peace' in Christ's name and that they should not therefore attack the pagan Turks. 'No whit, my lord', Baldwin replies:

> for with such infidels,
> In whom no faith nor true religion rests,
> We are not bound to those accomplishments,
> The holy laws of Christendom enjoin:
> But as the faith which they profanely plight
> Is not by necessary policy,
> To be esteemed assurance for ourselves,
> So what we vow to them should not infringe
> Our liberty of arms and victory.[73]

Defending God's honour, like that of the king, is presented as outweighing any other honourable concern. In *2 Henry IV*, however, as in *Tamburlaine, Part Two*, this self-justification of deceit does not in the end come across as entirely morally satisfying. As Hadfield points out, 'The Christian perfidy misfires, and they are overwhelmingly defeated by the Turks in battle in the next Act – a sign that God was really on the side of the Turks, that he was eager to punish the Christians for breaking oaths, or that he is indifferent to human actions'.[74] Lancaster's rhetorical justifications of bad faith in *2 Henry IV* also prove damaging. The legitimacy of Henry IV's kingship remains in question, even after his death. At the end of the play, the Archbishop and his followers are successfully suppressed 'underneath the yoke of government', but there is news that Northumberland and Bardolph are planning to revive the revolt.[75] The king's deteriorating health seems to represent a similar decline in his reputation. The guilt that he feels for usurping the throne and the anxiety that he feels about keeping the crown and passing it on to his son casts a long shadow on Westmoreland's and Lancaster's seeming confidence in their defence of what they consider to be just and honourable.

In keeping with the so-called 'Tudor myth', Shakespeare minimizes Lancastrian treachery. His source material, in some contrast, presents a fuller view of the event. *Holinshed's Chronicles* report the negotiation between Lancaster and the rebels through Thomas

Walsingham's account; Shakespeare follows Walsingham's description of the scene until the rebels are arrested, but Holinshed tells readers that 'other[s] write somewhat otherwise of this matter':

> Herevppon as well the Archbiſhop as the Erle Marſhall, submitted themselues vnto the king, and to his sonne the lorde Iohn that was there preſent, and returned not to their armie. Wherevpon their troupes scaled and fled their waies: but being pursued, manie were taken, many slaine, and many spoiled of that they had about them, & so permitted to go their waies ... The archbishop suffered death verie constantlie, insomuche as the common people tooke it, he dyed a martyr, affirming that certaine miracles were wrought as well in the field where he was executed, as also in the place were he was buried: and immediately vpon such bruits, both men and women began to worship his dead carcasse, whom they loued so much when he was aliue, till they were forbidden by the Kings freendes, and for feare gaue ouer to visit the place of his sepulture.[76]

This account departs from Walsingham's description, which includes a mention of the exchange of peace tokens but says nothing about a submission, the slaughter of the disbanded rebels and the people's reaction to the Archbishop's death or his martyrdom. Lancaster's and Westmoreland's convictions in Shakespeare's play, however persuasive they may seem to those who believe in the righteousness of God and king, are clearly not of the kind that all of Shakespeare's contemporaries would accept.[77]

Shakespeare's omission of the slaughter and the people's disapproval of Lancaster's treatment of the rebels can be interpreted as an attempt to perpetuate the Tudor myth. It is also possible that his audiences did not need the more detailed and explicit description of this betrayal that could be found in the *Chronicles* in order to draw their own conclusions. In the late 1590s when the play was first being staged, news of violence from the Irish war was widely circulated. Throughout Elizabeth's reign, several similar instances of dissimulation and treachery practised on her Irish subjects were reported. O'Neill listed some of these incidents in the ceasefire documents; he believed that Ireland was 'being destroyed, unbeknownst to [her], by the rapacious activities of soldiers and captains and was in process of being divided up by officials, lawyers and court clerks'.[78] In Shakespeare's play, Westmoreland's and Lancaster's actions appear to be motivated solely by their loyalty to the king. Where historical drama gives only one explanation, history provides another. Shortly after Hotspur's death at Shrewsbury, his post, the Wardenship of the East March, was left vacant and was quickly filled by Westmoreland. A reposting took place soon after, and Westmoreland was put in charge of the West March; the Wardenship of the East March was then given to none other than Prince John of Lancaster. The North, a traditional Yorkist stronghold, where the people 'knew no prince but a Percy', was carved up and transformed into Lancastrian territory, a kind of colonization, resembling the Tudor conquest of Ireland.[79]

Jane Yeang Chui Wong is Assistant Professor of English at Nanyang Technological University (Singapore). Her primary research area is in sixteenth-century British literature and history. She is especially interested in how changes in state and foreign policies shaped early modern literature and historiography. Ireland figures prominently in her research; her current project focuses on the representation of dissent and conflict among Elizabeth's colonial administrators between the 1570s and 1603.

Notes

1. William Shakespeare, *The Second Part of Henry the Fourth (1597–8)*, 4.1.331–34. All references to Shakespeare's plays are from *The Oxford Shakespeare: The Complete Works*, ed. Stanley Wells, Gary Taylor, et al. (Oxford: Clarendon Press; New York: Oxford University Press, 2005).
2. *The Life of Henry the Fifth (1598–9)*, 4.6.35–37. See also Conal Condren, 'Understanding Shakespeare's Perfect Prince: *Henry V*, the Ethics of Office and the French Prisoners', in *The Shakespeare International Yearbook* 9, ed. Graham Bradshaw, T. G. Bishop and Laurence Wright (Farnham, UK: Ashgate Publishing, 2009), 195–213; Theodor Meron, *Bloody Constraint: War and Chivalry in Shakespeare* (New York: Oxford University Press, 1998), especially 132–49; and John Sutherland and Cedric Watts, *Henry V, War Criminal? And Other Shakespeare Puzzles* (Oxford: Oxford University Press, 2000), 108–16.
3. A. R. Humphreys, ed., *King Henry IV, Part 2*, 'Introduction', xv (London: Bloomsbury Arden Shakespeare, 2014), xi–xci.
4. See R. W. Hoyle, *The Pilgrimage of Grace and the Politics of the 1530s* (Oxford: Oxford University Press, 2001), 31; as well as H. C. Darby, 'Domesday England', in *A New Historical Geography of England before 1600* (Cambridge: Cambridge University Press, 1976), 41.
5. Steven Ellis, 'Civilizing Northumberland: Representations of Englishness in the Tudor State', *Journal of Historical Sociology* 12, no. 2 (1999): 105. Details on some of the common traits of the development of marcher culture in Wales, Ireland and Northern England can be found in Paul Courtney, 'The Marcher Lordships: Origins, Descent and Organization', *The Gwent County History* 4 (2008): 47–69; Ralph A. Griffiths, 'Lordship and Society in the Fifteenth Century', *The Gwent County History* 4 (2008): 241–79; and Christopher Maginn, 'English Marcher

Lineages in South Dublin in the Late Middle Ages', *Irish Historical Studies* 34, no. 134 (2004): 113–36.
6. John Hardyng, *The Chronicle of John Hardyng*, ed. Henry Ellis (London: F. C. and J. Rivington, 1812), 380.
7. Alastair J. Macdonald, 'John Hardyng, Northumbrian Identity and the Scots', in *North-East England in the Latter Middle Ages*, ed. Christian D. Liddy and Richard H. Britnell (Woodbridge, UK: Boydell, 2005), 42.
8. Steven Ellis, *Ireland in the Age of the Tudors 1447–1603: Expansion and the End of Gaelic Rule* (Essex, UK: Addison Wesley Longman Limited, 1998), 108.
9. Raphael Holinshed, *Chronicles of England, Ireland and Scotland* (1587). Volume VI, *Ireland* (New York: AMS Press, 1965), 277.
10. Christopher Maginn, '"Surrender and Regrant" in the Historiography of Sixteenth-Century Ireland', *Sixteenth Century Journal* 38, no. 4 (2007): 955–74.
11. Holinshed, *Chronicles*, Volume VI, 181.
12. K. J. Kesselring, *Mercy and Authority in the Tudor State* (Cambridge: Cambridge University Press, 2003), 195.
13. Ciaran Brady, *The Chief Governors: The Rise and Fall of Reform Government in Tudor Ireland, 1536–1588* (Cambridge: Cambridge University Press, 1994), 73–74.
14. Hiram Morgan, 'The 1597 Ceasefire Documents', *Dúiche Néill: Journal of the O'Neill Country Historical Society* (1997): 1–21. I am indebted to Prof. Morgan's immensely helpful commentary and transcription of this document. His arrangement of the documents into five 'enclosures' provides a clear overview of the negotiation process and development.
15. Morgan, 'Ceasefire Documents', 3.
16. Ibid.
17. Ibid., 8.
18. Marcus Tullius Cicero, *De Officis*, trans. Walter Miller (London: William Heinemann Ltd., 1913), 27. See also Steven Shapin, *A Social History of Truth: Civility and Science in Seventeenth-Century England* (Chicago, IL: Chicago University Press, 1994), esp. 3–64.
19. Lodowick Bryskett, *A discourse of ciuill life containing the ethike part of morall philosophie. Fit for the instructing of a gentleman in the course of a vertuous life (1606)*, Early English Books Online Text Creation Partnership (EEBOTP), 63, doi: http://quod.lib.umich.edu/e/eebo/A17081.0001.001/1:4?rgn=div1;view=fulltext.
20. Ibid.
21. Ibid., 15, 16. O'Neill's complains, that his messages may not reach the queen (without interference from her officers), were prevalent throughout the early modern period, when the governance of Ireland was largely in the hands of English lord deputies. The implications of ruling Ireland by proxy through a viceregal system are discussed more fully in Willy Maley's chapter, '"And nought but presed gras where she had lyen": Royal Absenteeism and Viceregal Verses' in his *Salvaging Spenser: Colonialism, Culture and Identity* (Basingstoke: Macmillan Press, St. Martin's Press, 1997), 99–117.
22. The two instances specifically mentioned in O'Neill's book of grievances include the entrapment and massacre of innocent Irish citizens at Mullaghmast in 1578, and the siege of Smerwick during the second Desmond Rebellion in 1580. Vincent Carey, 'John Derricke's "Image of Ireland", Sir Henry Sidney, and the Massacre at Mullaghmast, 1578', *Irish Historical Studies* 31, no. 123 (1999): 305–27.

23. John Blades notes that Rumor has both thematic and dramatic functions in the play; Rumor 'resembles Janus, the Roman god of doorways and beginnings, and although he links both parts of Henry IV, he effectively obstructs the flow between them since he breaks the continuity by standing outside the two plays, mediating the experiences before it has happened'. John Blades, *Shakespeare: The Histories* (Houndsmills, Basingstoke, UK: Palgrave Macmillan, 2013), 123. In the induction, 'the potential of language for deception is accented, and once more, as in the motifs of counterfeiting and true and false of [*Henry IV*] *Part I*, common-sensical notions of an easily distinguished difference between truth and rumour are assumed'. Hugh Grady, *Shakespeare, Machiavelli, and Montaigne: Power and Subjectivity from Richard II to Hamlet* (Oxford: Oxford University Press, 2002), 181.
24. *1 Henry IV*, 1.3.160–61.
25. Ibid., 1.3.179–80.
26. *2 Henry IV*, Induction, 24; 26; 29–30.
27. Keith M. Botelho, *Renaissance Earwitnesses: Rumor and Early Modern Masculinity* (New York: Palgrave Macmillan, 2009), 4.
28. *2 Henry IV*, 1.1.24.
29. Bardolph's inability to 'adjudicate' in the opening scene of *2 Henry IV* is soon remedied with Morton's arrival, as he reports to Northumberland: I am sorry I should force you to believe / That which I would to God I had not seen. / But these mine eyes saw him [Percy] in bloody state (1.1.105–7). In Northumberland's response to Bardolph, the word 'tongue' is mentioned six times, each time in reference to news that may or may not be accurately reported, and other times insisting that the ear, of all parts of the body, is the most unreliable place to find truth.
30. *2 Henry IV*, 1.1.26.
31. Botelho, *Renaissance*, 5, 21.
32. For Botelho, *earwitnessing* in early modern England is a process that requires the 'sifting and distilling of information that comes to the ear, ... an active concept that entails engaging the ear in the pursuit of truth and carefully adjudicating ambiguous information'. Ibid., 2.
33. Thomas Vicary, *The Anatomie of the Bodie of Man* (London, 1548, 1577), 35, quoted in Botelho, *Renaissance*, 2.
34. Botelho, *Renaissance*, 3.
35. Francis Bacon, *The Essayes or Counsels, Civill and Morall*, ed. Michael Kiernan (Cambridge, MA: Harvard University Press, 1985), 64. See also Robert Zaller, *The Discourse of Legitimacy in Early Modern England* (Stanford, CA: Stanford University Press, 2007), esp. 23–30; and John Guy, 'The Rhetoric of Counsel in Early Modern England', in *Tudor Political Culture*, ed. Dale Hoak (Cambridge: Cambridge University Press, 1995), 292–310.
36. *2 Henry IV*, 4.1.67–79.
37. Ibid., 4.1.88–89.
38. Morgan, 'Ceasefire Documents', 16.
39. Ibid.
40. Ibid., 2.
41. Ibid.
42. *2 Henry IV*, 4.1.102–5.

43. Ibid., 4.1.129–30; 135; 131–32.
44. Queen Elizabeth, 29 December 1597, *Carew MS*, v. 601, 147r, quoted in Brendan Kane, *The Politics and Culture of Honour in Britain and Ireland, 1541–1641* (Cambridge: Cambridge University Press, 2010), 97.
45. Morgan, 'Ceasefire Documents', 4.
46. *2 Henry IV*, 4.1.146.
47. Ibid., 4.1.160.
48. Ibid., 4.1.161–63.
49. Ibid., 4.1.195–202.
50. Royal commissions and delegated royal authority have profound effects on the bonds of trust between rebels and monarch. Rebels like O'Neill were careful not to confuse the authority of crown representatives with the queen's authority. His agreement to parley with the Earl of Ormond (the queen's lieutenant-general) indicates that he trusted the latter but also that the terms offered could be trusted, and thus he could hope to receive some 'measure of justice'. Morgan, 'Ceasefire Documents', 15.
51. *2 Henry IV*, 4.1.176.
52. Ibid., 4.1.248–56.
53. Lancaster's speech complicates and blurs the distinctions between substitutes (stand-ins) and counterfeits (imitations), especially after the king sends out counterfeits of himself at the battle of Shrewsbury in *1 Henry IV*. He seems to imply that 'substitutes' are so called because they are approved and endorsed by the king, and thus seen as a kind of 'proper' replacement for that which cannot be present, whereas 'counterfeits' are false and untrue, and associated with ideas of deception and cheating. 'Substitutes' connote good faith by virtue of religious and royal sanction, and 'counterfeit' is associated with bad faith for lack of sanction.
54. *2 Henry IV*, 4.1.261–68.
55. Ibid., 4.1.280–93.
56. Ibid., 4.1.307–10.
57. Ibid., 4.1.324.
58. Jon R. Syder, *Dissimulation and the Culture of Secrecy in Early Modern Europe* (Berkeley, CA: Berkeley University Press, 2012), 5–6.
59. A historical overview that examines the cultural and sociological aspects of the phenomenon can be found in Craig Muldrew, *The Economy of Obligation: The Culture of Credit and Social Relations in Early Modern England* (New York: St. Martin's Press, 1998).
60. Tim Stretton, 'Conditional Promises and Legal Instruments in *The Merchant of Venice*', in *Taking Exception to the Law: Materializing Injustice in Early Modern English Literature*, ed. Donald Beecher et al. (Toronto: University of Toronto Press, 2014), 72.
61. Syder, *Dissimulation*, 5. See also Perez Zagorin, *Ways of Lying: Dissimulation and Conformity in Early Modern Europe* (Cambridge, MA: Harvard University Press, 1990), his 'The Historical Significance of Lying and Dissimulation', *Social Research* 63, no. 3 (1996): 863–912, and Andrew Hadfield, 'Lying in Early Modern Culture', *Textual Practice* 28, no. 3 (2014): 339–63.
62. *2 Henry IV*, 4.1.292.
63. John Kerrigan, 'Oaths, Threats and *Henry V*', *The Review of English Studies* 63, no. 261 (2012): 554–55.

64. Ibid., 555.
65. Morgan, 'Ceasefire Documents', 15.
66. Kerrigan, 'Oaths, Threats and *Henry V*', 554.
67. *2 Henry IV*, 4.1.335–41.
68. Edmund Spenser, *A View of the Present State of Ireland*, ed. Andrew Hadfield and Willy Maley (Oxford: Blackwell, 1997), 103. Grey's recall from Ireland is often associated with the episode in Smerwick, and it is frequently assumed that Elizabeth ordered his recall because of his excessive violence in Ireland. These assumptions are generally derived from Spenser's 'defense' of Grey both in the *View* and in his allegorical representation of Grey in the figure of Artegall in Book V of the *Faerie Queene* ('The Legend of Justice'). It should be noted that Grey was not indeed recalled for the bloodshed at Smerwick but for his mismanagement of funds. In fact, Catherine G. Canino has called attention to the immediate responses to the massacre in court; Grey was praised for the work he did at Smerwick and even received thanks and congratulatory greetings from the queen. See Catherine G. Canino, 'Reconstructing Lord Grey's Reputation: A New View of the *View*', *Sixteenth Century Journal* 29, no. 1 (1998): 3–18.
69. Morgan, 'Ceasefire Documents', 21.
70. See Grey's report to the queen in *Calendar of the State Papers, Ireland, 1574–1585* (London: Longmans, Green, Reader, & Dyer, 1867), 92–103.
71. Canino, 'Reconstructing Lord Grey's Reputation'.
72. *2 Henry IV*, 4.1.347–49.
73. Andrew Hadfield, 'Literature and the Culture of Lying before the Enlightenment', *Studia Neophilologica* 85 (2013): 137.
74. Ibid., 138.
75. *2 Henry IV*, 4.3.10.
76. Raphael Holinshed, *Chronicles of England, Ireland and Scotland* (1587). Volume III, *England* (New York: AMS Press, 1965), 38.
77. Annabel Patterson's *Reading Holinshed's Chronicle* (Chicago, IL: Chicago University Press, 1994) has been immensely influential in changing the way we think about early modern historiography and how the most ambitious historiographical project of the early modern period accommodated subversive interpretations of history even though the Elizabethan authorities were highly sensitive to writings that were perceived to undermine the legitimacy of the queen and her government. More recent assessments related to this topic can be found in Paulina Kewes, Ian W. Archer and Felicity Heal, eds., *Oxford Handbook of Holinshed's Chronicles* (Oxford: Oxford University Press, 2013).
78. Morgan, 'Ceasefire Documents', 21, 8. For an overview of the colonization projects in early modern Ireland, especially the political implications of land grants, and agricultural and economic reforms, see Michael MacCarthy-Morrogh, *The Munster Plantation: English Migration to Southern Ireland, 1583–1641* (Oxford: Clarendon Press, 1986), and John Patrick Montaño, *The Roots of English Colonialism in Ireland* (Cambridge: Cambridge University Press, 2011).
79. Ellis, *Ireland in the Age of the Tudors*, 108; Andy King, '"They have the Hertes of the People by the North": Northumberland, the Percies and Henry IV, 1399–1408" in Gwilym Dodd and Douglas Biggs (eds.), *Henry IV: The Establishment of the Regime, 1399–1406.* (Woodbridge: York Medieval Press in association with Boydell Press, 2003), 139–160, here 146.

Chapter 3
Shakespeare's Unjust Wars

Franziska Quabeck

Towards the end of *Troilus and Cressida*, Thersites captures the essence of the play in a single cynicism: 'If the son of a whore fight for a whore, he tempts judgement' (5.7.21–22).[1] Thersites means tempting fate, i.e. the Gods, but his words equally address the audience. We judge. And in this play, we cannot help but judge the incredible futility of what is allegedly the most glamorous war of all time. In Shakespeare's retelling, this legendary conflict is a cynical endeavour in which both parties are keenly aware of the futility of their actions. The war is clearly unjust; as Shakespeare's characters never tire of pointing out, its cause is not worthy. What, then, is a worthy cause? And what costs would be justified in pursuing it? Throughout Shakespeare's plays, whenever the subject of war comes up, characters soon turn to consider claims for its justice and, especially, proportionality. Working through a welter of contradictory statements, ranging from Jack Cade's bloodthirsty wish to butcher citizens like cattle to Henry VI's blessing of peacemakers,

Notes for this section begin on page 80.

the different voices gradually develop a complex, relatively consistent framework for assessing the ethics of war.

Over the past half-century, the striking variety of Shakespeare's characters' statements on war has led to very different conclusions as to what, if any, coherent perspective on war can be seen as generally upheld across his oeuvre as a whole. Despite Norman Rabkin's influential appeal to understand Shakespeare's *Henry V* as 'both/and', rather than 'either/or', critics have tended to see Shakespeare either as glorifying war or else as condemning it altogether. Depending on the play in question, either opinion can seem equally strong *prima facie*. Early English history plays seem more militarist; later plays such as *Troilus and Cressida* more pacifist. The most notable attempt to date to resolve this dilemma, other than Rabkin's, is that of Steven Marx, who sees Shakespeare as changing his mind over the course of his career. Marx identifies a 'Marlovian militarism' and 'glorification of violence' in Shakespeare's early work which gives way over time to consistent pacifism; *Troilus and Cressida* in particular marks an irreversible turning point.[2]

The juxtaposition of militarism and pacifism which Shakespeare's plays present is in keeping with the range of opinions about the morality of war available in the work of contemporary philosophers such as Erasmus and Machiavelli. The influence of Machiavellian *Realpolitik* is manifest in Shakespeare's Machiavels, York and Richard III, as well as other characters such as Iago, Edmund and Macbeth. Erasmus's relative pacifism is less often cited as a possible influence. As Marx suggests, however, Erasmus's *Complaint of Peace* was a seminal text. Machiavelli advises the ruler not to occupy himself 'with anything else except war and its methods and practices'.[3] Erasmus argues, in contrast, 'There is scarcely any peace so unjust, but it is preferable, on the whole, to the justest war'.[4]

The other notable attempt to read Shakespeare as a pacifist is that of R. S. White, who rejects Marx's biographical narrative of a change of heart. As an alternative, White sees conflicting statements about war in Shakespeare's plays as a strategy: Shakespeare's 'radical ambiguity'. Shakespeare deliberately juxtaposes opposing perspectives, but nonetheless, White argues, can be seen to favour pacifism in the end.[5] J. R. Hale sticks closer to Rabkin's 'undecideability'. Like White, he foregrounds Shakespeare's ambiguity; unlike White, however, he sees Shakespeare as holding opinions pro and contra in equal balance. Thus, Shakespeare is able to 'play it safe': 'no "view" on war emerges from the evenhandedness with which he has his characters express sentiments appropriate to their roles'.[6] Theodor Meron grants that 'each of Shakespeare's dramatic characters expresses distinct, individual attitudes, and is not a spokesperson for Shakespeare'; nevertheless, Meron cannot resist the temptation to conclude that the playwright ultimately shows that 'wars are not only tragic and bloody, but also futile'.[7]

Many of Shakespeare's plays suggest that under certain circumstances, at least, war can be excessively gruesome and therefore unjust. This concession to the particulars of a situation does not necessarily suggest a general partiality for pacifism, however. The only one of Shakespeare's characters who is unequivocally pacifist is Henry VI. The statements from other characters that Marx, White and others marshal as evidence of Shakespeare's pacifism are not, like Henry VI's, directed against war *tout court*, but instead against the injustice of particular wars. Moreover, they tend to focus on a specific kind of injustice: a disproportion between the cause and the costs of a war. This disproportionality is not a necessary condition for a war to be unjust, but it is sufficient.

Kenneth Muir has claimed that civil wars in Shakespeare are regarded as 'an evil to be avoided at all costs', more than any other kind of war, an assumption he attributes to the legacy of the Wars of the Roses. Elizabethans saw the Tudor era as in contrast a time of peace and welcome reconciliation.[8] Civil war was also understood as an evil, however, because its costs were seen as out of keeping with its intended effect. Shakespeare's first tetralogy foregrounds the horrors of civil war, not merely to condemn the Houses York and Lancaster, but also to reveal how its cost in suffering exceeds and undermines its own rationale. Unchecked violence in the name of revenge leads to a general disregard, even contempt, for human life. As Warwick states, 'Measure for measure must be answered' (*3H6*, 2.6.55). As characters slaughter each other pell-mell, and Henry VI stands by, feckless, it becomes increasingly clear that the violence on stage is out of all proportion to the *casus belli*.

In *1 Henry VI*, the matter of the initial quarrel between Richard Plantagenet and the Duke of Somerset, the one that leads to the plucking of the roses, red and white, is never revealed or explained to the audience. Warwick dismisses it as trivial: 'nice sharp quillets of the law' (*1H6*, 2.4.17). Yet it is this off-stage dispute, too minor even to be spelled out, which gives the war itself its name. Henry VI appeals to heaven: 'Wither one rose, and let the other flourish' (*3H6*, 2.5.101).

But which one? Henry VI does not seem to care; the two warring factions have become indistinguishable. The stage tableau which immediately follows, in which a son realizes he has killed his father and a father his son, stands as a metonymy of civil war itself. Each side is too close to the other to claim any kind of moral high ground. Picking up the body of his son, the father exclaims, 'I'll bear thee hence; and let them fight that will, / For I have murder'd where I should not kill' (*3H6*, 2.5.121–22). The language of this nameless soldier introduces a precise distinction between killing and 'murder', one that speaks to the crux of the difference between just and unjust war.

As an approach to war in Shakespeare, just war theory breaks down the 'either/or' dilemma, offering a perspective that is neither militarist nor pacifist. It includes arguments that both Marx and White employ in their arguments for Shakespeare's pacifism, yet also posits that war can be justified, given certain crucial conditions. Since the turn of the century, the collocation 'just war' has found a place in Shakespeare scholarship. In 2000, John Mark Mattox published an analysis of Henry V as a just warrior; references in Shakespeare criticism to 'just war' increased notably in the following years.[9] Michael Hattaway claims that 'the Battle of Bosworth in *Richard III* may be the only example of a just war in the canon'.[10] Nicholas Grene states that 'when an armed force appears under the command of Richmond, it is to be welcomed as the just war to end the cycle of violence';[11] Simon Barker refers to Richmond's 'lukewarm version of the just war ethic'.[12] This increasing interest in Shakespeare's take on the justice of war is reflected in R. A. Foakes' observation that 'Shakespeare seems especially interested in ... the emerging question whether there can be a just war',[13] as well as Paolo Pugliatti's study of the 'revival of the just war doctrine at that particular time and that particular place'.[14] What is a just war, however, according to this theoretical model? What might conceivably constitute a justified cause for war?

Just war theory derives from Cicero, by way of St. Augustine, as well as St. Thomas Aquinas, and proposes that on certain conditions a war can be just. It strives to discern and delimit a middle way between strict pacifism, which holds that all violence against other persons is unjust, and realism, which maintains that war is not liable to moral judgement.[15] War in just war theory is not seen as exempt from ethical consideration; wars and people's actions in wars can be judged from a moral standpoint. These two aspects, however, are necessarily distinct. In his classic treatise on just war theory, Michael Walzer explains, 'It is perfectly possible for a just war to be fought unjustly and for an unjust war to be fought in strict accordance with the rules'.[16] The distinction made is, in other words, between *jus ad bellum* and *jus in bello*. For a war to be just, just war theorists generally agree on key criteria that must be fulfilled. Steven Lee sets out a useful catalogue: 'For a war to be just, it must (1) have a *just cause*; (2) be declared by a *legitimate authority*; (3) be fought with a *rightful intention*; (4) show *proportionality* in the balance between the good and harm it does; (5) be a *last resort*; and (6) have a *reasonable chance of success*'.[17]

The triad of just cause, right intention and legitimate authority holds its ground within discussion of just war theory to this day. Formulated by St. Thomas Aquinas, it can be seen throughout Shakespeare's plays. In *3 Henry VI*, Warwick claims: 'York in justice puts his armour on' (2.2.130). In *Richard III*, Richmond states: 'God, and our good cause, fight upon our side' (5.3.241). Henry IV claims in the first part of the play series: 'God befriend us as our cause is just!' (5.1.120). Hotspur utters in the same play the belief that 'the arms are fair, / When the intent of bearing them is just' (5.2.87–88). In the second part of the series, the Archbishop explains that he has 'in equal balance justly weigh'd' their cause for war against the costs and finds their 'griefs heavier than their offences' (4.1.67–69), but Westmoreland claims that *their* 'cause is best' (4.1.156). Henry V asks whether he may 'with right and conscience' (1.2.96) make his claim on France, and in conversation with his soldiers claims that his cause is just and 'his quarrel honourable' (4.1.126). These references are merely exemplary; as I have tried to show elsewhere, Shakespeare's plays engage in extended discussions of the justice of war in all its aspects.[18]

The father-son tableau in *3 Henry VI* brings together several aspects of just war theory in a single image. As the father and the son bring their dead kin on stage and lament the atrocities of a particularly gruesome civil war, they point to the central principles of *jus ad bellum* and *jus in bello* as well as the logical distinction between the two: 'I'll bear thee hence and let them fight that will, / For I have murdered where I should not kill' (2.5.121–22). As the father carries his dead son off the stage, he draws, in effect, upon four principles of just war theory. (1) He is aware that in just warfare, the soldier's actions are typically described as legitimate killings, due to their duty as subjects to the king. (2) He refers indirectly to the logical distinction between *jus ad bellum* and *jus in bello*, which frees him from the responsibility for the justice of the war itself. (3) He has observed that the present civil war, one that asks soldiers to kill their own kin, is unjust. (4) The injustice of the war means his actions should be understood as murder.

Richmond's speech before the Battle of Bosworth in *Richard III*, a later play, continues the debate. Shakespeare does not simply ascribe the justice of Richmond's cause to the necessary deposition of a tyrant, but takes care to cover all three of the conditions posited by St. Thomas Aquinas. Richmond is presented as a legitimate authority who has come to free the country from a tyrant. His cause is just, since the war is designed to re-establish peace and avert more evil done by Richard. He declares his right intention; his motivation, he explains, is Richard's 'cold corpse on the earth's cold face' (5.3.267). He thus avoids the impression of a personal interest in the crown.

The necessary logical distinction between *jus ad bellum* and *jus in bello* occurs again in *2 Henry IV*. Infamously, Prince John defeats the rebels at Gaultree by promising to fulfil their demands, only to arrest and execute them as soon as they have agreed to the truce. 'Is this proceeding just and honourable?' they ask. 'Is your assembly so?' he replies (4.2.110–11). Prince John argues that the rebels deserve no just treatment for their unjust aggression. Yet his own action could be considered unjust, since he 'breaks faith'. Alexander Leggatt wondered what irritated him more, 'John's deviousness or his victims' behaviour'.[19]

Like *Richard III*, *Henry V* devotes considerable attention to the question of the prerequisites for a just war. Yet the contrast is telling. Richmond's speech before the Battle of Bosworth proves that his war is fully justified. Henry V's references are hollow, insincere and dubious, driven by a desperate desire to avoid moral responsibility for the war he leads in France. Even though it proves ironic, however, Henry V's speech on the need for proportionality in war is entirely in keeping with the precepts of just war theory.

> For God doth know how many now in health
> Shall drop their blood in approbation
> Of what your reverence shall incite us to.
> Therefore take heed how you impawn our person,
> How you awake our sleeping sword of war:
> We charge you in the name of God take heed.
> For never two such kingdoms did contend
> Without much fall of blood, whose guiltless drops
> Are everyone a woe, a sore complaint
> 'Gainst him whose wrongs gives edge unto the swords
> That makes such waste in brief mortality. (1.2.18–28)

Henry stresses the need to ensure that the costs of a war are proportionate to its cause. If its rationale is too insignificant or too misguided to merit risking the lives of thousands of soldiers, then a war is unjust, and the aggressor who provokes it is morally blameworthy. Henry's seemingly sincere plea here is echoed by Williams' response much later in the play, when the common soldier points out in more humble, direct language that '[if] the cause be not good, the King himself hath a heavy reckoning to make when all those legs and arms and heads chopped off in a battle shall join together at a latter day' (*H5*, 4.1.132–35).

Hamlet addresses the same question of proportionality in war in a short scene that is usually cut in performance. During his encounter with the otherwise anonymous Captain who leads Fortinbras' troops, Hamlet contemplates the 'imminent death of twenty thousand men' (4.4.60) that 'go to their graves like beds' (4.4.62). The *casus belli* in this case is woefully, pointedly inadequate. The Captain freely admits that the territory they are trying to win has 'no profit but the name' (4.4.19). Hamlet twice refers to it dismissively as a 'straw' (4.4.26, 55). Hamlet's difficulty keeping the numbers straight – first two thousand, then twenty thousand men – emphasizes the metric required by the principle of proportionality. Whether the inconsistency is a mistake (as Harold Jenkins muses in his edition of the play) or else reflects Hamlet's desire for hyperbole (as Ann Thompson and Neil Taylor suggest), the emphasis is clearly on the proportion between the cause and cost of warfare.[20] The disparity between the meagre *casus belli* and the death toll it entails means that Fortinbras' endeavour is fundamentally immoral. Hamlet admires it as a form of decisive action, even though misguided; the problem of proportionality that Hamlet introduces here, however, will be taken up again with even greater force, and a more obvious polemical edge, in *Troilus and Cressida*.

Steven Marx grounds his argument for Shakespeare's pacifism in Erasmus's discussion of the need for a balance between the cause and costs of a war in his *Complaint of Peace*.

> There is scarcely any peace so unjust, but it is preferable, on the whole to the justest war. Sit down before you draw the sword, weigh every article, omit none, and compute the expence of blood as well as treasure which war requires, and the evils which it of necessity brings with it; and then see at the bottom of the account whether after the greatest success, there is likely to be a balance in your favour.[21]

Erasmus's line of thought here reappears in Henry V's speech against 'waste' in warfare. And as this parallel might suggest, Erasmus is not best understood as a pacifist, strictly speaking. Pacifism rejects any form of violence between human beings. Erasmus, however, allows that waging war might conceivably be justified. In keeping with just war theory, his appeal to 'sit down' and 'compute the expence of blood' emphasizes a moral obligation to weigh the cost of a war against its costs *ante bellum*. His reference to a 'balance' between the two stresses proportionality as a necessary condition for just war. As Michael Walzer insists, the objective of war, what Erasmus calls 'the greatest success', must be a better state of peace. Like a present-day just war theorist, Erasmus argues that the justice of a war depends on the relation between its justification and its consequences. Modern just war theory, as Walzer sets it out, defines a better state of peace as 'more secure than the *status quo ante bellum*, less vulnerable to territorial expansion, safer for ordinary men and women and for their domestic self-determinations'. Crucial here is a sense of relative rather than absolute success. As Walzer explains, 'The key words are all relative in character: not invulnerable, but less vulnerable; not safe, but safer. Just wars are limited wars; there are moral reasons for the statesmen and soldiers who fight them to be prudent and realistic'.[22]

As Steven Lee points out, however, the justice of a *casus belli* is understood as a deontological rather than teleological category. Waging war is only just as a defensive response to aggression.[23] War can never be declared just in hindsight; if the consequences are positive, but the reason for declaring war is unjust, the war must still be regarded as an unjust war. In this kind of deontological evaluation, the criterion of proportionality is crucial. A war is just only if it is fought with the intention of averting an evil great enough to justify its cost in human suffering. As Lee writes, 'a war fails to satisfy the proportionality criterion when the harm it brings about is disproportionate to the good it achieves, in terms of reasonable expectations at the time the war started'.[24] These evaluations make it necessary to 'be prudent', in Walzer's terms, and to 'weigh every article', as Erasmus has it, in a careful consideration of cause and cost. Steven Lee again provides a useful catalogue, this time of factors to be weighed: '(1) the resisted evils; (2) the created evils; and (3) a comparison of the two in terms of some metric'. 'The third', he points out, 'requires a calculation comparing the first and the second, balancing or weighing them against each other, determining where the greater evil lies'.[25] It is the 'metric' aspect that makes the calculation of cause and costs particularly difficult. As Jeff McMahan observes, there are no explicit guidelines in the laws of war for establishing this metric: 'ad bellum proportionality is so difficult to calculate that it is simply not possible to formulate a sufficiently determinate principle for purposes of codification. Any statement of a jus ad bellum proportionality requirement would have to be so vague as to be legally unenforceable'.[26] However difficult the legal formulation of proportionality may be, however, its moral ramifications are reasonably clear. It matters a great deal, in principle, whether the number of soldiers whose lives are at stake in a given conflict is two thousand or twenty thousand. Hamlet's confusion on this point draws attention to a salient problem.

Troilus and Cressida confronts us with a war whose cost is egregiously disproportionate to its cause. The emphasis on the problem of proportionality in the representation of the Trojan War is especially clear in three elements of the play: the debate among the Trojans, featuring Hector's notorious *volte-face*; Diomedes, as the voice of proportionality; and Thersites, as the voice of injustice. Like Henry V and Hamlet, Hector argues, at least initially, that war should be waged if and only if its cost in human life is outweighed by the benefits of its success:

> Since the first sword was drawn about this question,
> Every tithe soul 'mongst many thousand dismes
> Hath been as dear as Helen – I mean, of ours.
> If we have lost so many tenths of ours
> To guard a thing not ours, nor worth to us
> (Had it our name) the value of one ten,
> What merit's in that reason which denies
> The yielding of her up? (*TC*, 2.2.18–24)

Hugh Grady sees Hector here as 'the voice of a traditional ethical rationality'.[27] His opponents at this point, Troilus and Paris, two younger men, are less rational; they argue, in effect, that the war is worth fighting because they are fighting it. The logical fallacy may seem obvious, but it is sometimes overlooked, in favour of Troilus's insistence on the importance of honour. A. P. Rossiter complains, 'Critics have been taken in by his "chivalrous passion" and never noticed that his argument is nonsense, and meant to be seen as nonsense'.[28] It helps here to recall Troilus's first appearance in the play, in which he is just as weary of the war as everyone else. Here, as Michael Bielmeier observes, 'for a moment Troilus sees the situation for what it is – a massive murderous engagement over one woman with questionable morals'. Only later, he notes, and 'for reasons unexpressed', 'Troilus dismisses his questioning and suggests that the effect justifies the cause'.[29] Troilus's inconsistency and irrationality are ultimately overshadowed, however, by his interlocutor, Hector, in his sudden 'resolution to keep Helen still' (2.2.192).

Extant explanations of Hector's change of heart here can be grouped into more or less three different modes of thought. The first is that the abrupt change of tack reveals the degree to which Hector is obsessed with honour. Even though he recognizes the moral shallowness of the war in which he is engaged, he cannot resist following an obsolescent, chivalric code of conduct. As Kenneth Muir has it, 'Hector ... does not realize that chivalry is dead. Indeed, as the Elizabethans would be acutely aware, all the Trojans are doomed ...'.[30] S. J. Lynch argues that 'Hector indulges in an excessive desire for honor';[31] Tom McAlindon, that he shows an 'irrational but typically chivalric procedure';[32] Thomas West, a 'passion for glory';[33] Mark Sacharoff, like Heather James, that Hector is an 'irrevocably doomed hero'.[34] Hector's dedication to anachronistic values leads to his demise as a tragic hero in a war that, for the wrong reasons, he does not in the end oppose. R. A. Foakes insists that 'as Hector is chiefly responsible for this, so he suffers for it'.[35]

A second line of thought looks beyond Hector himself to a more general trend towards hypocrisy in the play. As J. Oates-Smith, Douglas Cole and others argue, *Troilus and Cressida* shows the tragic consequences of men acting contrary to their beliefs. Camille Slights writes, 'The scenes do not contrast two schemes of value; they are complementary dramatizations of the failure of men to live up to their values'.[36] Scholars such as these who emphasize the insincerity of the values at the heart of the play argue that Shakespeare's exposition of those alleged heroes is deliberately ironic. This view is congruent with the demystification thesis of the legend of Troy, and it has been the dominant view in recent years. A third and still more recent perspective takes this argument about *Troilus and Cressida* to a further extreme, seeing in its ostensible discussions of ethics sheer arbitrariness and wilfulness. As Paul Yachnin puts it, Hector is only 'playing at conciliar debate'.[37] John Bayley sees the play as a whole as merely giving the impression of philosophic debate, in order to stimulate an intellectual audience.[38] W. R. Elton maintains that, at best, Hector is the voice of 'a conventional method of legal dialectic'.[39] R. S. White takes the extreme position that any scrutiny of Hector's *volte-face* is futile: 'There is no rational reason why Hector suddenly changes sides, and given the general tone at which the play is pitched it seems irrelevant to look for deep psychological reasons, and impossible to find them. He just does, and no explanation is offered. ... The fate of Troy is changed on a whim'.[40] White is surely right in insisting that we not look for psychologically comprehensible reasons.

Hector's *volte-face*, however, is more than a caprice. The question to ask is why Shakespeare stages the Trojan council scene in the first place, given that the outcome is necessarily determined by the *Odyssey* as the hypotext. Given that the play dramatizes the Siege of Troy, Hector cannot possibly win the debate.[41] There is no need, in terms of plot, for Shakespeare to include this ethical, relatively abstract debate on the need for proportionality in war, as distinct from and opposed to the imperatives of honour. The question therefore is not why Hector changes his mind; the question is why Shakespeare stages the debate at all, given its foregone conclusion. In brief, he uses it to stress the immorality of a war, however legendary, fought for the wrong reasons at the cost of thousands of human lives.

As if to further stress the injustice of the Trojan War, not only the Trojans, but the Greeks as well, argue against the validity of their *casus belli*. Diomedes dismisses the value of Helen, as a prize:

> She's bitter to her country: hear me, Paris –
> For every false drop in her bawdy veins
> A Grecian's life has sunk; for every scruple
> Of her contaminated carrion weight
> A Trojan hath been slain. Since she could speak,
> She hath not given so many good words breath
> As for her Greeks and Trojans suffer'd death. (*TC*, 4.1.69–75)

Here again, the emphasis lies on the calculation of cause and cost, represented figuratively in quantitative terms. Diomedes' 'scruple' echoes Hector's 'tithes' and 'dismes'; such metaphors help make the disproportion as concrete, as self-evident, as possible. The difference between the two speeches lies in Diomedes' specific reference to unjust casualties on both sides. The juxtaposition of 'Grecian' and 'Trojan', 'Greeks and Trojans', as if interchangeable, builds an implicit argument for peace, like Henry VI's in his appeal to heaven, irrespective of where victory may ultimately fall.

Hector and Diomedes both stress that no one sat down before the Trojan War, as Erasmus urges, and considered whether its potential benefits would outweigh its probable cost. As Thersites observes, in his quasi-choric commentary, 'All the argument is a whore and a cuckold; a good quarrel to draw emulous factions and bleed to death upon' (*TC*, 2.3.74–76). Thersites' ironic turn of phrase, 'good quarrel', recalls the laconic diagnosis of the Prologue: 'Menelaus' queen / With wanton Paris sleeps; and that's the quarrel' (Prologue 9–10).[42] *Troilus and Cressida* shows that when the cause and costs of a war are not duly considered, tragedy unfolds, and that these actions are necessarily held to be morally blameworthy. This war cannot be considered other than unjust, in the end; a judgement the play anticipates and confirms through its constant reference to the war's disproportional violence, far exceeding the merits of its cause.

Richard III, *Henry V*, *Hamlet* and *Troilus and Cressida* engage in a deliberate discourse on the ethics of war, one that is in keeping with the just war tradition and that lays special emphasis on the question of the proportionality of violence as a means to peace as an ostensible end. The plays observe the distinction between just and unjust wars and reflect on key questions of just war theory: just cause, right intention, legitimate authority and, above all, the principle of proportionality. This consideration is not the same as a general condemnation of war. Rather than rejecting violence altogether, the plays posit carefully-limited conditions for a just war. In the representation of warfare, unethical behaviour is the norm; almost all of the wars the plays depict are unjust, violating one prescribed principle of just war theory or another, with the notable exceptions of Richmond's war against Richard, as well as Malcolm's war against Macbeth. The two more radical extremes of pacifism and militarism are not adequately complex to capture this more nuanced ethics of war. Instead, in the spirit of authors such as Cicero and St. Augustine, as well as St. Thomas Aquinas, the plays ask us to judge individual instance of warfare on the basis of particular circumstances. Just war theory provides a general framework for evaluating the ethics of war case by case.

Franziska Quabeck is a lecturer in English Literature at Westfälische Wilhelms-Universität Münster. She is the author of *Just and Unjust Wars in Shakespeare* (de Gruyter, 2013) and *Oddities: Kazuo Ishiguro's Unauthentic Narrators* (unpublished manuscript), as well as editor of the collection *Just War Theory in Literature: Facts and Fictions* (Palgrave Macmillan, forthcoming).

Notes

1. Unless otherwise indicated, all references to Shakespeare's plays are to *The Arden Shakespeare Complete Works*, ed. Richard Proudfoot, Ann Thompson and David Scott Kastan (Walton-on-Thames: Thomas Nelson and Sons Ltd, 1998).
2. Steven Marx, 'Shakespeare's Pacifism', *Renaissance Quarterly* 45, no. 1 (1992): 49–95, here 59.
3. Machiavelli, *The Prince*, ed. Quentin Skinner and Russell Price. Cambridge Texts in the History of Political Thought (Cambridge: Cambridge University Press, 1988), 52.
4. Marx, 'Shakespeare's Pacifism', 53.
5. R. S. White, 'Pacifist Voices in Shakespeare', *Parergon* 17, no. 1 (1999): 135–62, here 143.
6. J. R. Hale, 'Shakespeare and Warfare', in *William Shakespeare. Vol. I: His World*, ed. John F. Andrews (New York: Charles Scribner's Sons, 1985), 85–98, here 97.
7. Theodor Meron, *Bloody Constraint: War and Chivalry in Shakespeare* (Oxford: Oxford University Press, 1998), 7, 8.
8. Kenneth Muir, 'Shakespeare and Politics', in *Shakespeare in a Changing World*, ed. Arnold Kettle (New York: International Publishers, 1964), 65–83, here 66.
9. John Mark Mattox, 'Henry V: Shakespeare's Just Warrior', *War, Literature & the Arts* 12, no. 1 (2000): 30–53.
10. Michael Hattaway, 'The Shakespearean History Play', in *The Cambridge Companion to Shakespeare's History Plays* (Cambridge: Cambridge University Press, 2002), 3–24, here 14.
11. Nicholas Grene, *Shakespeare's Serial History Plays* (Cambridge: Cambridge University Press, 2002), 92.
12. Simon Barker, *War and Nation in the Theatre of Shakespeare and His Contemporaries* (Edinburgh: Edinburgh University Press, 2007), 128.
13. R. A. Foakes, *Shakespeare and Violence* (Cambridge: Cambridge University Press, 2003), 83.
14. Paola Pugliatti, *Shakespeare and the Just War Tradition* (London: Ashgate, 2010), 5.
15. Michael Walzer, *Just and Unjust Wars: A Moral Argument with Historical Illustrations* (New York: Basic Books, 2003), 3. Just war theory usually refers to 'realism' as another term for militarism.
16. Walzer, *Just and Unjust Wars*, 21.
17. Steven P. Lee, *Ethics and War* (Cambridge: Cambridge University Press, 2012), 70 [italics in original].

18. See Franziska Quabeck, *Just and Unjust Wars in Shakespeare* (Berlin: Walter de Gruyter, 2013).
19. Alexander Leggatt, *Shakespeare's Political Drama: The History Plays and the Roman Plays* (London: Routledge, 1988), 87.
20. See *Hamlet*, ed. Harold Jenkins. The Arden Shakespeare Second Series (London: Methuen & Co. Ltd., 1982), 346n60 and *Hamlet*, ed. Ann Thompson and Neil Taylor. The Arden Shakespeare Third Series (London: Bloomsbury, 2006), 371n59.
21. Qtd. in Marx, 'Shakespeare's Pacifism', 53.
22. Walzer, *Just and Unjust Wars*, 121, 122.
23. Lee, *Ethics and War*, 77, 78.
24. Ibid., 72.
25. Ibid., 86.
26. Jeff McMahan, 'Proportionality and Necessity in *Jus in Bello*', in *The Oxford Handbook of the Ethics of War*, ed. Helen Frowe and Seth Lazar (forthcoming). Available online at http://jeffersonmcmahan.com/publications/ (accessed 2 December 2015).
27. Hugh Grady, *Shakespeare's Universal Wolf: Studies in Early Modern Reification* (Oxford: Clarendon Press, 1996), 89.
28. A. P. Rossiter, '*Troilus* as "Inquisition"', in *Troilus and Cressida: A Casebook*, ed. Priscilla Martin (London: Macmillan, 1976), 100–21, here 112; see also Vivian Thomas, *The Moral Universe of Shakespeare's Problem Plays* (London: Croom Helm, 1987), 87; and Harold Goddard, *The Meaning of Shakespeare Vol. 2* (London: The University of Chicago Press Ltd, 1955), 25.
29. Michael G. Bielmeier, 'Ethics and Anxiety in *Troilus and Cressida*', *Christianity and Literature* 50, no. 2 (2001): 225–45, here 227.
30. Kenneth Muir, '*Troilus and Cressida*', in *Aspects of Shakespeare's Problem Plays*, ed. Kenneth Muir and Stanley Wells (Cambridge: Cambridge University Press, 1982), 96–107, here 102.
31. S. J. Lynch, 'Hector and the Theme of Honor in *Troilus and Cressida*', *The Upstart Crow: A Shakespeare Journal* 7 (1987): 68–79, here 71.
32. Tom McAlindon, 'Language, Style and Meaning in *Troilus and Cressida*', *PMLA* 84, no. 1 (1969): 29–43, here 31.
33. Thomas G. West, 'The Two Truths of *Troilus and Cressida*', in *Shakespeare as Political Thinker*, ed. John E. Alvis and Thomas G. West (Wilmington, DE: ISI Books, 2000), 143–62, here 150.
34. Mark Sacharoff, 'Tragic vs. Satiric: Hector's Conduct in II, ii of Shakespeare's *Troilus and Cressida*', *Studies in Philology* 67, no. 4 (1970): 517–31, here 527. Compare also Heather James's comment: 'The problem is that Hector cannot maintain his distinguished role as the ethical Trojan after he has been tempted by his equally attractive role as the chivalric one: in the Trojan council, he insists upon his ethics and even cites Aristotle on the subject – anachronism intended – and then, warming to Troilus' speeches on honor, formally exchanges one traditional role for the other and issues a highly romantic challenge to single combat'. Heather James, *Shakespeare's Troy: Drama, Politics and the Translation of Empire* (Cambridge: Cambridge University Press, 1997), 98.
35. R. A. Foakes, '*Troilus and Cressida* Reconsidered', *University of Toronto Quarterly* 32, no. 2 (1963): 148.

36. Camille Slights, 'The Parallel Structure of *Troilus and Cressida*', *Shakespeare Quarterly* 25, no. 1 (1974): 42–51, here 45; see also J. Oates-Smith, 'Essence and Existence in Shakespeare's *Troilus and Cressida*', *Philological Quarterly* 46, no. 2 (1967): 167–85, here 175; and Douglas Cole, 'Myth and Anti-Myth: The Case of *Troilus and Cressida*', *Shakespeare Quarterly* 31, no. 1 (1980): 76–84, here 81.
37. Paul Yachnin, 'Shakespeare's Problem Plays and the Drama of His Time: *Troilus and Cressida, All's Well That Ends Well, Measure for Measure*', in *A Companion to Shakespeare's Works, Vol. IV: The Poems, Problem Comedies, Late Plays*, ed. Richard Dutton and Jean E. Howard (Malden, MA: Blackwell, 2006), 46–68, here 55.
38. John Bayley, 'Time and the Trojans', *Essays in Criticism* 25, no. 1 (1975): 55–73, here 72.
39. W. R. Elton, *Shakespeare's* Troilus and Cressida *and the Inns of Court Revels* (Aldershot: Ashgate, 2000), 104.
40. R. S. White, '*Troilus and Cressida* as Brechtian Theatre', in *Shakespearean Continuities*, ed. John Batchelor, Tom Cain and Claire Lamont (Basingstoke: Macmillan, 1997), 221–37, here 237.
41. As Douglas Cole has noted, 'we know beforehand that the Trojans will fight on for Helen – the myth of the story demands it'. Cole, 'Myth and Anti-Myth', 81.
42. William Shakespeare, *Troilus and Cressida*, ed. David Bevington. The Arden Shakespeare Third Series (London: Thomson Learning, 2006).

Chapter 4

Sine Dolore

Relative Painlessness in Shakespeare's Laughter at War

Daniel Derrin

An old tension lies at the heart of Christian thinking about war. How does a Christian individual, ruler or state balance the imperative of peace against the necessity of engaging in war, with all of its horror? More specifically, how does a Christian society balance the need and means for war against a duty not to exult in it or to enjoy constructing an 'honourable' selfhood through the destruction of others? Shakespeare's laughter at war, I argue here, addresses that tension.

Among the theological traditions that influenced thinking about war in Shakespeare's world, there were of course pacifist approaches; however, Augustine's seminal ideas about 'just war' were much more commonly adopted.[1] For Augustine, there were exceptions to the commandment 'thou shalt not kill', including the case of 'just wars' waged 'by God's authority'.[2] It is, he notes (influentially) in

Notes for this section begin on page 98.

De Civitas Dei, 'the iniquity of the opposing side that imposes upon the wise man the duty of waging wars'.[3] The Roman Empire may have grown, even by means of just wars, Augustine admits, and yet that expansion is far from being a kind of felicity:

> Let everyone, therefore, who reflects with pain upon such great evils, upon such horror and cruelty, acknowledge that this is misery. And if anyone either endures them [wars] or thinks of them without anguish of soul, his condition is still more miserable: for he thinks himself happy only because he has lost all human feeling.[4]

Augustine here registers two levels of war's pain. Not only are the effects of war a great evil, but so is the very fact that Christians must sometimes engage in it. The fallen world is a tragic world. Soldiers can only address this tension, Augustine suggests, by fighting with the aim of creating a larger peace, and with the realization that 'bodily strength is a gift of God' not to be used 'against God'.[5] From an Augustinian perspective, a Christian is never justified in using the opportunity of war to exult in the pleasures of self-definition that military 'honour' can afford, as Shakespeare's Hotspur, Bertram, Antony, Coriolanus (and family) do, yet must bravely engage in war when the need arises, as Shakespeare's Paroles and Falstaff do not.

Each of those characters can be seen as comic distortions of an ideal Christian balance. At the same time, that balance itself has always sat uneasily with the political necessity of keeping men on the field, preferring death to 'dishonour'. Such characters – and the amusement Shakespeare generates with them – are partly situated, then, by the gap between ancient Christian and ancient Roman discourses of war. Christian discourse, and its criticizing laughter, locates a warrior's proper subjectivity somewhere between a Hotspur and a Falstaff, or a Bertram and a Paroles. At the same time, a warrior shaped by both Christian and Roman discourses of war is often in a position to be deeply attracted at some level both to the valour of a Hotspur or Bertram and to the love of bare life shown by a Falstaff or Paroles. That duality of attraction and repulsion, created within the laughter these figures generate (so far as it is generated by Shakespeare himself), is a duality difficult to theorize; it goes right to the heart of the differences between Aristotelian and Freudian approaches to laughter. Where Freud generally sees 'the joke' as an expression of the desire to free up repressed aggressive impulses, Aristotle sees 'the laughable' as an expression of scorn for the ugly.[6] Freud explains laughter's pleasure and Aristotle its proximity to pain. Both are important insights that cannot be reconciled easily; we are attracted to the laughable and repelled by it.

The complexity of that attraction-repulsion duality cannot be fully addressed here. What I want to do is draw on and develop one particular aspect of the discourse of laughter within the Aristotelian tradition in the sixteenth century, an aspect which is particularly relevant to laughter in the context of war. It is the idea that a comic space creates a kind of emotional distance, a relative painlessness, from that which is elsewhere simply troubling or horrifying. Renaissance thinkers often repeat the idea that the *ridiculus* (the laughable) is that type of 'deformity' or 'turpitude' that is '*sine dolore*' (lacking pain).[7] Such 'emotional distance' resonates in part with Henri Bergson's famous contention that laughter involves an 'absence of feeling'; however, I think it is unhelpful here to go as far as to call it, with Bergson, 'a momentary anesthesia of the heart'.[8] How can 'the heart' not be involved in a laughter at war that teeters on the edge of its great pain? John Morreall has recently identified within the 'comic vision of life' an 'emotional disengagement', as opposed to the *engagement* that tragic visions create.[9] The emphasis here, however, will be on the emotional 'distance' of the comic rather than its 'disengagement' because I want to locate Shakespeare's laughter at war near the contiguity of the tragic and comic without relying too much on those generic categories at the expense of a historical philosophy of laughter.

In characterizing Shakespeare's laughter at war as an exploitation of 'relative painlessness' (*sine dolore*), I want to avoid two problems. One is the tendency to see comical scenes – such as Hotspur's and Falstaff's reflections on 'honour' in *1 Henry IV* or the gulling of Paroles in *All's Well That Ends Well* – as mere light-hearted and ideologically impotent 'comic relief'.[10] Second, I want to avoid conceiving of the comical scenes merely as 'undercutting' or subverting military ideals, as is often done in attempts to politicize laughter: the scenes as much *express* military ideals, to the extent that they encourage laughter at instances where the ideals are *de*formed. Ros King describes how Shakespeare's characters, including Paroles, apparently subvert ideals of conducting war espoused in William Garrard's *The Art of War* (1591): 'in all cases', claims King, 'Shakespeare comically undercuts the military ideal'.[11] Yet the question remains: on what basis can we decide whether Shakespeare is using Paroles to 'undercut' ideals or, rather, encouraging critical laughter at Paroles for failing to uphold them in the slightest? Both 'comic relief' and 'undercutting' are inadequate models for analysing how Shakespeare's laughter at war engages Christian philosophical debate about its demands and its horrors. Those models do not fully address the emotional and moral significance (and complexity) of what is attractive and repulsive about his literary individuals.

An alternative approach is needed. Crisscrossing Europe in the sixteenth century was a complex and interrelated set of discourses for discussing laughter and the laughable, spanning humanist and medical intellectual circles.[12] *De Ridiculis*, by the Italian philosopher Vincenzo Maggi (Vincentius Maddius c.1498–c.1564) is a suitable point of entry because it usefully brings together some of the key Aristotelian and Platonic concepts being relied on here.[13] Maggi first identifies Aristotle's idea that the laughable (*ridiculum*) is 'a certain fault or turpitude or deformity without pain (*sine dolore*)'.[14] The classic Aristotelian example is the comic mask: distorted but not in pain or causing pain.[15] However, Maggi moves immediately to note that it is with good reason that Aristotle added the phrase 'sine dolore': 'for if a person sees a face distorted from convulsion, they will not be moved to laughter but to pity, unless they are inhuman'.[16] There is a qualitative emotional difference between pity and laughter, to be sure, yet the difference (the relative pain or pleasurable distance) is located for Maggi in the relations between amused subject and laughable object. Laughter may begin where pain begins to stop but the one who laughs and the one who pities may yet be looking at the same face. What is horrible can be intimately related to what is, at another remove, laughable. This is particularly relevant to Shakespeare's laughter at war.

Another fundamentally important consideration is the centrality of laughable 'ignorance'. Maggi understands laughable 'turpitude' and 'deformity' – Latin terms derived from Cicero's glosses on Aristotle's comments in *Poetics* – in Platonic terms. He sees what is laughable as a kind of deviation from *natura*, from how things 'really' ought to be. For Maggi, turpitude may be of the body (*corporis*) or an external condition (*extrinsecus*). The more relevant category here, though, is turpitude or deformity of the mind (*animi*). To explain *turpitudo animi*, Maggi's Platonic cast of mind draws him to consider varieties of 'ignorance'. Maggi first notes Plato's interest in different kinds of ignorance in his dialogue *Sophist* and moves on to consider one particularly laughable kind. It occurs in a situation in which 'we know absolutely nothing about the thing we are ignorant of'.[17] That situation can be particularly funny when it is an ignorance 'of those things which are commonly known by others [*quae communiter ab aliis sciuntur*] and which are evident from their own natures'.[18] Maggi gives an example that might be found in many a Roman comedy: 'if some old guy really believes that it is not indeed his moneybag that the prostitute has fallen in love with'.[19] The exemplary senex's magnanimous delusions are a laughable failure of the Delphic injunction to know oneself and how things actually are.[20] Thus, for Maggi, what seems like wilful ignorance of what is commonly known and recognized very often raises a laugh.

One potentially laughable aspect of Martius Coriolanus's attitude to war and personal glory, for Shakespeare's Christian audience, is his complete ignorance of a Christian way of seeing war in relation to virtue. Of course, to begin here with *Coriolanus* is not to begin with a particularly funny play, in part precisely because its mimetic power is its capacity to create an early Roman world where such an Augustinian mode of self-understanding is obviously irrelevant. There is something akin to Coriolanus in Hotspur. Yet the scenes with Hotspur in act one scene three of *1 Henry IV* are much funnier than the foreignness of *Coriolanus*, partly perhaps because Hotspur's subjectivity is made to be located more clearly within a *quae communiter ab aliis sciuntur*, a what-is-commonly-understood-by-others.

In part, the tragic structure of *Coriolanus* revolves around the hero's ignorance of the delicacy and oratorical skill a patrician leader needs to keep the *civitas* together. That ignorance is connected with his virtually cartoonish commitment to military valour for the sake of his own renown. It is not just his career that is at stake. His hyperbolic personal valour displaces ordinary incentives for war, such as expansion and defence, by making them a secondary concern, and together with his deep ignorance of the political arts of civility, such a 'valour' eventually threatens the very survival of Rome. None of those developments are very funny.

However, one small scene changes into comic gear and does so without providing any 'relief'. In act one scene three, Volumnia (Martius's mother), Virgilia (his wife) and Valeria (another Roman lady) discuss Martius – before he comes home to be dubbed 'Coriolanus' – as well as Martius's and Virgilia's young son who has 'comically' shredded a butterfly after toying with it repeatedly.[21] I want to suggest that our sense that this is a comic scene – even if we do not find it very funny – is attributable to the fact that it is structured as a space *sine dolore*, through the prism of the boy, without losing for one moment its empathetic but critical focus on the broader culture of war in ancient Rome.

Even before the comic image of the boy emerges, Volumnia herself highlights the 'deformation' – from an early modern Christian point of view – of her own identity as mother, all in the pursuit of an honour stirred by 'renown' (1.3.11). It is almost but not quite disingenuous. Shakespeare is posing the question: is this deformation of 'natural' motherhood funny, disturbing, or something in between? Virgilia expresses a natural fear of her husband's death (1.3.18). Volumnia counters that fear by suggesting that in such a scenario she would simply remake her maternal feelings so as to be happy with the 'issue' of 'good report' in place of an actual son (1.3.20–21). Now perhaps in a kind of trance, Volumnia exults in a vivid image of her son destroying bodies 'Like to a harvest-man that's tasked to mow', wiping the blood off his brow as he goes (1.3.38). In response, Virgilia expresses her visceral disgust for the blood that signifies the cost of renown: the ruination of other people's bodies (1.3.40). Volumnia counters the emotional power of that blood-signification with a grotesque comparison between the 'loveliness' of the 'breasts of Hecuba / When she did suckle Hector' and 'Hector's forehead when it spit forth blood / At Grecian sword, contemning' (1.3.42–45). The comically absurd comparison underscores the discomfort one might feel towards Volumnia's economy of renown. It is not perhaps accidental that her apparent willingness to exchange one particular life-defining part of herself (a first-born son) for another (a 'good report') is precisely the kind of exchange that Shakespeare's Falstaff and his Paroles will not make.

The ladies' friend Valeria now comes on stage and their reflection on Martius continues with reference now to 'the father's son' (1.3.59). Valeria says she saw the boy:

> o' Wednesday ... run after a gilded butterfly, and when he caught it, he let it go again, and after it again, and over and over ... Or whether his fall engaged him, or how 'twas, he did so set his teeth and tear it! O, I warrant, how he mammocked it! (1.3.60–67)

Volumnia comments: 'one on's father's moods' (1.3.68). The image of the boy involves the same 'mood' of absorption and exultation in powerful violence as that of the father mowing down bodies. However, boy is associated with father even more specifically: through levels of 'ignorance', made comic in the image of the boy because of its lower stakes, and thus relative emotional distance. The association between boy and man is made not merely through their ignorance of (and contempt for) the suffering of other beings, butterflies or men. It is also an ignorance of the larger 'purpose' in violence that a Christian civilization – thinking in Augustinian terms – takes for granted. Coriolanus, and the boy who figures him more comically, have 'lost all human feeling', to use Augustine's words. The egotistical (and thus more broadly pointless) cruelty towards the butterfly renders (*sine dolore*) Coriolanus's own self-absorbed cruelty both to his country and ultimately to himself. Coriolanus's valour serves a 'renown' that he cannot even protect precisely because he is ignorant of the political arts of civility. That ignorance comes to a tragic and immensely moving end in the final confrontation scene of act five scene three. Volumnia finally persuades her son to desist from his attack on Rome partly by pointing out that his total self-absorption in personal valour, expressed as revenge, will actually bring about its own self-denial through a notoriety for having destroyed his own country. The scene is anything but funny, though its stakes are prefigured in the comic image of the boy who will grow up to be the same kind of threat. Intriguingly, Coriolanus, finally moved by his mother, immediately observes: 'the heavens do ope, / The gods look down, and this unnatural scene / They laugh at' (5.3.184–86). Of course, the gods have the benefit of further remove.

One might link Coriolanus's ignorance to the more laughable ignorance of Hotspur by means of an intriguing observation of Enobarbus in *Antony and Cleopatra*. At the end of act three, Enobarbus, fearing the many consequences of his master Antony's waning star, has decided to 'seek some way to leave him' (3.13.202–3). Enobarbus states his reason: 'I see still / A diminution in our captain's brain / Restores his heart' (3.13.199–201). By way of further explanation, he describes Antony's attitude to war such that it is characterized as just such a distortion of Augustine's Christian balance, a distortion which has been seen in Coriolanus and shall be in Hotspur: 'When valour preys on reason, / It eats the sword it fights with' (3.13.201–2). That is to say, valour can absorb a person to the point of ignoring the very understanding that would preserve it, which everyone else can see. Thus it rusts itself. Unaccountable valour deconstructs its own meaning. This is a failure of the Delphic injunction 'know thyself', a state of ignorance that might be rendered tragic, comical or tragi-comical, depending on the pain it causes.

Hotspur is a case in point. As Roberta Barker has shown, he has been read as tragic hero and comical fool, and can be read as both simultaneously.[22] In a much discussed scene of *1 Henry IV*, act one scene three, Hotspur, angry at having to give up his prisoners to King Henry, incoherently expresses both his rage at Henry's former courtesy now turned to cold regality and his fantasies about leaping 'To pluck bright honour from the pale-faced moon' (1.3.200) or diving to the bottom of the sea to 'pluck up drownèd honour by the locks' (1.3.203). His overblown apprehensions are the more funny because they are spoken in clear ignorance of the fact that his uncle and father are patiently waiting to discuss 'matter deep and dangerous' (1.3.188), things which will actually answer to the younger man's perturbations. Alexander Leggatt points out the absurdity of Hotspur's unconscious self-criticism in these lines, for 'an honour that has to be fetched from the moon or the depths of the sea is an honour that is lost'.[23] Audiences have also no doubt laughed for centuries at Hotspur's puerile fantasy of tormenting King Henry – vexed already with Mortimer's claim to the throne – by yelling 'Mortimer!' (1.3.221) in the sleeping king's ear or by teaching a starling to speak nothing but that name 'To keep his anger still in motion' (1.3.224). These are what Vincenzo Maggi would have called 'laughable deformities' of the norms of the adult male sapiens.

However, there are levels of ignorance, too, that should be added. It is not just that Shakespeare's Hotspur (so far as he is comical) ignores his father and his uncle or that he embodies an ignorance of the outdatedness of chivalric honour codes. It is also that he ignores (in so far as he is both comical and tragical) the 'form of what he should attend' (1.3.208), which is the fact that if he is going to survive politically, and establish the honour he desires, he must attend to the kind of policy that his uncle Worcester is trying to propose. This is a comical ignorance of *quae communiter ab aliis sciuntur*, a what-is-commonly-understood-by-others, glimpsed tellingly in his speedy and narrow gloss on Worcester's machinations as a 'noble plot' (1.3.273).

While Shakespeare makes something of the same ignorance a part of Hotspur's downfall in the later acts of the play, it remains comic here because of the framing that renders it *sine dolore*. Later on, Hotspur's self-declared inability to 'flatter' and his defiance of 'the tongues of soothers' (4.1.6–7) means that he cannot distinguish when to use those arts and when to use the force of arms. His enthusiasm for the self-definition offered by the use of arms emerges in his reading of his father's absence as a 'lustre' (4.1.77) to be derived rather than the military disadvantage that most others see. The myopia is underscored later by Vernon (4.3.20). At this level, he is comparable with Coriolanus. However, act one scene three remains on the comic side of the spectrum because of the safety built into it. Although Hotspur is, as his father puts it, 'drunk with choler' (1.3.127), there is no real fear that he will 'hazard' (1.3.126) his head by going after the king to refuse the return of the demanded prisoners. In addition, responding to Hotspur's assurance that his rant is over, 'I have done' (1.3.252), Worcester's bemused mockery – 'Nay, if you have not, to't again. / We'll stay your leisure' (1.3.253–54) – signals that the scene is moving towards an expense of spirit rather than any climactic (and dangerous) confrontation. And yet it is the same 'deformity'.

E. M. W. Tillyard influentially characterized Hotspur as 'honour exaggerated', an 'excess' of 'military spirit', contrasting him with Falstaff's military 'defect', 'dishonour'.[24] However, Falstaff's famous reflection on 'honour' – 'Can honour set to a leg? No. Or an arm? No. Or take away the grief of a wound? No. Honour hath no skill in surgery, then? No. What is honour? A word ... Therefore, I'll none of it. Honour is a mere scutcheon. And so ends my catechism' (5.1.131–40) – is often regarded sympathetically as a part of Shakespeare's questioning of chivalry and the honour code rather than as a comic distortion that expresses its ideals. As Franziska Quabeck notes, the sympathy is plausible partly because 'Falstaff rises after Hal's exit and triumphs over the dead honourable knight [Hotspur]' and so his parodic 'catechism on the uselessness of honour seems to be confirmed as the more reasonable approach'.[25] Furthermore, his disreputable behaviour as a warrior – not only by misusing 'the King's press damnably' (4.2.13) but also by stabbing an already dead Hotspur in the leg (5.4.126–27) – seems to be a part of Shakespeare's questioning of the honour code Hotspur stands for; it has been overtaken by a living embodiment of the refusal to condone its meanings and priorities. Quabeck suggests that what is going on here is that if Shakespeare is expressing 'disillusionment with chivalry' as James Shapiro and Thomas Merriam have debated, he is not, however, therefore disillusioned with 'just conduct' in war.[26] Military values tied up with *jus in bello* (right conduct in war) have not in some simple way been 'undercut'.

There are a range of laughable deformities displayed in the honour speech that might have amused audiences across the centuries about Falstaff and his 'catechism'. These, too, are structured in a way that keeps audiences a step or two from pain, from *dolore*. Falstaff deforms, laughably, the virtue of bravery in a Christian kingdom by rationalizing his own cowardice in a manner that parodies not only a 'catechism' but perhaps also a scene from book XI of the *Iliad* in which Odysseus convinces himself successfully to stand firm on the side of honour against the impulse to survive, as Steven Doloff has suggested.[27] Christopher McDonough has argued that Falstaff's reference to honour as 'a mere scutcheon' – actually a piece of 'armament' itself and not just a 'decorative device' – situates him 'squarely in the classical motif of the *rhipsaspis* or "shield-tosser"', a pathetic, if empathetic, scenario in which the soldier gives in to 'the instinct for self-preservation' despite its shame.[28] Much of the 'honour speech' is funny – to the extent that an audience wishes to see Falstaff in terms of such laughable 'deformity' – because it is *sine dolore*: Falstaff's equivocations are only a moderate threat to his captain's enterprise. Indeed, Shakespeare does not position the outcome of the battle by making it a result of who has the right kind of honour. Hal simply beats Hotspur. Hal's political acumen does not help him, nor does Hotspur's exulted selfhood, when arm meets arm. The battle itself seems less about who has the *winning* attitude to war and more about what the right attitude to war itself should be.

Rather than decide who of Hotspur and Falstaff is the more disreputed (and disreputable) or who is the more human character and who the more comic, I wish to pose them as 'contraries' of a particular kind, contraries that deepen Shakespeare's laughter at war.[29] Whereas Tillyard's purpose in contrasting Hotspur and Falstaff as comic distortions was to bring out Prince Hal as the real hero of military virtue – an Aristotelian 'middle quality between two extremes' – my purpose is to show how the ideal Christian ethical balance in a soldier's attitude to war emerges in their midst, rather than simply Hal as a specific embodiment of balance.[30] It is a middle ground distanced from both extremes of exultation and dishonour, yet is constituted in the reciprocity of their laughability, making them 'contraries' of a unique kind.

It is not the 'contrariety' that Robert Weimann and Douglas Bruster link with clowning, where a clown embodies the heterogeneity especially of author's pen embodied in actor's voice.[31]

Weimann and Bruster refer to the 'discourse of the contrarious' in the period as they develop their account of clowning, in which contrariety on stage is seen as a sort of 'transport' between author and actor.[32] In making that claim, they quote from Sidney's *Apology for Poetry*, especially his understanding of the contrariety between 'laughter' and 'delight'.[33] Weimann and Bruster see in this Sidnean difference the contrariety they theorize in the 'transport' between clowning's embodied unpredictability and author's written word. That is to say, unscripted 'laughter' threatens with unpredictability – they read Sidney as saying – the proper bounds of decorous comedy, which ought to produce 'delight'. That may be so. However, Sidney goes on immediately to explain the difference between the two emotional responses, of delight and laughter, in a way that introduces another kind of contrariety relevant to this discussion. Sidney says: 'for delight we scarcely do but in things that have a conveniency to ourselves or the general nature; laughter almost ever cometh of things disproportioned to ourselves and nature'.[34] To laugh at something, Sidney suggests, is to respond to something contrary, or disproportioned, to one's own ideals. To delight in something is rather the opposite.

Though Sidney keeps those orientations, laughter and delight, fundamentally separate, he inadvertently gives us a means of thinking about the contrariness of Hotspur and Falstaff, in relation to Augustine's conception of a properly balanced approach to Christian war. At one level, Shakespeare has made Hotspur and Falstaff contraries because each is a laughable deformity of one particular side of the Christian balance, Hotspur of too much military exultation, and Falstaff of cowardice and self-regard. However, a further aspect must be observed. In each of the two characters, what the Christian military subject of Shakespeare's audience may laugh at as being 'disproportioned' to himself and 'nature' is an expression of the same perspective that lends a delighting 'conveniency' to the other character – using Sidney's terms. In other words, what is laughably deformed about Falstaff is informed by the humanity and virtuous nobility of Hotspur. Likewise, what is laughably deformed about Hotspur is informed by the humanity and critical acumen of Falstaff. Each one's particular insight into the ideal Augustinian-Christian balance is an insight directly linked to the laughable deformity of the other. Laughter at and delight in these characters cross over rather than just coincide. The clever balance of repulsion and attraction in effect forges a middle space. Shakespeare invites laughter in both directions so as to create a middle ground that resonates with a balanced Christian view of war as necessary but thoroughly repulsive, and thus tragic. Shakespeare's laughter at war engages a Christian philosophy of war, not just particular 'values' of chivalry, honour, bravery, et cetera.

In *All's Well That Ends Well*, Shakespeare refigures that crisscrossing laughter at-and-with Hotspur-Falstaff, with their contrary military failures. This happens via his clever pairing of Bertram and Paroles, in the interlinked scenes of acts three and four. Through that pairing, Shakespeare makes Bertram himself the point of focus for considering the ideal Augustinian middle ground. Helen Wilcox has pointed out that integral to the play's 'tragi-comedy of war' is the fact that Shakespeare 'leaves us unsure of the grounds' for its particular conflict; the effect is that the ideals of 'soldierly honour' 'are firmly cast in the past'.[35] For Wilcox, Shakespeare makes an 'unflinching mockery' of the 'whole world of war' in the play, a mockery heavily dependent on the interpenetrating 'languages of war and sexual desire'.[36] In this play, laughter at Paroles and his failure to uphold military ideals is interlinked with Bertram in a different manner from that we have seen, for Bertram is not a Hotspur in the same way that Paroles is like to Falstaff. Bertram's shocked laughter at Paroles becomes a potential agent in his own self-realization, in so far as it invites him towards a more balanced approach to war via the legitimate claims of the social.

The pairing of Bertram and Paroles is central to that dynamic. As Robert Miola has shown convincingly, the two are 'moral identical twins', two sides of the same coin not least because they split the Roman *miles gloriosus* (braggart soldier) figure into two halves: Bertram embodies his 'amorous pretensions' while Paroles does his 'military' ones.[37] There are many other parallels spanning the two characters and the ordeals they face in the play. Most obviously, Shakespeare interlinks the scenes in which Bertram is caught by Helen's bed trick and Paroles is caught by Bertram's men. The 'smoking' (shaming and exposure) of Paroles prefigures that of Bertram in the play's final act.[38] Also, at the beginning of act four scene three, with the plot to expose Paroles in place, the first and second Lords Dumaine discuss the despicable behaviour of Bertram while they wait for him to return in order to follow through with the plot against Paroles. First they make abstract observations about human imperfection and ignorance with Bertram in mind. The second lord, for instance, says that we are 'merely our own traitors' and, with reference to Bertram, that 'he contrives against his own nobility' (4.3.22, 25–26). A few lines down, the first lord wishes explicitly that in the gulling to come, Bertram 'might take a measure of his own judgments' (4.3.34), to which the second lord responds with: 'We will not meddle with him till he come, for his presence must be the whip of the other' (4.3.36–38). If the proliferation of ambiguous pronouns here is deliberate, the effect is to jam the references to Bertram and Paroles together and emphasize the mutuality of the coming comedy that will 'meddle' and 'whip'.

The pairing clearly associates the comic shaming of Paroles with the (possibly comic) shaming of Bertram. Miola suggests that the 'daring strategy' of making 'a comic butt' into a 'romantic lead is not without risks, as the history of dissatisfaction with Bertram for failing to be a Romeo ... shows'.[39] Yet Paroles' laughable faults are clear enough. Under pressure, he wilfully ignores his 'friends', such as they are – though, of course, this is the sort of conflict in which, as the French king says, the young men 'freely ... have leave / To stand on either part' (1.2.14–15). Like Falstaff, Paroles is also obviously a coward. In accordance with an ideal 'Drumme' – a vulnerable military position involving the use of a drum to communicate commands and good linguistic skills to parley with the enemy side – Paroles 'has a smack of all neighbouring languages' (4.1.16).[40] Yet, contrary to the Drum's responsibility not to 'bewray any secrets known' if caught by the enemy, Paroles is immediately willing to use any of the languages he knows to do just that once he believes he is caught (4.1.72–74).[41] At the same time, though, and again like Falstaff, he is in tune with a certain kind of realism that the exultation of war, in its turn, ignores: 'Simply the thing I am / Shall make me live' (4.3.334–35). Just like the fat knight, this gives him an attraction parallel to his laughable deformity.

Bertram's ignorance of Paroles and, by extension, of himself is the primary structure through which Paroles' comic shaming is made to reflect back on Bertram. In both cases, what is ridiculous about them is structured cleverly within *quae communiter ab aliis sciuntur*, what-is-commonly-understood-by-others. As Bertram's fog of ignorance about Paroles clears, so begins the slower clearing of his foggy relationships with others. Accordingly, his manner of referring to Paroles softens slightly from 'What a past-saving slave is this!' (4.3.143) to 'I could endure anything before but a cat, and now he's a cat to me' (4.3.242–43). The reflexivity of 'he's a cat to me' is also a step along from the earlier confidence of 'He can say nothing of me' (4.3.119–20), and recalls the lord Dumaine's comment mentioned before (4.3.36–38) about the one half of Bertram-Paroles whipping the other. Bertram recognizes in Paroles a laughable ignorance of the underpinning responsibilities of the social bonds, which construct Paroles' identity. As that happens, Bertram himself is presented with the possibility of seeing – through his laughter at Paroles' distasteful ignorance and military infidelity – his own infidelity in love and his own ignorance of the possibilities created by familial and social bonds. The semantic duality of 'honour' in reference to sex and war here is key. Bertram's mother wants him to be informed that 'his sword can never win / The honour that he loses' (3.2.95–96). Miola describes the link clearly: 'The word "honour" suggests the military standard Bertram upholds and the amorous one he violates, unmarking and marking him as a comic butt like Paroles'.[42] This is precisely why 'the love of war and the war of love' that Wilcox documents 'are interlinked in the play'.[43] Military ignorance figures amatory ignorance and thus one kind of laughable ignorance (Paroles) is meant to illuminate and expose the other (Bertram). Whether or not illumination actually happens – one can play Bertram in different ways after all – the invitation for Bertram to see himself anew, through the prism of Paroles' laughability, is there. It is an invitation to see the relationship between his military and his erotic selfhood in a more balanced relationship with claims of family and society, which underpin who he is. To see himself in that way would be to step outside the very ignorance that links him with Coriolanus as a distortion of the Augustinian approach to war.

Looking, with a laugh, *at* the prism of Paroles' deformed ignorance is plausibly much funnier to Bertram than looking through that prism to glimpse himself. This is because the former vision is relatively *sine dolore*. In the final act, the emotional distance of laughing at Paroles falls away and Bertram is forced even further by others to confront his own uncomfortable reality. Just as Shakespeare links laughter at Paroles with an invitation to Bertram to balance out the meaning of his own military selfhood, so he invites the Christian subject within his audiences towards a balanced view of war.

I have argued that Shakespeare's laughter at war evokes and responds to the difficulty faced by Christian societies that must at the same time engage in war – and keep men on the field – without eating the 'swords' they fight with by culturally endorsing military exultation. The laughter at Coriolanus, the laughter in-between Hotspur and Falstaff, and the laughter of Bertram at Paroles each generate and work (rhetorically) to intensify the desire for balance proposed by Augustine. They normalize balance and intensify desire for it by means of the interlocking forces arranged between the characters of laughing at, laughing with and, perhaps, laughing *from*.

Shakespeare's means of doing this involves different modes of constructing a laughter of 'relative painlessness', distanced from the painful and tragic reality of war, though in no way the less focused on its imbalances for being *sine dolore*. Shakespeare maintains a *relative* painlessness in his laughter at war in several ways. He displaces pain at shredded human bodies by refocusing, for instance, on the image of mammocked butterflies instead, and yet he keeps laughter on the verge of pain by focusing, too, on laughable ignorance that is sometimes close to military consequence (Falstaff misusing the king's press) and sometimes less so (Paroles losing the drum).

Furthermore, a laughter of relative painlessness in the context of war also implicitly frames itself within the larger consolations of Augustinian theology. The ending of the 'comedy' *All's Well That Ends Well* is unsatisfactory perhaps precisely because it leaves us merely with hope, rather than assurance, that harmony, forgiveness and expanded vision will follow on from the uncomfortable confrontation. Augustine finishes *De Civitas Dei* with just the same inarticulate hope for *comoedia divina*. Writing 'Of the eternal felicity of the City of God', in which 'there will be no evil' and 'no good thing will be lacking', he admits 'I cannot even imagine it'; though of course he is without any doubt that it will come.[44] This is a thirst for the transformation of the cosmos, away from the sound and fury of perpetual war, that tale told by idiots, away from the tragic signification of nothing and towards the ending of a comedy, in which 'we will neither cease from work through idleness nor be driven to it by need'.[45] Shakespeare's laughter at war, as it looks backward, is like Hamlet's jesting with death in the graveyard, a jesting without which we human beings could not 'face the truth of our absurdity'.[46] His laughter within war, as it looks forward with theological vision, is like to the desire for a good 'end' to the comedy.

Daniel Derrin teaches at the Department of English Studies at Durham University. He has been a Junior Research Fellow and Teaching Fellow at Durham University, an S. Ernest Sprott Fellow at the University of Melbourne, as well as an Associate Investigator with the Australian Research Council Centre of Excellence for the History of Emotions 1100–1800. His publications have focused on Shakespeare, Francis Bacon and John Donne. He is now working on two books on the topic of early modern humour.

Notes

1. For a discussion of the range and influence, see Paola Pugliatti, *Shakespeare and the Just War Tradition* (Farnham: Ashgate, 2010), 9–52.
2. For the commandment, see Exodus 20:13 and Deuteronomy 5:17; see also Augustine, *The City of God against the Pagans*, ed. R. W. Dyson (Cambridge: Cambridge University Press, 1998), 1.21.
3. Augustine, *City of God*, 19.7.
4. Ibid.
5. Quoted in Pugliatti, *Just War*, 15.
6. I shall say more about the Aristotelian approach further on. For Freud's approach, see Sigmund Freud, *The Joke and Its Relation to the Unconscious*, trans. Joyce Crick (London: Penguin, 2002); and for discussion of the ideas therein, John Morreall, *Taking Laughter Seriously* (Albany, NY: State University of New York Press, 1983), 27–37.
7. A prominent example features in the treatise *De Ridiculis* by Vincenzo Maggi (Maddius), to which I shall return. The treatise was published in the volume: Vincenzo Maggi and Bartolomeo Lombardi, *In Aristotelis Librum de poetica communes explanationes* (Venice, 1550).
8. Henri Bergson, *Laughter: An Essay on the Meaning of the Comic*, trans. Cloudesley Brereton and Fred Rothwell (New York: Macmillan, 1921), 4–5.
9. John Morreall, 'The Comic Vision of Life', *British Journal of Aesthetics* 54, no. 2 (2014): 125–40, here 127.
10. A useful discussion of comic relief as a neoclassical 'chimera' may be found in Robert Hornback, *The English Clown Tradition from the Middle Ages to Shakespeare* (Cambridge: D. S. Brewer, 2009), 12–13.
11. Ros King, '"The Disciplines of War": Elizabethan War Manuals and Shakespeare's Tragicomic Vision', in *Shakespeare and War*, ed. Ros King and Paul J. C. M. Franssen (New York: Palgrave Macmillan, 2008), 15–29, here 16.
12. For a sense of the richness, see Daniel Ménager, *La renaissance et le rire* (Paris: Presses Universitaires de France, 1995), as well as Quentin Skinner, 'Hobbes and the Classical Theory of Laughter', in *Leviathan after 350 Years*, ed. Tom Sorell and Luc Foisneau (Oxford: Oxford University Press, 2004), 139–66.
13. The treatise was positioned in the middle of Maggi and Lombardi's co-publication *In Aristotelis Librum de poetica communes explanationes* (Venice, 1550). The book appeared in the context of a spate of new commentaries on and editions of

Aristotle's *Poetics* across the first half of the sixteenth century: see Bernard Weinberg, *A History of Literary Criticism in the Italian Renaissance*, 2 vols. (Chicago, IL: University of Chicago Press, 1961), vol. 1, 349–423.

14. '*Ridiculum igitur peccatum et turpitudinem ac deformitatem quondam esse sine dolore*' (302).

15. The relevant comments may be found in Aristotle, *Poetics*, ed. and trans. Stephen Halliwell, Loeb Classical Library (1995; Rpt. Cambridge, MA: Harvard University Press, 1999), chapter V (1449a). Aristotle's word, translated by Latin-speaking scholars as '*sine dolore*', or sometimes '*absque dolore*' was '*anôdunon*'.

16. '*Nam si quis faciem ex convulsione distortam viderit, non ad risum, sed ad misericordiam (nisi prorsus inhumanus sit) commovebitur*' (302).

17. '*cum de re quam ignoramus nihil omnino scimus*' (304).

18. '*de iis quae communiter ab aliis sciuntur et quae natura sua sunt evidentes*' (304).

19. '*ut si quis senex ... non autem suam crumenam ab aliqua meretrice adamari crederet*' (304).

20. Plato himself links laughable ignorance to failures with respect to the Delphic injunction in *Philebus*, trans. J. C. B. Gosling (Oxford: Clarendon Press, 1975), 47–50 (48c–50b).

21. References to Shakespeare's plays are to the scenes and line numbers of the Oxford Shakespeare: William Shakespeare, *The Complete Works*, 2nd edition, ed. Stanley Wells and Gary Taylor (Oxford: Clarendon Press, 2005).

22. Roberta Barker, 'Tragical-Comical-Historical Hotspur', *Shakespeare Quarterly* 54, no. 3 (2003): 288–307.

23. Alexander Leggatt, *Shakespeare's Political Drama: The History Plays and the Roman Plays* (London: Routledge, 1988), 85.

24. E. M. W. Tillyard, *Shakespeare's History Plays* (1944; rpt. London: Chatto and Windus, 1948), 265.

25. Franziska Quabeck, *Just and Unjust Wars in Shakespeare* (Berlin: De Gruyter, 2013), 213.

26. See James Shapiro, *1599: A Year in the Life of William Shakespeare* (London: Faber and Faber, 2006), as well as Thomas Merriam, 'Shakespeare's Supposed Disillusionment with Chivalry in 1599', *Notes and Queries* 54, no. 252 (2007): 285–87.

27. Steven Doloff, 'Falstaff's "Honour": Homeric Burlesque in *1 Henry IV* (1597–8)', *Notes and Queries* 55, no. 2 (2008): 177–81.

28. A *rhipsaspis* is a soldier who has left his shield on the field because it is heavy and impedes flight. See Christopher M. McDonough, '"A Mere Scutcheon": Falstaff as *Rhipsaspis*', *Notes and Queries* 55, no. 2 (2008): 181–83.

29. Quabeck, *Just and Unjust Wars*, 211, points to the 'humanity' that Shakespeare gives to Hotspur, in spite of Hal's jokes about the 'Hotspur of the North' (2.5.103), which lends him part of his tragic pathos.

30. Tillyard, *Shakespeare's History Plays*, 265.

31. See Robert Weimann and Douglas Bruster, *Shakespeare and the Power of Performance: Stage and Page in the Elizabethan Theatre* (Cambridge: Cambridge University Press, 2008).

32. Ibid., 29.

33. Ibid., 29–30. See Philip Sidney, *An Apology for Poetry, or the Defense of Poesy*, ed. Geoffrey Shepherd, rev. R. W. Maslen (Manchester: Manchester University Press, 2002), 112.

34. Sidney, *Apology*, 112.
35. Helen Wilcox, 'Drums and Roses? The Tragicomedy of War in *All's Well That Ends Well*', in King and Franssen, *Shakespeare and War*, 84–95, here 86.
36. Ibid., 88–89.
37. See Robert S. Miola, *Shakespeare and Classical Comedy* (Oxford: Clarendon Press, 1994), 122, 130.
38. For a useful discussion, see ibid., 129–31.
39. Ibid., 135.
40. See the discussion of Paroles as a 'Drum' in Nick de Somogyi, *Shakespeare's Theatre of War* (Aldershot: Ashgate, 1998), 179–83.
41. Giles Clayton, *The Approoved Order of Martiall Discipline* (1591), 17, quoted in Somogyi, *Shakespeare's Theatre of War*, 180.
42. Miola, *Shakespeare and Classical Comedy*, 130.
43. Wilcox, 'Drums and Roses?', 89.
44. Augustine, *City of God*, 22.30.
45. Ibid.
46. Indira Ghose, 'Jesting with Death: Hamlet in the Graveyard', *Textual Practice* 24, no. 6 (2010): 1003–18, here 1012.

Chapter 5
The Better Part of Stolen Valour
Counterfeits, Comedy and the Supreme Court

David Currell

> Elizabethan soldiers *were* proud people in a country that was proud
> of them, but they were also physically and emotionally scarred
> people in a country that exploited them, disparaged them, and
> grumbled at having to maintain them.
> Indeed, nothing about war changes much.
> —Adam McKeown, *English Mercuries*

Adam McKeown's *English Mercuries* treats the literature by and of early modern English veterans, framing this literature as powerfully illuminating veteran experiences in the contemporary United States.[1] I aim to use the same historical juxtaposition to reflect upon the relationship between military service and martial storytelling, but where McKeown has an eye on deep truths, I am interested in shallow lies. A lie could create the obverse of McKeown's devalued veteran: an impostor who misappropriates the honour due to the valorous by counterfeiting a military identity. Counterfeit soldiers

---

Notes for this section begin on page 114.

raise social questions that are also inherently literary questions. The phenomenon turns on fiction-making, and these fictions in turn rely on the deep mutual implication of the codes of honour which condition public life in militarist societies and the generic codes which give literary currency to the true and counterfeit coins. Honour's at the stake – and the state takes an interest.

'The better part of valour is discretion', says Falstaff after resurrecting himself from a counterfeited death, just before the shock of seeing the genuinely dead Hotspur.[2] David Scott Kastan notes that here '*part* means "quality" not "portion"' and this gloss appropriately conveys Falstaff's valuing of good judgement in a living body above good repute in an inanimate one. Yet the abjured quantitative sense (i.e. 'a majority of [a reputation for] valour rests on judicious self-preservation') is not entirely beyond Falstaff's, or the play's, connotative scope. This scene ends with Hal undertaking to connive in Falstaff's false boast, permitting him to appropriate the 'grace' due to Hal himself for killing Hotspur (5.4.157–58). Shakespeare's extraordinary reimagining of the *miles gloriosus* (braggart soldier) archetype shares the last laugh. Falstaff's 'discretion' helps him to a reputation for valour, constituting, in the circumstances, not merely its 'better part' but its entirety. Honour and valour are qualities that persistently raise such quantitative issues: can the general fund of honour grow and shrink, or does it obey a kind of conservation law? Should we conceive of the apportionment, circulation and exchange of honour on some economic model? If honour circulates, can it therefore be misappropriated, or even 'stolen'? Falstaff's career will prove an important touchstone in discussing how honour intersects with truth and falsehood, imposture and reality, civilian and military life – and how the buck stops with the Chief Justice.

This nexus of questions came into play during a recent legal episode in the United States that grew from an effort to bring the legal code closer to the spirit of *2 Henry IV* than *1 Henry IV*.[3] The Stolen Valor Act of 2005 (Pub. L. 109-437, 120 Stat. 3266–67) criminalized falsely claiming to have been awarded US military honours, with enhanced penalties for specific high honours, such as the Congressional Medal of Honor.[4] Xavier Alvarez was indicted under this law for falsely claiming, at a 2007 meeting of the Three Valley Water District Board in Claremont, California, to be a veteran of the United States Marine Corps and to have received the Congressional Medal. Alvarez's challenge to the constitutionality of the law was rejected by a District Court but upheld by the Court of Appeals. The case ultimately reached the Supreme Court, which, in *United States v. Alvarez* (132 S. Ct. 2537), struck down the Act on First Amendment grounds by a vote of 6-3 on 28 June 2012. Three opinions were published: the majority opinion, authored by Justice Anthony Kennedy joined by three other Justices (Ruth Bader Ginsberg, John Roberts and Sonia Sotomayor); Justice Stephen Breyer's concurring opinion, joined by Justice Elena Kagan; and a dissent by Justice Samuel Alito, joined by Justices Antonin Scalia and Clarence Thomas.[5] The texts of these opinions conveniently condense the chief points in briefs and oral argument presented by the government, respondent and *amici curiae*, and constitute a rare and illuminating public assessment of the social and legal doctrines hedging the value placed on the marks of honour accorded to acts of valour by the United States. The immediate context is judicial, but the occasion also evokes an engagement by the Justices with contemporary and historical military and political culture.[6]

I have so far used the related words *valour* and *honour* without explicit distinction or definition. This is true also of the Stolen Valor Act. Falstaff, whose 'catechism' on honour is almost as famous as his proverb on valour, can help:

> What is honour? A word. What is in that word 'honour'? What is that 'honour'? Air. A trim reckoning. Who hath it? He that died o'Wednesday. Doth he feel it? No. Doth he hear it? No. 'Tis insensible then? Yea, to the dead. But will it not live with the living? No. Why? Detraction will not suffer it. Therefore I'll none of it. Honour is a mere scutcheon. (5.1.133–40)

We'll return to some of Falstaff's later questions, but it would be well to start at the beginning: what is honour?

Falstaff's first answer suits a critical excavation: a word. Both as noun and verb, *honour* carries multiple valences, but an initial scheme might show the nominal and verbal forms of the word creating a kind of circuit: honour is an attribute or possession, and what makes a claim to possess it legitimate and credible are the actions of the community to recognize this attribute.[7] Another sense of 'honour' is created by a sort of abstraction from this social situation: the proper functioning of a dynamic of possession and respect itself constitutes the 'honour' of the community as a whole. These senses are collocated within a passage in which Justice Kennedy endorses the historical rationale of the Congressional Medal of Honor:

It is right and proper that Congress, over a century ago, established an award so the Nation can hold in its highest respect and esteem those who, in the course of carrying out the 'supreme and noble duty of contributing to the defense of the rights and *honor* of the nation', *Selective Draft Law Cases*, 245 U.S. 366, 390 (1918), have acted with extraordinary *honor*. And it should be uncontested that this is a legitimate Government objective, indeed a most valued national aspiration and purpose. This does not end the inquiry, however. Fundamental constitutional principles require that laws enacted to *honor* the brave must be consistent with the precepts of the Constitution for which they fought. (2–3; emphases added)

The passage stresses mutuality and circulation: the Medal of Honor (honour *qua* military decoration) is properly awarded 'to honor' (*qua* social performance) those who have displayed 'extraordinary honor' (*qua* personal attribute). At once preceding and reconstituted by this very process is the state interest, the 'honor of the nation'.

This national dimension is in significant ways an early modern legacy, although the classical models of honour reactivated and scrutinized in early modern texts stressed the striving, achievement and recognition of (aristocratic) individuals, whose economistic concept of honour took it as a scarce, finite resource to be won from competitors and recognized by the community through the external signifiers of possessions and privileges. Homeric epic is an indispensable guide to these codes; paradigmatic to humanist social and literary codes (albeit often via moralization or imitation), the poems establish a complex lexicon distinguishing various senses of 'valour' and 'honour'.[8] 'Valour' is used by Richmond Lattimore and many other anglophone translators for Homeric *alkē* (often in the formula *thouridos alkēs* [furious valour]), but it is also a frequent choice for *aretē*, a word encompassing the set of excellences idealized in the Homeric hero.[9] By the exercise of *aretē* in agonistic competition on the battlefield or in athletics, Homeric warriors accrue *timē* (honour) or *geras* (portion of honour – also an occasional translator's choice for *timē*). What one hero gains comes at another's expense and cannot be shared without division (and, therefore, arithmetic diminishment). The plot of the *Iliad* centres on Achilles' perceived loss of *timē* at the hands of Agamemnon, who takes from him the slave Briseis, part of an earlier distribution of spoils (proportional to the *aretē* of the participants in the raid by which she was enslaved) against the rules of what is understood by Achilles as a zero-sum game. What is ultimately at stake for the Homeric hero is *kleos* –

'fame', but more specifically the species of fame obtainable by celebration in epic poetry. Behind the Iliadic narrative of 'stolen *timē*' lies an ideology of 'stolen valour'. Community recognition, in the form of both material and immaterial rewards, must accurately reflect military accomplishments. The moral of the *Iliad* is that the disturbance of this equation by Agamemnon's force destroys the incentive for heroic action. The moral burden of the government's case in *Alvarez* is that the disturbance of this equation by fraud is equally destructive.

In *1 Henry IV*, Hotspur is the spokesperson of this mentality.[10] Incensed by the king's withholding of his prisoners, Hotspur promises Northumberland and Worcester that 'Yet time serves wherein you may redeem / Your banished honours and restore yourselves / Into the good thoughts of the world again' (1.3.179–81), preliminary to the following avowal of honour as scarce, emulous and exclusive:

> By heaven, methinks it were an easy leap
> To pluck bright honour from the pale-faced moon,
> Or dive into the bottom of the deep,
> Where fathom-line could never touch the ground,
> And pluck up drowned honour by the locks,
> So he that doth redeem her thence might wear,
> Without corrival, all her dignities. (200–206)[11]

The expression 'time ... may redeem' (179) and the repetition of 'redeem' at 205 echo Prince Hal's soliloquy on 'redeeming time' (1.2.207), and when they ultimately encounter on the battlefield at Shrewsbury, Hal joins Hotspur in espousing the value of an honour that can brook no 'corrival':

HOTSPUR	My name is Harry Percy.
PRINCE	Why then, I see
	A very valiant rebel of the name.
	I am the Prince of Wales, and think not, Percy,
	To share with me in glory any more.
	Two stars keep not their motion in one sphere,
	Nor can one England brook a double reign
	Of Harry Percy and the Prince of Wales.
HOTSPUR	Nor shall it, Harry, for the hour is come
	To end the one of us, and would to God
	Thy name in arms were now as great as mine.
PRINCE	I'll make it greater ere I part from thee,
	And all the budding honours on thy crest
	I'll crop to make a garland for my head. (5.4.60–72)

The long arc of Hal's eclipse of Hotspur and rejection of Falstaff partly involves an appropriation of the former's code of honour. But Shakespeare represents this appropriation as undertaken on behalf of a patriotic-nationalist rather than an aristocratic-individualist ideology. The nationalist perspective informs the night thoughts that Hal (now Henry V) shares on the emptiness to him personally of 'general ceremony'.[12] Publicly the next morning, of course, he tells a different, Homeric story: 'The fewer men, the greater share of honour' (4.3.22) – but this is rhetoric to repurpose the code towards a nationalist end. For Henry, as for the Supreme Court, activating or retaining the nation's investment in honour – a mechanism that classically functioned without the active participation of a general populace – has become a crucial political prerogative in the face of sceptics like Michael Williams.

The special problem of the Stolen Valor Act is protecting against counterfeiters the value of honour as 'social capital' in which a nation at war is expected to invest. The Act was defended on the basis that persons such as Xavier Alvarez, publicly lying about having received the Congressional Medal of Honor in 'a pathetic attempt to gain respect that eluded him' (Kennedy 1), threatened the entire system and even threatened to deplete the common stock of honour held, by a sort of double-entry accounting, simultaneously by the nation as a whole and by a tiny heroic elite. All three opinions in *United States v. Alvarez* recognize a danger of honour suffering 'dilution' (Breyer 7–8). In the dissenting opinion, this proposition is taken to a seemingly extraordinary conclusion: 'the proliferation of false claims about military awards blurs the signal given out by the actual awards by making them seem more common than they really are, and this diluting effect harms the military by hampering its efforts to foster morale and esprit de corps' (Alito 6). That an impression of heroism as more common or more commonly rewarded within the armed forces than is truly the case should injure morale appears thoroughly counter-intuitive, until read from the perspective of a Hotspur aspiring to a precious honour as far beyond mortal grasp as the moon or the ocean floor.

A philosopher of scarcity, Justice Alito is exercised by a potential *inflation* of honours. This was the rubric under which Laurence Stone analysed patterns of ennoblement from 1558 to 1641, the period of the extraordinary Elizabethan shortage and the equally extraordinary (and partly reactive) Jacobean glut in aristocratic creations.[13] The political challenge posed to Elizabeth's parsimonious monopoly in the granting of such honours by Essex's systematic practice of knighting his soldiers on the field is a part of the story well known to historians and Shakespeareans (these are the 'Empress' and 'General', of course, of *Henry V* 5.0.30). Especially interesting to us, however, is Stone's recounting of an example of how public humiliation was mandated to punish forty-seven fraudulent claimants of coat arms in Staffordshire in 1583:

> These names being writtne on a sheet of paper with fower great letters, was carried by the Bayliffe of the Hundred & one of the Heraulds men to the chiefe towne of that Hundred; where in the cheife place thereof the heraulds men redd the names (after crye made by the Bayliffs and the people gathered) & then pronounced by the said bayley every mans name severally contayned in the said Bill; that done, the Bayley sett the said Bill of Names on a post fast with waxe where it may stand drye ... in the cheifest place of the said towne.[14]

This effort yokes versions of the two practical recommendations of the *Alvarez* decision: public ridicule and public records.[15] Such exercises try to ward off Falstaff's contention that honour is 'a mere scutcheon' – that is, a mere matter of carpentry and paint (or metalwork and ribbons) – the scandalous spectre of the superstructural scarcity erected on these common materials being challenged in this phrase as itself a mere confidence trick.

Censorious treatment of this scandal was meted out on the public stage as well as in the public square.[16] A counterfeit or upstart was frequently the foil for comic plots concluding with the expulsion or reduction of this unwanted or unworthy element, the tighter to bond those fitted for the new social equilibrium. City comedy and those Shakespearean histories structured significantly around comic plots reprise this pattern of exposure, judgement and expulsion; though my emphasis on *1 Henry IV* has hitherto given greater scope to Falstaff's vitalist subversions of honour, these only make more devastating his rejection and sentencing in *2 Henry IV*. Yet the dead Falstaff left epigoni, and at the end of *Henry V* the humiliated Pistol announces he will creep back over the Channel to a life of petty theft ('To England will I steal, and there I'll steal'), including traffic in stolen valour: 'And patches will I get unto these cudgeled scars, / And swear I got them in the Gallia wars' (5.1.84–86).

Pistol's proposed perjury condenses a number of social anxieties aroused by the repatriation of veterans in Elizabethan England

and the concomitant literary transmutation of those anxieties into comedy.[17] Avatars of Xavier Alvarez are not far to seek near the heart of Elizabethan political culture and its disciplinary apparatus. Rory Rapple quotes Gabriel Harvey's 1578 flattery of the Earl of Oxford as 'Achilles ... come to life again' and drily notes: 'there is no evidence that the earl of Oxford, too small to be an Achilles, had any martial experience whatsoever'. Rather, the earl's enduring cultivation of the legend of his Netherlands service 'appears to have arisen out of a day trip to survey the Spanish army lines in the Low Countries while on his Continental adventures'.[18]

The farcical vanity of the earl might be contrasted with the high stakes and tragic consequences of an analogous imposture on the part of the Catholic activist John Ballard, the 'militant ... real animus' behind the Babington Plot, which led to his death and ultimately that of Mary, Queen of Scots.[19] An underground priest, Ballard in early 1586 used his pastoral circuit to agitate for an uprising of recusant nobles to coincide with Mary's liberation.[20] Ballard gained universal notoriety and was the first of the conspirators publicly executed during the two-day extravaganza devoted to their dispatch on 20 and 21 September 1586.

Receiving striking emphasis in contemporary testimony and historiography on Ballard is his disguise in England: a counterfeit soldier. William Camden describes Ballard returning from meetings in Paris thus: 'At Whitsontide this Priest ariued in *England*, apparelled in Silks, in the habite of a Souldier, and by a borrowed name called himselfe Captaine *Foscue*. Hee consulted at *London* about these things with *Anthony Babington* of *Dethicke in Darbyshire*'.[21] His erstwhile prison-mate and travelling companion, Anthony Tyrrell, describes a rendezvous thus:

> About Bartholomew-tide, we met together in London, where Foscue had his attendants as thick as might be, every gentleman calling him Captain; insomuch that in every tavern and inn in London he was called Captain Foscue; and every man thought, that knew him, that he with a great band should have gone over with my Lord Leicester.

In Tyrrell's summary assessment: 'a man vainglorious and desirous of his own praise, and to be meddling in things above his reach'.[22] It is the very model of a *miles gloriosus*: affecting the title 'Captain', the dandified dress ('He wore a fine cape laced with gold, a cut satin doublet and silver buttons on his hat'), the sumptuous dining, the hangers-on, and the breezy boasts of foreign service never rendered or intended ('he with a great band should have gone over with my Lord Leicester'). This picture is complicated, however, because Ballard was, so to speak, not a counterfeit but the counterfeit of a counterfeit; this braggadocio was a ruse covering a different kind of courage (the spy risking death for his beliefs). The key point is that Ballard acting the *miles* was playing a socially legible role – legible, in part, because Elizabethan culture was also well read in a dramatic tradition on the point of being transformatively revivified by actors playing *miles* roles reimagined by Shakespeare and Jonson.

Before a final word on their creations, some of the sociological and literary strands raised so far can be usefully condensed via the ethical analysis of valour and imposture in Aristotle, the crucial intermediary between Homer and humanism.[23] A key passage is Aristotle's discussion of courage at *Nicomachean Ethics* 1115a6–17b22.[24] The approach is both quantitative and qualitative. The framework within which Aristotle discusses *andreia* (courage) as the proper disposition towards fear relies on measurement. Courage itself represents a proper alignment between *phobos* (fear) and *tharros/tharsos* (confidence), and in relation to courage, a person is *thrasus* (rash) or *deilos* (cowardly) by virtue of excessive or deficient confidence in the face of what inspires fear.

The subsequent discussion, however, disrupts this schema in interesting ways. Among evil things properly feared are *adoxia* (dishonour, ill repute); one who does not fear it is *anaiskhuntos* (shameless), yet, adds Aristotle, '*legetai d' hupo tinōn andreios kata metaphoran*' [some people apply the term courageous to such a man by analogy] (1115a15). Here the basis of the analogy is the absence of fear, although the criterion of propriety is lacking. Aristotle later enumerates five more 'metaphorical' senses of courage current in everyday usage, ranked by diminishing proximity from the presumed 'pure' form, and beginning with *andreia politikē* (citizen courage). Citizen soldiers are 'courageous' *dia ta ek tōn nomōn epitimia kai ta oneidē kai dia tas timas* [because of the legal penalties and the reproach, and because of the honours] (1116a19). Aristotle confirms citizen courage as the normative form of courage in Homeric epic in citing Hector's famous fear of dishonour from the Trojans and Trojan women should he retreat, though it save his life. Even these kinds of interest, however, appear to contaminate or qualify *andreia* per se. Yet Aristotle has earlier specified the pure form of *andreia* partly through the following argument: courage concerns fear; the most fearful thing is death; the noblest death is the greatest with respect to which courage may be manifested; battle is where life is defended through valour (*alkē*), or lost most nobly (*kalon*). The final point is clinched thus: '*homologoi de toutois eisi kai hai timai hai en tais polesi kai para tois monarkhois*' [this conclusion is borne out by the principle on which public honours (*timai*) are bestowed in republics and under monarchies] (1115a32). The gap between the uses of *timē* in the argument is never closed.[25]

Even more unexpected is Aristotle's move dialectically to identify rashness and cowardice: *dokei de kai alazōn einai ho thrasus kai prospoiētikos andreia ... dio kai eisin hoi polloi autōn thrasudeiloi* [the rash man is generally thought to be an impostor, who pretends to courage which he does not possess ... hence most rash men really are cowards at heart] (1115b29–32). The identification is condensed into Aristotle's splendid portmanteau *thrasudeilos*. As an observed social and military phenomenon, Aristotle claims, the apparent boldness of one who is *thrasus* is exhibited only in confidence-inspiring contexts, not terror-inspiring ones. By over-performing the former, the rash man perpetrates an imposture, and is thereby not only *thrasudeilos*, but also an *alazōn* (impostor).

Alazōn is a term developed explicitly in the *Nicomachean Ethics* as its own vice of excess with respect to regard for one's own merits (1127a13–b31). *Alazoneia* (boastfulness) is paired with *eirōneia* (self-deprecation), but is the more deplorable vice. Again, ethics is bound up in social performativity, and therefore theatrical performativity can function as an ethical laboratory. In drama, '*alazōn*' denotes the class of boasters of which the braggart soldier is the archetype.[26] *Alazōn* is, moreover, the title of the lost Greek original from which Plautus adapted his *Miles Gloriosus* (as the Plautine text records).[27] In Plautus's play, the *miles gloriosus* Pyrgopolynices is made the gull of a plot cooked up by the clever *seruos* Palaestrio to reunite the *adulescens* Pleusicles with Philocomasium, the girlfriend trapped in Pyrgopolynices' Ephesian house. The soldier ends the play without slave, woman or the military accoutrements of which he is violently stripped. In fact, he is a minor presence up to the denouement, with the great exception of the memorable opening scene – the pattern of innumerable imitations in the ancient world, Renaissance and beyond – in which a cynical parasite teases from the *miles* a comical series of vaunts, including an escalating kill count that leaves Falstaff and Hal's parody of Hotspur in the shade (42–49). He is nothing if not '*magnidicus*' (big-talking; 923). Along the way, the play has more fun with military vocabulary and Homeric allusions than can be explicated here, but the ending is of special interest. Palaestrio has convinced Pyrgopolynices to release Philocomasium by leading him to believe that his beauty and valorous reputation have seduced his neighbour's wife (non-existent, but counterfeited by the *meretrix* Acroteleutium). Apprehended as an adulterer after Philocomasium has made her escape, Pyrgopolynices proves he is *thrasudeilos* as well as *alazōn*, as he is stripped, beaten and threatened with castration. The arrest and punishment are extra-legal, and the worst of it only play-acting, yet a Latin pun on *testes* (testicles/witnesses) foregrounds the question of justice (see 1416, 1422, 1426). By keeping an oath not to avenge his punishers, Pyrgopolynices will be saved from literal emasculation: '*et si intestatus non abeo hinc, bene agitur pro noxia*' [And if I don't go away from here without the power to bear witness as a man, I'm getting off lightly] (1416). But Pyrgopolynices' entire counterfeit projection of masculinity is implicated, and the play ends with him acknowledging his foolishness, accepting judgement and addressing the audience directly to solicit applause.[28]

The *miles gloriosus* fascinated dramatists of the late Tudor and early Stuart period, who experimented with different methods and severities of exposure. Ben Jonson's *Every Man in His Humour* presents a sophisticated set of refractions. Two counterfeit soldiers appear: Captain Bobadil, a classical *miles* type, but also Brainworm, a clever manservant who disguises himself as the destitute veteran Fitzsword and is the hub of the comic plots. In knowingly adopting the false identity, Brainworm shares something with John Ballard: he can call himself 'a true counterfeit man of war', inventing an outlandish European, Levantine and Mediterranean service record.[29] Like Alvarez and Falstaff, Brainworm and Bobadil both come before a Justice. Justice Clement, the comic reconciler, briefly reprises the cowing of Pyrgopolynices in his encounter with Bobadil, who is most willing to be cowed. Brainworm's behaviour in this scene of exposure is more striking. Facing severe legal penalties for a part of his plotting, he removes his disguise and declares: 'I will not lose, by my travail, any grain of my fame certain' (5.1.130–31). Nor does he: though 'fame' recalls Homeric *kleos*, Brainworm's renunciation of his pretence does not merely cancel a false reputation but earns him a better one. Neither ridiculed nor committed, Brainworm is invited to supper. The braggart remains an object of Jonsonian contempt, yet Jonson valorizes a sort of comic heroism consisting in skilfully woven fiction that threatens to destabilize the relationships between truth, valour and justice.

Shakespeare found a particular value and complexity in the *miles* type, developing characters with a special capacity for interrogating and ironizing the plots of heroism and honour in which they are embedded. Setting aside his experiment with the 'Spanish braggart' type in *Love's Labours Lost*, Shakespeare's central adaptations run from the Bastard Falconbridge in *King John*, through Falstaff (both *Henry IV* plays and *The Merry Wives of Windsor*) and Pistol (*2 Henry IV* and *Henry V*), to Parolles in *All's Well That Ends Well*.[30] Across this genealogy, the Shakespearean types exhibit a systematic diminishment in birth and military rank as they retain sympathetic and attractive qualities, including their rhetorical vitality (with a falling off in Parolles, ironizing his name). Falstaff represents a kind of optimization point along these vectors. An unabashed liar, as when he continually inflates the number of assailants at Gad's Hill, he is nevertheless afforded the space to contest his own definition as a counterfeit:

> Counterfeit? I lie; I am no counterfeit. To die is to be a counterfeit, for he is but the counterfeit of a man that hath not the life of a man. But to counterfeit dying when a man thereby liveth is to be no counterfeit but the true and perfect image of life indeed. (5.4.114–18)

'To die is to be a counterfeit' – but this follows the catechism 'Who hath [honour]? He that died o'Wednesday'; Falstaff effects a transvaluation of these values and finds 'life' the more precious commodity (cf. 5.3.59–60). Parolles, in a speech widely taken to encapsulate an ethos of private identity and self-sufficiency arising in the early modern period, only makes the trade more explicit in resolving to 'live / Safest in shame' (4.3.326–27).[31]

Parolles speaks of the soldier 'who knows himself a braggart' (323). Between Hal and Falstaff rests a mutual knowingness. The difficulty, and the challenge to the honour system, lies in the confidence with which an audience can judge the honour of one who stands up at the Three Valley Water District Board or the bridge over the Tenoise. *Henry V*, part of which is set near the latter location, reflects especially on this question. Captain Fluellen, advocate of the 'true disciplines of wars ... the Roman disciplines' (3.2.72–73), reports to Captain Gower that the bridge was held by the Duke of Exeter, 'as magnanimous as Agamemnon, and a man that I honour with my soul, and my heart, and my duty, and my life, and my living, and my uttermost power'; he follows up, however, with an asseveration that Pistol is a soldier 'as valiant a man as Mark Antony' (3.6.5–9, 13–14). Fluellen's first impression demonstrates how diagnoses of valour are prone to false positives. Pistol is ultimately exposed, but the play as a whole is exercised by the paradoxical demand that honour in a nationalist context exhibit at once both scarcity and universality. Henry's Agincourt speech promises inclusion irrespective of class or military rank; as many critics have noted, however, the night scene, the careful accounting of the quantity and quality of the slain in the aftermath of battle, and the politicking of Act 5 all belie the 'band of brothers' rhetoric.

Reading the *miles gloriosus* tradition in light of the Stolen Valor Act crystallizes two enduring social problems: the valuation of honour, especially military honour, and the accommodation of the veteran soldier. One instrument by which valuation and accommodation alike are effected is the literary system of genres, which, the case suggests, in this domain at least remains as articulated with the social system as in Homeric or Renaissance culture. 'More speech', the First Amendment antidote to Alvarez endorsed by the Supreme Court's decision, is functionally a call for more satire in the vein of Plautus, Shakespeare and Jonson: Falstaff is spared the Fleet but must still be fleered. Will it remain a laughing matter? In 2013 Congress passed a modified version of the Stolen Valor Act. The amended law seeks to address the *Alvarez* decision by adopting a wholly economistic view of honour, re-criminalizing an imposture that causes harm through the acquisition of money or tangible benefits (who steals my valour steals trash, but he who filches money...). The new formulation is thoroughly Aristotelian.[32]

The challenge of counterfeit valour was intricately worked through during a massively generative phase of early modern drama already informed by cultural, philosophical, legal and political debates that continue to roil. In disagreeing over whether there is a vital national interest in punishing 'bar stool braggadocio' (Breyer 8), or whether 'ridicule' (Case Syllabus 3) is the necessary and sufficient response, the dissenting and majority opinions in *United States v. Alvarez* contest the question of whether the civil repercussions of US militarism belong to epic or comedy.[33] Either way, it is Falstaff's kind of lie, not Henry's, that turns up in the dock and on the docket. Indeed, nothing about war changes much.

David Currell is Assistant Professor of English at the American University of Beirut, where he teaches early modern drama and poetry. His work has appeared in *English Studies*, *Shakespeare Survey* and collections including *Fall Narratives* and *Critical Insights: Macbeth*. He is coeditor of *Digital Milton* (Palgrave Macmillan, 2018).

Notes

My thanks to Loran Peterson for his research assistance. An earlier version of part of this chapter was presented to the seminar 'Theater and Judgment in Early Modern England' at the Annual Meeting of the Shakespeare Association of America in St. Louis. My thanks to seminar convener Kevin Curran and respondents Heather Hirschfeld and Richard Strier for their generous feedback.

1. Adam McKeown, *English Mercuries: Soldier Poets in the Age of Shakespeare* (Nashville, TN: Vanderbilt University Press, 2009). The text used as epigraph to this chapter appears on page 62.
2. *King Henry IV, Part 1*, ed. David Scott Kastan (London: Thomson, 2002), 5.4.118–19. Subsequent parenthetical references are to this edition.
3. I take an obvious poetic licence in putting it like this, and would suggest further that the court keep its Shakespearean pretensions in check in light of the reported Oxfordian consensus that had quite recently united its liberal and conservative wings (Jess Bravin, 'Justice Stevens Renders an Opinion on Who Wrote Shakespeare's Plays', *The Wall Street Journal*, 18 April 2009).
4. I retain US spellings of *valor* and *honor* in the names of the Stolen Valor Act and Congressional Medal of Honor and where relevant in direct quotation.
5. Parenthetical references in this chapter are to the slip opinion (http://www.supremecourt.gov/opinions/11pdf/11-210d4e9.pdf), by author and page (each of the three opinions is separately paginated). For representative media coverage of the case, see Robert Barnes, 'Supreme Court to Review Stolen Valor Act, Which Outlaws Lying about Military Honors', *The Washington Post*, 18 February 2012; and James Dao, 'Lying about Earning War Medals Is Protected Speech, Justices Rule', *The New York Times*, 28 June 2012.
6. Legal commentary on the Stolen Valor Act has registered these wider historical contexts. For an analysis that begins from medieval and early modern heraldry laws, see Ramya Kasturi, 'Stolen Valor: A Historical Perspective on the Regulation of Military Uniform and Decorations', *Yale Journal on Regulation* 29, no. 2 (2012): 419–36.
7. David Graeber, following Maurice Bloch, notes an analogy between the (at least) dual senses of 'honour' and the term *hasina* in the language and culture of central Madagascan kingdoms. The quality of *hasina* was treated as inhering in the ruling elite, but was capable of effecting benefits which the community could activate through the ceremonial granting to a king of a tributary coin. This coin was also termed *hasina* and was valued not for its material attributes but as a sign of the *hasina* of the recipient. In short, 'having *hasina* – in the sense of intrinsic superiority (which Bloch labels "*hasina* mark 1") – is like having honor; giving the

coins ("*hasina* mark 2") is like honoring people'. See *Toward an Anthropological Theory of Value: The False Coin of Our Own Dreams* (New York: Palgrave Macmillan, 2001), 234.

8. Douglas Cairns asserts the value of the comparative analysis of Homeric epic within the interdisciplinary study of honour in the first half of his stimulating essay, 'Honour and Shame: Modern Controversies and Ancient Values', *Critical Quarterly* 53, no. 1 (2011): 23–41. Far from being relevant only in relation to the pre-developed Mediterranean contexts central to an earlier generation of scholarship on honour, Homeric epic remains a useful source for chronologically and geographically diverse contexts approached through contemporary paradigms.

9. Liddell and Scott's *Greek-English Lexicon* glosses '*goodness, excellence,* of any kind, in *Hom.* esp. of *manly* qualities' (s.v. *aretē*). In post-Homeric Greek, excellence in an activity or in moral virtue becomes the dominant sense (as frequently in Plato). This paragraph is indebted to Gregory Nagy's studies of Homeric motivation and the epic's function in the distribution of praise and blame, especially *The Best of the Achaeans: Concepts of the Hero in Ancient Greek Poetry* (Baltimore, MD: Johns Hopkins University Press, 1979).

10. See David Quint, 'Bragging Rights: Honor and Courtesy in Shakespeare and Spenser', in *Creative Imitation: New Essays on Renaissance Literature in Honor of Thomas M. Greene*, ed. David Quint, Margaret W. Ferguson, G. W. Pigman III and Wayne A. Rebhorn (Binghamton, NY: Medieval and Renaissance Texts and Studies, 1992), 405–14.

11. As this chapter juxtaposes epic and comedy, I take notice in passing of the mocking imitation of Hotspur's hyperbole in Francis Beaumont's *The Knight of the Burning Pestle* (1608). Called on to show his theatrical talents, the apprentice Rafe (a boy in a play written for a boys' company) hypermetrically gilds Hotspur's rhetorical lily: 'By heaven, methinks it were an easy leap / To pluck bright honour from the pale-faced moon, / Or dive into the bottom of the sea, / Where never fathom line touched any ground, / And pluck up drowned honour from the lake of hell'. Quoted from Michael Hattaway, ed. (London: Methuen, 2002), Ind. 81.

12. *King Henry V*, ed. T. W. Craik (London: Thomson, 1995), 4.1.236. Subsequent parenthetical references are to this edition.

13. Laurence Stone, *The Crisis of the Aristocracy, 1558–1641* (1965; repr. with corrections Oxford: Clarendon Press, 1979), 65–128.

14. British Library Harley MSS. 1173, f. 85, quoted in Stone, *Crisis of the Aristocracy*, 68.

15. The United States government acted quickly in the wake of the *Alvarez* decision to implement the Justices' suggested recourse of a public database of military honours recipients, accessible at the felicitous url valor.defense.gov.

16. See in this connection an intriguing exchange across the majority and dissenting opinions concerning theatre. The majority struck down the Act chiefly because it criminalized lies without sufficient qualifications to satisfy the First Amendment. It might therefore, Justice Kennedy speculates, potentially criminalize a 'theatrical performance' (10). The dissent takes cognisance of this argument but dismisses it (Alito 2). Shakespeare was certainly alive to the parameters and perils of performativity, of actors pretending to be characters pretending to be heroes: 'Oldcastle died a martyr, and this is not the man' (*2 Henry IV*, ed. A. R. Humphreys [1981; repr. London: Thomson, 2003], Ep. 31–32).

17. See Mark Thornton Burnett, 'Tamburlaine: An Elizabethan Vagabond', *Studies in Philology* 84, no. 3 (1987): 308–23 on late Elizabethan perceptions of discontented veterans as a threat to social stability. The comic Pistol invites formal contrast with the tragic Coriolanus: 'It is a part / That I shall blush in acting ... To brag unto them "Thus I did, and thus", / Show them th'unaching scars which I should hide, / As if I had received them for the hire / Of their breath only' (2.2.143–49). *Coriolanus* addresses several issues pertinent to this chapter, but as it were through the looking-glass: the protagonist practises a normative 'classical' valour (Cominius: 'It is held / That valour is the chiefest virtue and / Most dignifies the haver. If it be, / The man I speak of cannot in the world / Be singly counterpoised' [2.2.81–85]; Volumnia: 'O, he is wounded, I thank the gods for't' [2.1.118]) so inflexibly he would destroy the community that under-honours him. Quoted from Peter Holland, ed. (London: Bloomsbury, 2013).
18. Rory Rapple, *Martial Power and Elizabethan Political Culture: Military Men in England and Ireland, 1558–1594* (Cambridge: Cambridge University Press, 2009), 73.
19. Charles Nicholl, *The Reckoning: The Murder of Christopher Marlowe* (London: Jonathan Cape, 1992), 148.
20. For an account, see John Hungerford Pollen, S. J., *Mary Queen of Scots and the Babington Plot* (Edinburgh: T. and A. Constable, 1922), lxxiii–clxix.
21. William Camden, *Annales: The True and Royall History of the famous Empresse Elizabeth* (London, 1625), 130–31. On the captain persona, see also Alan Gordon Smith, *The Babington Plot* (London: Macmillan, 1936), 3–7.
22. Nicholl, *The Reckoning*, 148.
23. For an account of honour in Aristotle's thought that addresses the complex interdependency of honour, the concept of 'nobility'/'fineness' (*kalon*) and the rhetoric of praise and blame, see Alexander Welsh, *What Is Honor? A Question of Moral Imperatives* (New Haven, CT: Yale University Press, 2008), 23–39.
24. *The Nicomachean Ethics*, ed. and trans. H. Rackham (1934; repr. Cambridge, MA: Harvard University Press, 1982). Subsequent parenthetical references are to this edition. The similar treatment at *Eudemian Ethics* 1228a23–30a36 differs slightly in length and sequence of presentation.
25. For a consonant analysis of this puzzle, developed in relation to Aristotle's concept of 'shame', see David Roochnik, 'Courage and Shame: Aristotle's *Nicomachean Ethics* III.6–9', *Etica & Politica / Ethics and Politics* 17, no. 2 (2015): 214–32.
26. 'A deceiving or self-deceived character in fiction, normally an object of ridicule in comedy or satire, but often a hero in tragedy. In comedy he most frequently takes the form of a *miles gloriosus* or a pedant' (Northrop Frye, *Anatomy of Criticism: Four Essays*, ed. Robert D. Denham [1957; repr. Toronto: University of Toronto Press, 2006], 331). See also Richard Janko, *Aristotle on Comedy: Towards a Reconstruction of Poetics II* (1984; repr. London: Duckworth, 2002), 216–18.
27. *Miles Gloriosus*, in *Plautus III*, ed. and trans. Wolfgang de Melo (Cambridge, MA: Harvard University Press, 2011), lines 86–87. Subsequent parenthetical line references are to this edition.
28. On this ending as striking a socially harmonious note, see Alison Sharrock, *Reading Roman Comedy: Poetics and Playfulness in Plautus and Terence* (Cambridge: Cambridge University Press, 2009), 255–56, 260.

29. *Every Man in His Humour*, in *The Roaring Girl and Other City Comedies*, ed. James Knowles (Oxford: Oxford University Press, 2001), 2.2.19–20, 51–61. The play was originally published in 1598 with an Italianate setting; Knowles' edition, to which subsequent parenthetical citations refer, is based on the revised, English setting that first appeared in Jonson's 1616 Folio.
30. For the 'Spanish braggart' tradition in Spain and Italy and Don Adriano as an Anglicized continuation, see Daniel C. Boughner, 'Don Armado and the *commedia dell' arte*', *Studies in Philology* 37, no. 2 (1940): 201–24, and the wider treatment in Boughner's *The Braggart in Renaissance Comedy: A Study in Comparative Drama from Aristophanes to Shakespeare* (1954; repr. Westport, CT: Greenwood, 1970). For the suggestion that the characterization of Othello is also informed by the *miles gloriosus* archetype, see Frye, *Anatomy of Criticism*, 37; and Wolfgang Riehle, 'Shakespeare's Reception of Plautus Reconsidered', in *Shakespeare and the Classics*, ed. Charles Martindale and A. B. Taylor (Cambridge: Cambridge University Press, 2004), 112.
31. *All's Well That Ends Well*, ed. G. K. Hunter (London: Methuen, 1959). For an exemplary citation of Parolles as inverting the classical ethos, see Bernard Williams, *Shame and Necessity* (Berkeley: University of California Press, 1993), 101–2. On Shakespeare's 'thoroughly Plautine' handling of Parolles, see Robert S. Miola, *Shakespeare and Classical Comedy: The Influence of Plautus and Terence* (Oxford: Clarendon Press, 1994), 129.
32. 'The man who pretends to more merit than he possesses for no ulterior object seems, it is true, to be a person of inferior character ... but he appears to be more foolish than vicious. When, on the other hand, a man exaggerates his own merits to gain some object, if that object is glory or honour (*timē*) he is not very much blamed, but if he boasts to get money or things that fetch money, this is more unseemly (*askhēmonesteros*)' (*Nicomachean Ethics* 1127a9–14). This recourse may still leave the statute's language contestably broad; see James Santiago, 'Is Honor Tangible Property?', *University of Michigan Journal of Law* 46, no. 1 (2012): 109–14; and David Hommel, 'Saving Private Ryan's Valor: The Stolen Valor Act and Lies about Military Medals', *The Jurist*, 16 April 2014.
33. As a final context for this prescription of satire, see some recent cogitations about whether satire on military themes remains possible in the contemporary United States that appeared in mainstream fora: Stephen M. Walt, 'Two Chief Petty Officers Walk into a Bar...', *Foreign Policy*, 7 April 2014; and James Fallows, 'The Tragedy of the American Military', *The Atlantic*, January/February 2015. The usually disavowed or ignored function of satire in protecting establishment institutions is raised in a non-military UK context by Jonathan Coe, 'Sinking Giggling into the Sea', *The London Review of Books*, 18 July 2013; Coe's essay implicitly challenges Walt's construction of a post-Second World War golden age of mass media military satire.

Chatper 6
Hamletism in the Spanish Civil War, 1936–39

Jesús Tronch

The Spanish Civil War broke out on 18 July 1936, when reactionary factions of the army rebelled against the young progressive Second Republic, then governed by a broad left-wing coalition.[1] Spain and the Spaniards were split between those loyal to the Republic and its democratic values and those supporting the self-denominated *nacionales*, who established a parallel regime led by General Franco. The Republic drew in military aid from the Soviet Union, Mexico and volunteers in the International Brigades, and the Nationalists from Nazi Germany and Fascist Italy. The struggle was seen as the contention between democracy and fascism, later to be staged in World War II. Franco's regime was finally recognized by the United Kingdom and France on 27 February 1939 and by the United States on 1 April 1939, when the last loyal forces surrendered, and the war was effectively over. The aftermath, like the three-year armed conflict, was traumatic, with thousands in prison, executed or exiled.

Notes for this section begin on page 132.

Within this historical context, I will consider manifestations of the cultural phenomenon of Hamletism, understood as ineffectuality, vacillation or irresolution in social and political commitment,[2] an exploration that seeks to contribute to the reception of Shakespeare in wartime. I first comment on uses of the type in a newspaper article and in an essay published in 1937, then suggest resonances of political irresolution apropos of a theatre production of *Hamlet* performed in Valencia in 1937, and finally analyse the fictionalization of Hamletism in the novel *El diario de Hamlet García* [*The Diary of Hamlet García*], written by Catalan journalist and writer Paulino Masip (1899–1963) during his exile in Mexico.[3]

Hamletism in periodicals

The Spanish Second Republic, established in April 1931 after the constitutional monarchy had lost its democratic credibility, initially aroused hopes of social justice but proved to be politically unstable amidst an inherited economic crisis. Social tensions increased and became polarized to the extent of bringing the country to great violence, especially after a broad left-wing coalition won elections in February 1936. In many areas of Republican Spain, the war unleashed a 'revolution' that put into practice socialist and anarchist principles of labour and political organization, begrudgingly tolerated by a Republican government necessarily focused on the war.[4]

By 1936, *Hamlet* had a long tradition of being quoted and employed figuratively in Spanish newspapers and journals, usually as a symbol of the hesitant individual or collective unable to take action, especially in the political arena.[5] Salient examples of Hamletism in the pressing circumstances of the civil war are seen, for instance, in one of Paulino Masip's articles in *La Vanguardia* in 1937, as well as in José Bergamín's contribution to the 2nd International Congress of Writers in Defence of Culture, published in the monthly review *Hora de España* in August 1937.

During most of the war, the Barcelona-based newspaper *La Vanguardia* had become the 'official' periodical of the democratic ideals of the Republic. Its editor between 1937 and 1938, Paulino Masip, usually editorialized about the war and the ensuing 'revolution' in a front-page article, to the extent that he has been described as 'one of the Republic's ideologues'.[6] A recurrent and explicit aim of his exhortations was to stir the 'inertia' of some citizens and to dispel the moral qualms and problems of conscience the 'revolution' posed to them. In one of his war articles, Masip replied to the physician Gregorio Marañón, one of the most significant intellectuals of twentieth-century Spain, in light of a letter Marañón had sent to the press explaining his discontent with the Communist-oriented Republic.[7] Masip described Marañón's letter as *una bellaquería* (an act of villainy) and reproached him for his ambiguous attitude. In another article, Masip explained how he developed from an initial fear of social revolution to glad acceptance of it, once civil war was underway.[8]

Masip particularly employed Hamlet in his 'Letter to a sceptical Spaniard',[9] addressed to the non-committal citizen who, much unlike the common people, who he saw as more willing to take action against the Nationalist faction, was overburdened by 'specific data, figures and maps', trapped in short-sighted intellectualism and mental reclusion. Masip urges his sceptical addressee to have the faith that the times demand, follow his instinctive impulses and 'burn' the ballast of logical reasoning. He presses him towards the inescapable dilemma of being either a paralysed intellectual 'lizard' or a Phoenix reborn from its ashes, and compares him to Hamlet as the paradigmatic example of an individual who knows where righteousness lies and loves it passionately but lacks the intuitive impulse driven by faith necessary in order to fight on its behalf. He denounces the sceptical Spaniard as an 'errant and indecisive soul, a tardy Hamletian spirit' whose willpower dies out in a book-crammed room and exhorts him to get out and immerse himself in the groans, panting, songs and horror in the streets, where he can acquire the faith he lacks.

Hora de España was a literary and artistic monthly publication of essays, poetry and criticism 'in the service of the people's cause'. First published in Valencia, then in Barcelona, between January 1937 and October 1938, and funded by the 'Ministerio de Propaganda', it became the review of the prime and pride of Spanish intellectuals sympathetic to the Republic.[10] One of its frequent contributors was the essayist, poet and playwright José Bergamín (1895–1983), chairman of the Alliance of Anti-Fascist Intellectuals and of the 2nd International Congress of Writers in Defence of Culture, held in Valencia in July 1937. The August issue of *Hora de España* contains contributions to this conference by, among others, Antonio Machado, Malcolm Cowley, Tristan Tzara, Stephen Spender and José Bergamín.[11] Bergamín addresses the problems of Spanish culture in that time of war. After objecting to the notion of a 'problem', he uses Hamlet's phrase 'To be or not to be' as encapsulating the throbbing and living question of a culture threatened by destruction; the question is to exist or not to exist at a time of extreme danger, as people became more aware of their precarious situation. For Bergamín, Hamlet is not a symbol of intelligence but rather its caricature, the tragic caricature of an intellectual. He complains that there is a 'Hamletic intellectualism that feeds on itself in that vacillating endeavour of problematizing itself' and argues that the essence of intelligence is the faculty of deciding rather than hesitating. Understanding Hamletism as the personal isolation of the intellectual, Bergamín deplores it as 'the worst evil in our century' and judges as despicable traitors the more or less 'Hamleticized' pseudo-intellectuals who distance themselves from the people and remain 'neutral'.

Hamletism in a Valencia theatre production of *Hamlet*

Four months after the publication of Bergamín's denunciation of Hamletism in *Hora de España*, Shakespeare's *Hamlet* was staged in Valencia. Not many Shakespearean productions seem to have been staged in Spain during the civil war. Consulted sources record performances of four Shakespeare plays. *Hamlet* premiered on 8 December 1937, and *La fiera domada*, an adaptation in Spanish, by Elena Arcediano and Maximiliano Thous, of *The Taming of the Shrew*, premiered on 5 July 1938, both at the Teatro Eslava in Valencia by the theatre company led by Salvador Soler and his wife Milagros Leal. A Catalan version of *The Taming of the Shrew* (*La feréstega domada*) premiered on 17 September 1938 by Maria Vila and Pius Daví, at the Teatre Català de la Comèdia in Barcelona, and was revived on 28 October. *Othello* appeared in Spanish with Enrique Borrás' company in Barcelona in 1938 at the Barcelona Liceu playhouse, announced on 25 October in the newspaper *La Vanguardia*.[12] In addition, a Catalan tragedy by Víctor Balaguer, *Coriolà*, based on Shakespeare's *Coriolanus*, was staged at the Institució del Teatre on 20 June 1937.[13]

For the *Hamlet* production, local newspapers confirm a premiere on 8 December 1937, as well as subsequent performances during 9–22, 24–25 and 27 December.[14] The advertisements in the newspaper *La Correspondencia de Valencia* title the production '*Prince Hamlet* by Shakespeare' and advertise it as an 'Artistic Solemnity', with Salvador Soler as *responsable escénico* (stage director) and Milagros Leal as 'leading actress'. The performance must not have taken longer than three hours, since on some double-show evenings it was put on at six, prior to a second play at ten. Newspaper advertisements from 11 December describe it as 'a great success', suggesting that the production was well received.[15] It enjoyed eighteen performances in fifteen days, an average success compared to the eighty-eight performances of Lope de Vega's *Fuenteovejuna*, but far from the popularity of vaudeville shows such as *La de Villadiego* (first published 1888) with 348 performances, and *Las tocas* (premiered 1938) with 572.[16]

From what we know about the company and Valencia theatrical life at that time, I will venture to explain why this Shakespearean production took place at that time. During the whole war, Valencia remained within the Republic. It was finally occupied by the *nacionales* only two days before their victory. Being far from the war front, the city became the loyalist capital between 6 November 1936, when the government fled a Nationalist-besieged Madrid, and 31 October 1937, when it moved to Barcelona. The management of playhouses and cinemas was taken over by the socialist trade union UGT and the anarchist CNT through the Comité Ejecutivo de Espectáculos Públicos (Executive Committee of Public Entertainment). Cooperatives were soon established as a model of business organization that freed theatre workers from the demands of *impresarios* and secured them regular work.[17]

Advocating a revolutionary theatre in tune with this social transformation,[18] the Committee created the Compañía Dramática Experimental (Experimental Theatre Company). Salvador Soler was 'responsible' for this subsidized company and started to perform at the Teatro Principal plays by George Bernard Shaw, Spanish Max Aub, and Russian Valentin Kataev.[19] The reality, however, of theatrical business soon dictated otherwise. In February 1937, after subsequent economic losses, the Committee could no longer subsidize the company and allowed Soler to choose the repertoire. Soler changed the name of the company to Compañía de Comedias[20] and started to perform plays for children, comedies and an occasional *flamenco* show,[21] in keeping with general trends in the theatres of Madrid and Barcelona. Companies soon realized that many actors lacked the training to perform ideologically committed plays and that audiences continued to demand the usual genres they had enjoyed before the war: melodramas, variety shows, *zarzuelas* (Spanish operetta), light and frivolous comedies, and *sainetes* (one-act comical pieces). In order to attract play-goers and keep theatre workers employed, companies had no option but to offer the bourgeoisie genres whose values the Republic ideologues ostensibly aimed to combat and whose plots provided spectators with an escape from their crude circumstances. In the case of Valencia, Marrast explains this indifference towards the war as an effect of the city's distance from the front.[22] Several voices from political parties and trade unions, as well as various intellectuals, criticized the repertoire as out of tune with the historical moment. They saw it as preserving a bourgeois decadence at odds with the values of the threatened Republic, and continuously called for a theatre of higher quality, as well as more in keeping with revolutionary principles.[23]

When Soler and Leal's company moved to the Eslava playhouse in October 1937, they started to stage more refined, critically acclaimed plays: in November, the classical *El Alcalde de Zalamea* (*The Mayor of Zalamea*) by Pedro Calderón de la Barca, and *Los intereses creados* (*The Bonds of Interest*) and *Los malhechores del bien* (*Wrongdoers of Good*) by Nobel-Awarded playwright Jacinto Benavente, who lived in Valencia at that time.[24] In December, they turned to Shakespeare's *Hamlet*. In the same newspaper announcing the premiere of this *Hamlet*, Mario Pommercy called for a pedagogical theatre for the people and listed Calderón's *Mayor* among plays by Hauptman, Romain Rolland and Tolstoy as those that should be put on the stage. In 1938, Soler and Leal's company staged another Spanish classic, Calderón's *La vida es sueño* (*Life's a Dream*), followed by Beltrán and Sendín's *¡Qué más da!*, a play about the social transformations prompted by the war,[25] as well as, in July, the adaptation of *The Taming of the Shrew*.[26] When the Ministry of Education granted a subsidy to the company, it moved back to the Teatro Principal with the name Compañía Oficial de Arte Dramático. The company opened with a Quixote-based play by Elena Arcediano and Maximilano Thous and followed it with Calderón's *Mayor* and Lope de Vega's *Fuenteovejuna*, among others.[27] As Noelia Llidó points out, Soler and Leal followed Benavente's advice in December 1936 that theatre should be educational and popular, albeit experimental, comical and spectacular, but never indecent or coarse. As grounds for this sense of decorum, Benavente cites the classical drama of the Greeks and the Spanish Golden Age, as well as Shakespeare.[28]

The *Hamlet* production can be understood as one expression of Soler and Leal's efforts to raise the quality of theatre in Valencia. Soler and Leal stood among the few who attempted to dignify theatrical activity at a point in time in which neither classics nor ideologically committed plays secured enough income to prove sustainable.[29] A close look at the *Hamlet* season, for instance, reveals that Shakespeare's tragedy was performed the same evening as comedies such as *Amor a oscuras* (*Love in the Dark*) and *Papá soltero* (*Unmarried Dad*).[30] The choice of their second Shakespeare, the adaptation of the comical *Taming of the Shrew* in July 1938, may be seen as a concession to the taste of audiences and the rivalry of other companies which offered more attractive titles. From the context, we can understand why Soler and Leal resorted to Shakespeare in reply to the *intelligentsia*'s and political leaders' demand for a more dignified theatre repertoire. But why *Hamlet* and not *Othello* or *Romeo and Juliet*? These two plays were performed more often in Spain at the time.[31] Or why not a more overtly political tragedy, such as *Julius Caesar* or *Coriolanus*?

As the articles by Bergamín and Masip suggest, presenting the tragedy of Hamlet on the stage could be seen as holding a mirror up to 'the spirits of socially timid and non-committal' Spaniards, including but not limited to intellectuals, reminding them of their lack of 'involvement in the urgent affairs of the dramatic situation of Spain'[32] – a lack of involvement or escapism that spectators could find in playhouses such as the Teatro Principal where the famous actor Enrique Rambal was producing *Beso mortal* (*Fatal Kiss*), advertised as 'declared fit for public use by the French government'. On 10 December, the local newspaper *La Correspondencia de Valencia* censored 'the voluntarily inactive in the rearguard' as 'traitors' in its front-page headline.

Hamlet as the prototype of political hesitation also had an international resonance. Japan's invasion of China and the temporizing attitude of the USA and Britain regularly featured in newspapers in Valencia. On 16 December, three days after the fall of Nanking, *La Correspondencia de Valencia* printed the slogan, 'Either aggressive militarism is fought against or it will destroy the vacillating [nations]'. This conflict had clear connections with the situation of Spain. Like China, the Republic was suffering a foreign invasion, or so Republican rhetoric would have it, given German and Italian military aid to the rebel army led by Francisco Franco. Moreover, democratic powers such as France and Britain had signed the non-intervention agreement in August 1936. Since that agreement was repeatedly broken by Italy and Germany – and by the Soviet Union supporting the Republic – news of ineffective meetings of the Committee and of voices in support or against was a hot issue.

In the absence of any promptbook of Soler and Leal's *Hamlet*, we cannot know, for instance, whether Hamlet's anti-militaristic lines in his soliloquy in 4.4 (only in the 1604–5 quarto text) were cut, or whether Fortinbras appeared ominously at the end of the play signifying the demise of national sovereignty (the Republic of Spain) by a belligerent foreign power. Did the tragedy reflect what befalls a people who does not commit to the pressing needs of a state threatened by the force of arms? Did it cut the Fortinbras subplot (as was common in nineteenth-century adaptations and in the most recent adaptation, that of 1928 by Fernando de la Milla)[33] and offer instead a romanticized version of the Danish prince devoid of political echoes? Or, induced by the social revolution, did it present a humanistic Hamlet wearied of the 'philistinism of the bourgeoisie', following A. A. Smirnov's orthodox Marxist interpretation at that time?[34] If nothing else, Hamlet's contempt for the court 'revels' and his intervention in a politically incisive drama (*The Mousetrap*) can be seen as recreating the attitude of the political and intellectual leaders in Valencia, in their opposition to frivolous and escapist shows and their desire for a more committed, realistic theatre. Soler and Leal's *Hamlet* reflects the same kinds of conflicts and anxieties expressed in contemporary journalists' denunciation of Hamletism.

Reverberations of Hamletism in Masip's *El diario de Hamlet García*

Paulino Masip's novel *El diario de Hamlet García* has been praised as one of the best 'among those written by Spanish Civil War exiles'[35] and one of the best literary accounts of the civil war.[36] It unfolds a simple story: in a diary, Hamlet García, a middle-class citizen of Madrid who earns his living from private classes in philosophy, records his experiences, inner debates and reflections during the early stages of the civil war. The diary runs from 1 January 1935 to 30 October 1936, devoting three-quarters of its pages to life during the war. Departing gradually from an initial attitude of proud detachment, Hamlet García begins to realize that the war has shattered the 'fragile inner castle' that he had laboured to build (94), making his internal dilemmas and doubts more acute.[37] The painful reality of everyday life in Madrid eventually leads him to sympathize with the people's defence of the Republic, inasmuch as social justice is at stake (159), and to become more aware of his humanity through faint experiences of love, sexual desire, empathy and the need to communicate. The sirens of warning of air raids ultimately knock down the walls of his inner fortress and leave it bare and defenceless, at which point he finds himself feeling both anguished and liberated (264). He is torn between angst from without and agony from within as he wearily waits for his destiny in silence (272–77), between recognition of his failure and brief discoveries of his re-humanization (278). The diary finishes abruptly, and its editor tells readers that Hamlet García was wounded, taken to hospital in delirium, and after a long convalescence 'is now wandering about...'. Whether he engages at last with the world or remains tormented by doubts in isolation, readers are not told (279).

Through the diary entries, the first-person narrator registers and examines his inquiring and vacillating mind as it reacts to external events: a brief episode of jealousy and adultery between his wife Ofelia and her lover, the shop-keeper Claudio; his protection of the ingenuous and attractive sixteen-year-old pupil Eloísa; his grotesque encounters with his conservative relative Captain Sebastián; the contrasting attitude of his maid Cloti and of his Socialist disciple Daniel who joined the Republican militia; the vain infatuation with prostitute Adela, and above all the wartime life in Madrid with its social and political turmoil, including the baffled incredulity of the bourgeois, the enthusiastic idealism of men and women in the militia, the partisanship, the political debates, the plight of endangered civilians, their everyday life disrupted; and finally, the grief and terror caused by air raids which scatter corpses on streets. These experiences finally destroy his self-constructed worldview. Besides the immediacy of first-person narration and the frequent use of the present tense, Masip's style is characterized by flights of vivid images that reflect inner thoughts and feelings, as well as descriptions of the urban and human environment.

As in Shakespeare's tragedy, Masip's protagonist occupies most of the fictional space of the work. Its diary entries are like twentieth-century expansions of the prince's introspective monologues. Nonetheless, the novel also registers the voices, attitudes and feelings of a varied civilian population in wartime Madrid. Eugenio de Nora describes it as the meditations of a teacher of philosophy 'yoked together with features of local customs and manners';[38]

Pablo Corbalán, as a 'collective tragedy through the mirror of a solitary intellectual'.[39] In this sense, Masip follows the notion of *intrahistoria* put forward by the Spanish philosopher and writer Miguel de Unamuno,[40] whereby history is to be understood through the histories of ordinary individuals and not only through great political and military events and their major heroic protagonists. In this respect, Hamlet García is an anti-hero, one such ordinary Madrilenian. Although an intellectual, he does not belong to the cultural and social elite of Madrid. Instead, he is an 'ignored citizen',[41] with a rather unusual personality.

Masip's protagonist retains many significant traits of Shakespeare's Hamlet, but not without some significant discrepancies as well. Hamlet García's first words are 'No soy Príncipe de Dinamarca' [I am not prince of Denmark] (15), recalling a notable variant form of Hamletism: T. S. Eliot's J. Alfred Prufrock. He is not a Wittenberg student, but instead is a thirty-five-year-old 'itinerant teacher of Metaphysics', as he recurrently defines himself (15, 32, 34, 49, 106, 257). Absent-minded, paralysed between 'eagerness for truth and the horror of discovering it' ('el afán de verdad y el terror de descubrirla') (39), weary of life (57), moody, sceptical, hesitant, contemplative and static (94), he is told by other characters that he always has his head in the clouds, and constantly employs the term 'nebulous' in his descriptions of himself.

In addition to evoking Hamlet's personality, the novel also builds in a fair number of allusions. There are phrases that go back to the Shakespearean dialogue:[42] 'qué inútil y absurda la tuya' (57) recalls 'how weary, stale, flat and unprofitable' (1.2.133); 'es mejor dormir, dormir, dormir' (73) recalls the insistent 'to sleep' in the prince's famous monologue (3.1.59–64); 'hay algo más de lo que los ojos ven y los oídos oyen' (207), 'There are more things in heaven and earth, Horatio, / Than are dreamt of in your philosophy' (1.5.166–67); 'He aquí el problema', 'that is the question' (3.1.55). Like the prince's last word, 'silence' is the last word written in the diary (279). Sometimes Hamlet García himself recognizes connections to Shakespeare's Hamlet explicitly: 'as my homonym, the prince, would say' (81, similarly in 207); likewise, his explanation of the origin of his name (51). Ofelia is Hamlet's wife, and her adulterous lover is Claudio. Yorick's skull also participates in the protagonist's meditations (264).

In contrast to Shakespeare's Hamlet, however, Masip's is not a significant member of the ruling elite. Instead, he is a liberal *petit bourgeois* proudly disinterested in politics (60). His libido is inhibited; likewise, he feels no special duty to set right a world 'out of joint'. Theatre-goers hear Shakespeare's prince debate 'the question' only once (3.1.55) and reproach himself twice (the soliloquies in 2.2 and in 4.4, the latter only in the 1604–5 quarto text); readers of Hamlet García's self-account see much more often how he constantly doubts himself, reproaches himself and raises dilemmas, sometimes of no consequence, on the basis of niggling scruples.

One major discrepancy is the absence of any clear-cut revenge plot. Hamlet García is overwhelmed not by the task of avenging a fratricide against his father, but by the task of coming to terms with a fratricidal war. In keeping with Goethe's metaphor for Shakespeare's Hamlet,[43] the oak tree planted in Hamlet García's precious pot is not the moral imperative of domestic or familiar revenge, but instead the moral, political and vital dilemmas that social fratricide thrusts upon him. In contrast to the Shakespearean prince, who apparently decides that he has to act against his uncle – more clearly in the 1623 folio text – (5.2.64–70) and who finally takes violent action, Hamlet García only becomes gradually aware of his internal breakdown, his inability to keep aloof from external contingencies which he had thought that his philosophy had fortified him against. Towards the end, just as he is beginning to discover his humanity, although never in its full measure, he painfully recognizes that war perturbs him utterly (266): he 'lacks communication with the saps of earth and life' (269). Whereas Shakespeare's Hamlet dies, after having purged the corruption of Denmark, Masip's Hamlet remains alive, albeit wounded. After he recovers from his temporary madness, his tragic end is left uncertain.

By bringing together a very common Spanish surname, García, and the unique, iconic forename Hamlet, Masip creates a man-in-the-street version of the Shakespearean archetype, limiting its profile to that of the 'detached intellectual'. This anti-heroic Hamlet also partakes of the parodic. Placed in an extreme situation, one that prompts heroic virtues in ordinary people, the attitudes and responses of Masip's nebulous, socially inhibited Madrilenian Hamlet prove to be pathetic and at times grotesque.

Viewing the novel, as Sebastiaan Faber suggests, as narrating 'the Shakespearean dilemma faced by the intellectual in times of political turmoil',[44] and considering the unhappy end and parodic character of Masip's metaphysical Hamlet García, one can read the novel as a criticism of intellectuals opting out of politics in troubled times. More specifically, as Eugenio de Nora and Rafael Conte have proposed,[45] it can be seen as a criticism of intellectuals aligned with the Republic unwilling to become more involved in the ongoing civil war. Further support of this view comes from the insertion, in the final pages of the novel, of an episode in which the ineffective philosopher García meets his perfect foil, an old friend, José Lazcano, a parallel to Shakespeare's Laertes. Lazcano is a lecturer in history, much as García is in philosophy. Both are intellectuals; both liberal *petit bourgeois*; both were surprised by the outbreak of war in Madrid and separated from their families. Lazcano's attitude towards war, however, is diametrically opposed to García's. From the very first day, we discover, Lazcano took the Republic's side, without hesitation, and condemned the social classes that supported the rebels as enemies of Spain (267). To this purpose, the appropriation of Shakespeare's Hamlet as the archetype of those 'thinking too precisely on th' event' (4.4.41) is opportune.

The novel is not limited, however, to disapproval of inhibited intellectualism, or Hamletism. Masip constructs Hamlet García with such care, gives him so much space, provides such a detailed record of his inner struggle, that it becomes difficult to conclude that his only purpose is to expose the fatal consequence of the intellectual's isolation from society at a time when it demands commitment. The diary provides such detailed attention to the protagonist's reflections and doubts that it is rather a psychological study of an individual. For Sanz Villanueva, the novel is the analysis of an existence scourged by historical events; for Corbalán, it shows not only the intellectual's, but also the common man's rejection of a war thrust upon him, as well as his moral judgement on its origins and consequences.[46] If it criticizes the 'so-called intellectual disinterestedness', it does so because it 'ultimately leads to dehumanization'.[47] As Anna Caballé suggests, Masip's is a 'contemporary Hamlet – a human character of hesitation' confronted with 'a situation of extreme complexity and confusion in which only conclusive answers are valid'; he undergoes a journey of self-knowledge, discovering new meaning in life, as he observes how men and women, in solidarity and not in isolation, struggle for something they know and want to defend.[48] Hamlet García's constant hesitation is not just over his political commitment but rather over his vital commitment, his attitude towards life itself.[49]

Such a detailed record of daily experiences and inner feelings invites speculation that the novel is autobiographical. Yet what we know about Paulino Masip's life makes it difficult to identify him with his protagonist. There are elements in common: Masip and Hamlet García are about the same age, for instance. Both were surprised by the outbreak of the war in Madrid while their families were on holiday, Masip's in León,[50] Hamlet García's in Ávila (65), both cities having fallen on the Nationalist side. Yet the journalist and writer Paulino Masip is not the detached lecturer of metaphysics Hamlet García. Masip served the Republic assiduously through his work for different newspapers. His front-page columns in the newspaper *La Vanguardia*, written in Barcelona, where he was reunited with his family in 1937, unmistakably support the Republican cause. In his 'Letter to a sceptical Spaniard', he compares Hamlet to a sceptical intellectual and encourages the latter to take action in support of the people. On his journey to exile in Mexico after the war, Masip wrote *Letters to a Spanish Emigré*,[51] in which he showed concern for the moral attitude of the exiles and encouraged them to carry on the struggle for Spain under their new conditions.[52] In the third letter of this collection, one can see a sketch of the plot and of the anti-heroic ordinary man that he would later develop in the novel *El diario*.[53] Masip's overt political commitment was the polar opposite of his Hamlet's apathy, and suggests that his portrait of this character is meant as a polemical critique, rather than a memoir of private doubts.

Masip began to write *El diario* not during the war, but as soon as he arrived in Mexico as an exile.[54] And as Faber states, 'for the exile, the simple act of writing becomes expressly political'.[55] Masip's writing of *El diario* can be seen as part of his effort to fulfil what he regarded as the duty of an intellectual in those historical circumstances, a moral duty which he has his character José Lazcano explain explicitly to Hamlet García. At the onset of the war, Lazcano recounts, he faced the moral problem. What course of action could he take, if he rejected both participating in destructive violent action and complaining about that destruction? His solution was to commit himself to his creative work as an intellectual, 'to keep working as I have been working, to create while others destroy, to do something while others undo so that tomorrow, when all this is over, not only ruins will remain ... And that's why I work more passionately than ever' (268).[56] This kind of passion can be discerned in Masip's front-page columns in *La Vanguardia*.

Zeal for creative production often characterizes the initial work of exiles.[57] As Antonio Muñoz Molina points out, exiles such as Masip obsessively endeavoured to remember their experience in Spain, to reconstruct it and to bear witness to what they experienced.[58] Having written his moral *Letters to a Spanish Emigré*, Masip might well have felt that he had the moral duty to write about his war experience and about the dilemmas it posed to intellectuals like him. To that end, he drew upon the example of Shakespeare's Hamlet as an iconic character immersed in internal debates about vital and political questions. In less than two years, in March 1941, he finished his first full novel, *El diario de Hamlet García*.[59] Given Masip's liking for weak-willed, melancholy characters and for introspection into their inner selves,[60] he decided to write about how war intruded and disrupted the individual's everyday life, even the life of someone who struggled to keep aloof and unconcerned, and he did so by focusing, through the structure of a fictional diary, on the inner self of a citizen of wartime Madrid, one with the sensitivity of an intellectual, and with an initial disposition to remain unperturbed by external reality, however harsh and imposing it might prove. Hamletism was a ready model from which to shape his own hero.

That Hamlet is the forename of Masip's Madrilenian citizen, García, allows him not only to draw attention to his novel, associating it with a well-known name, but also to use it more effectively in a further-reaching effort to revive and maintain defeated Republicans' collective memory and fighting spirit. As Jay M. Winter and Emmanuel Sivan point out, this counterpoint is the opposition that literature provides in times, such as in Spain after the Nationalist victory, when 'the writing of history' has become 'a routine operation dedicated to the glorification of the regime'.[61] Masip was aware of an inflection point – what Susan Suleiman calls a 'crisis of memory'[62] – in the way the war was to be represented, and he wanted to hammer home his act of remembrance by endowing his war story with the prestigious aura of Shakespeare's best-known protagonist. As in Suleiman's case studies, in Masip's novel 'individual self-representation overlaps with ... collective self-representation; put another way, individual remembrance takes on collective significance'.[63]

Masip's novel is a site of resistance which gives an account of a reality that, after the defeat, was being utterly wiped out, rewritten by the victors. In Hamlet García's last meeting with his former pupil Daniel, now a member of the militia, Masip inserts a criticism of manipulation of news about the siege of the Alcázar of Toledo (275–76). The novel is an unofficial *lieu de mémoire* – recalling Pierre Nora's title[64] – for exiled Spaniards, a site of remembrance[65] which provides them with a commemoration of the suffering of civilians in the rearguard, as well as the rationale that inspired the Republican cause.[66] Masip uses his anti-heroic re-imagining of Shakespeare's *Hamlet* not only to criticize wartime Hamletism, but also to recall and reflect upon the dilemmas which the experience of war thrust upon him and other contemporary intellectuals, as well as the attitudes, feelings and anxieties of the civilian population of Madrid at the onset of the Spanish Civil War.

Jesús Tronch is *professor titular* (Senior Lecturer) at the University of Valencia, where he teaches English literature and creative translation. He is the author of *A Synoptic* Hamlet (Publicacions de la Universitat de València/SEDERI, 2002) and *Un primer* Hamlet (Fundación Shakespeare de España, 1994) and co-editor of bilingual English-Spanish editions of *Antony and Cleopatra* (Cátedra, 2001) and *The Tempest* (Cátedra, 1994) as well as a critical edition of *The Spanish Tragedy* for the Arden Early Modern Drama series (Bloomsbury, 2013). His essays and reviews have appeared in journals such as *SEDERI, Atlantis, Shakespeare Survey* and *Shakespeare Quarterly*, as well as numerous collections. At present, he is editing *Timon of Athens* for the Internet Shakespeare Editions.

Notes

Research for this chapter was supported by the EMOTHE project funded by the Spanish government, reference number FFI 2016-80314-P, which is part of the national network of excellence FFI2015-71441-REDC.

1. Historical details of the Spanish Civil War are taken from Hugh Thomas, *The Spanish Civil War*, 3rd edition (Harmondsworth: Penguin Books, 1977), and Michael Alpert, *A New International History of the Spanish Civil War*, 2nd edition (Basingstoke: Palgrave, 2004).
2. For the range of cultural meanings of Hamletism, see R. Foakes, *Hamlet versus Lear* (Cambridge: Cambridge University Press, 1993), 19–44.
3. Paulino Masip, *El diario de Hamlet García* (1944; repr. Madrid: Consejería de Educación; Visor Libros, 2000).
4. Thomas, 268–79; Stanley Payne, *The Spanish Revolution* (London: Weidenfeld & Nicolson, 1970), 215–61.

5. Jesús Tronch, 'Spain', in *Hamlet Handbook*, ed. Peter. W. Marx (Stuttgart: Metzler Verlag, 2014), 289–95. In January 2016 I updated my searches in the digital periodicals archive of the Biblioteca Nacional de España, the virtual library of historical periodicals of the Spanish Ministry of Education, and the online archives of the newspapers *ABC* and *La Vanguardia*. See also Helena Buffery, *Shakespeare in Catalan: Translating Imperialism* (Cardiff: University of Wales Press, 2007), 19–60.
6. Sebastiaan Faber, *Exile and Cultural Hegemony: Spanish Intellectuals in Mexico, 1939–1975* (Nashville, TN: Vanderbilt University Press, 2002), 94.
7. Paulino Masip, 'Respuesta al doctor Marañón', *La Vanguardia*, 19 February 1937, 1.
8. Paulino Masip, 'Diálogos de la retaguardia', *La Vanguardia*, 21 February 1937, 1.
9. Paulino Masip, 'Carta a un español escéptico', *La Vanguardia*, 16 September 1937, 1.
10. As described in the online 'hemeroteca digital' of the Biblioteca Nacional de España and by Francisco Mundi, *El teatro de la guerra civil* (Barcelona: PPU, 1997), 320.
11. José Bergamín, '[Discurso]', *Hora de España* 8 (1937): 30–36, here 31. In a later article, 'Larra, peregrino en su tierra', *Hora de España* 9 (1937): 17–30, Bergamín refers to the 'melancholy Hamletism' of the nineteenth-century Spanish journalist and satirist Mariano José de Larra (28).
12. Robert Marrast, *El teatre durant la guerra civil espanyola* (Barcelona: Institut del Teatre/Edicions 62, 1978), 201 and 176; Ricard Blasco, *El teatre al País Valencià durant la guerra civil, 1936–1939* (Barcelona: Curial, 1986), vol. 1, quoting the yearbook *Almanque de 'Las Provincias'* (1940); Mundi, *El teatro*, 53; María Dolores Cosme Ferris, 'El teatro en la ciudad de Valencia: reconstrucción de la cartelera valenciana (1936–1939)' (Ph.D. diss., Universitat de València, 2008). Mundi only mentions *Hamlet* in Valencia. Marrast does not record the *Shrew* adaptation in Valencia. Oddly enough, he states that the *Hamlet* production was 'the only Shakespeare play that, as far as we know, was performed in Spain during the civil war' (201). César Oliva echoes this statement, although qualified by 'probably', in *El teatro desde 1936* (Madrid: Alhambra, 1989), 24, and by 'seemingly' ['al parecer'] in *Teatro Español del siglo XX* (Madrid: Editorial Síntesis, 2002), 127. Keith Gregor's admirable, and professedly selective, survey, *Shakespeare in the Spanish Theatre: 1772 to the Present* (London: Continuum, 2010), does not cover the civil war period. The great Catalan actress Margarita Xirgu (1888–1969) produced *Hamlet* and performed the title role herself in 1938 during her exile in South America. See Ricard Salvat, 'Revisió necessària de les grans aportacions de Margarita Xirgu', in *Margarita Xirgu 1888–1969* (Madrid: Comisión Promotora 'Casa del Teatro', 1988), 9–29.
13. Marrast, *El teatre*, 148. This Catalan tragedy was published in 1876, and Balaguer did not publicize it by using the name of Shakespeare, as noted by Buffery, *Shakespeare in Catalan*, 127. According to Fernando Collado, this Shakespearean tragedy was included by the *Consejo Central de Teatro* in a list of plays to be performed at the Teatro de la Zarzuela in Madrid, alongside plays by García Lorca, Chekhov, Calderón de la Barca, Maeterlinck and Cervantes: Fernando Collado, *El teatro bajo las bombas en la guerra civil* (Madrid: Kaydeda, 1989), 290. I have not found any reference to a Spanish-language *Coriolano* in the above-mentioned digital archives.

14. For the premiere date, *La Correspondencia de Valencia*, 8 December 1937, 2; *El Pueblo*, 8 December 1937, 3; *La Hora*, 8 December 1937, 11; and *El Mercantil Valenciano*, 8 December 1937, 4; all of them announcing 'the magnificent tragedy by Shakespeare, Hamlet'.
15. Unfortunately, I have not found any review in the periodicals I have consulted, nor have I come across any information about the cast, text or setting. The Institute of Social History in Amsterdam, which holds the archives of the Spanish anarchist union CNT that ran the Teatro Eslava, does not have any material related to Soler and Leal's company. In a telephone conversation in July 2010, I asked Soler and Leal's only daughter, the famous theatre and film actress Amparo Soler Leal, about materials or memories related to her parents' work, and she was sorry not to have or remember anything. She said that her mother had to destroy material when the war was over.
16. Figures are from Cosme Ferris, 'El teatro en la ciudad de Valencia'. In her list of 524 plays arranged from the most to least performed, *Hamlet* ranks 200 from top. The *Shrew* adaptation was performed twenty-two times, and ranks 120.
17. Marrast, *El teatre*, 212.
18. Ibid., 120.
19. Blasco, *El teatre al País Valencià*, vol. 1, 126.
20. Noelia Llidó, 'Salvador Soler Marí y Milagros Leal: Trayectoria teatral y breve biografía', *Stichomythia* 10 (2010): 33–48, here 41.
21. Blasco, *El teatre al País Valencià*, vol. 1, 129. All the plays mentioned are in Spanish. Plays in the minorized Valencian or Catalan language were a small percentage, regularly performed at Nostre Teatre in Valencia (Blasco, *El teatre al País Valencià*, vol. 2, 69–125).
22. Marrast, *El teatre*, 201.
23. See, for instance, Manuel Altolaguirre, 'Nuestro teatro', *Hora de España* 9 (October 1937): 29–37, and Mario Pommercy, 'Teatro del pueblo y para el pueblo', *La Correspondencia de Valencia*, 8 December 1937, 1. Other voices are cited by Blasco, *El teatre al País Valencià*.
24. Benavente was wedding godfather to Salvador Soler and Milagros Leal (Llidó, 'Salvador Soler Marí y Milagros Leal', 38).
25. Josep Lluís Sirera defines this play as an alternative to both the revolutionary and the escapist drama, in his article '¡*Qué más da!* de Enrique Beltrán y Alfredo Sendín Galiana', *Stichomythia* 7 (2007): 213–17, here 217.
26. Marrast, *El teatre*, 201–2; Llidó, 'Salvador Soler Marí y Milagros Leal', 42. On the *Shrew* adaptation, see María Dolores Cosme Ferris, 'Intentos de renovación en el teatro durante la guerra civil', *Stichomythia* 10 (2010): 3–9.
27. Marrast, *El teatre*, 203.
28. Mascarilla, 'Teatros. Principal. Una breve charla de Jacinto Benavente', *El Mercantil Valenciano*, 4 December 1936, 4.
29. Marrast, *El teatre*, 212; Blasco, *El teatre al País Valencià*, vol. 1, 147.
30. See newspaper references in note 14.
31. See Gregor, *Shakespeare in the Spanish Theatre*, and Juan Francisco Cerdá Martínez, 'Shakespeare and the Renovation of Spanish Theatrical Culture (1898–1936)' (Ph.D. diss., Universidad de Murcia, 2010). José María Pemán's adaptation *Julieta y Romeo* was performed just before the war.

32. Tronch, 'Spain', 292.
33. Fernando de la Milla, trans. and adapt., *El príncipe de Dinamarca, versión libérrima de Hamlet* (Madrid: Prensa Moderna, 1928).
34. A. A. Smirnov, *Shakespeare: A Marxist Interpretation*, trans. Sonia Volochova (New York: The Critic's Group, 1936), 66.
35. Faber, *Exile and Cultural Hegemony*, 109.
36. Santos Sanz Villanueva, *Historia de la literatura española: 6/2 Literatura actual* (Barcelona: Ariel, 1984), 194; Pablo Corbalán, 'Prólogo', in Paulino Masip, *El diario de Hamlet García* (1944, repr. Barcelona: Anthropos, 1987), 7–18, 16; Anna Caballé, *Sobre la vida y obra de Paulino Masip* (Barcelona: Ediciones del Mall, 1987), 64.
37. Page numbers in parentheses are keyed to the 2000 edition of Masip's *El diario* (see note 3).
38. Eugenio G. de Nora, *La novela española contemporánea*, 2nd edition, vol. 3 (1962; repr. Madrid: Gredos, 1973), 77–78.
39. Corbalán, 'Prólogo', 14.
40. Caballé, *Sobre la vida y obra de Paulino Masip*, 57.
41. Corbalán, 'Prólogo', 15.
42. References to the text(s) of *Hamlet* are keyed to *A Synoptic 'Hamlet'*, ed. Jesús Tronch-Pérez (Valencia and Zaragoza: Publicacions de la Universitat de València/ SEDERI, 2002), in its turn following the widely used *Riverside Shakespeare*, ed. G. B. Evans (Boston, MA: Houghton Mifflin Company, 1974).
43. Johann Wolfgang Goethe, *Wilhelm Meisters Lehjahre / Wilhelm Meister's Apprenticeship*, 1796, trans. Eric Blackall (New York: Suhrkamp, 1989), book 4, chapter 13, 145–46.
44. Faber, *Exile and Cultural Hegemony*, 109.
45. De Nora, *La novela española contemporánea*, 31; Rafael Conte, 'La novela española en el exilio', *Cuadernos para el diálogo* 14 (1969): 36–37.
46. Sanz Villanueva, *Historia*, 194; Corbalán, 'Prólogo', 15.
47. Faber, *Exile and Cultural Hegemony*, 110.
48. Caballé, *Sobre la vida y obra de Paulino Masip*, 64 and 67.
49. Ibid., 68–96.
50. Ibid., 30.
51. Paulino Masip, *Cartas a un emigrado español* (México: Publicaciones de la Junta de Cultura Española, 1939). For the date of composition, see Caballé, *Sobre la vida y obra de Paulino Masip*, 34.
52. Caballé, *Sobre la vida y obra de Paulino Masip*, 34, 94.
53. Ibid., 36.
54. Corbalán, 'Prólogo', 8.
55. Faber, *Exile and Cultural Hegemony*, x.
56. In the Spanish original: 'Trabajar como venía trabajando: crear mientras los otros destruyen, hacer algo mientras los otros deshacen para que el día de mañana cuando esto acabe, no sean sólo ruinas lo que quede ... Y por eso trabajo con más pasión que nunca'.
57. Corbalán, 'Prólogo', 8.
58. Antonio Muñoz Molina, 'Nubes atravesadas por aviones: la novela fantasmal de Paulino Masip', in Paulino Masip, *El diario de Hamlet García* (Madrid: Consejería de Educación; Visor Libros, 2000), 7–12.

59. As he refused to have it published in Spain because he had to submit it to the regime's censorship (Corbalán, 'Prólogo', 7), the novel was not issued until 1944 in Mexico, and remained relatively unknown for the Spanish general readership until published in Barcelona in 1987 (Muñoz Molina, 'Nubes atravesadas por aviones', 8).
60. Caballé, *Sobre la vida y obra de Paulino Masip*, 27, 56.
61. Jay M. Winter and Emmanuel Sivan, eds., *War and Remembrance in the Twentieth Century* (Cambridge: Cambridge University Press, 1999), 7.
62. Susan Rubin Suleiman, *Crises of Memory and the Second World War* (Cambridge, MA: Harvard University Press, 2006), 1.
63. Ibid.
64. Pierre Nora, ed., *Les Lieux de mémoire*, 7 vols (Paris: Gallimard, 1984–92).
65. For Winter and Sivan's preference for the term 'remembrance' over 'memory', see their introduction to *War and Remembrance*, as well as Jay Winter, *Remembering War: The Great War between Memory and History in the Twentieth Century* (New Haven, CT: Yale University Press, 2006), 3, 276–77.
66. In her essay, 'El espectro de Hamlet: Hamletisme, Hamlet García, *Hamlet, Dramaturg*', in *Exilio y Universidad (1936–1955)*, ed. J. A. Ascunce et al. (San Sebastián: Saturraran, S.L., 2008), 842–59, Helena Buffery sees Masip's novel as an example of how Hamlet served as a starting point for exile writers 'to explore and question the role of the intellectual at a "time out of joint"' (843), and connects Masip with Ramon Vinyes and his play (in Catalan) *Hamlet, dramaturg* (1944) and with Salvador de Madariaga and his appraisal of the Shakespearean hero in his essay *On Hamlet* (1948).

Chapter 7
Where Character Is King
Gregory Doran's Henriad

Alice Dailey

There is something of a red herring in the title of the RSC's recent mega-event, 'King and Country: Shakespeare's Great Cycle of Kings'. Headlined by David Tennant in the role of Richard II, the four-play Henriad directed by Gregory Doran was staged in Stratford, London and China before its sold-out, month-long finale at the Brooklyn Academy of Music, where I saw it in April 2016. In addition to declaring kingship and nationality its key conceptual interests, the title describes a spectacle of significant scale – of greatness: the double greatness of Shakespeare and of this group of plays. What I encountered when I saw the cycle at the BAM Harvey was something quite different: a more modest, intimate group of productions that were less interested in a conceptual engagement with politics or monarchy than in an exploration of character. In a conversation with James Shapiro during the run at BAM, Doran, current Artistic Director at the RSC, explained that he is 'not a conceptual director'.

Notes for this section begin on page 154.

Recounting his training at the Bristol Old Vic Theatre School, he quoted the advice of his influential mentor, Rudi Shelley, who once wagged a reproving finger at him and intoned, 'Greg, don't want to be clever'. 'And you know', summarized Doran, 'that was the best piece of advice a classical theatre director could ever have'.[1]

'King and Country' was not 'clever', especially by comparison to the eight-play Histories cycle directed in 2007 by Doran's predecessor at the RSC, Michael Boyd.[2] While Boyd's cycle made elaborate use of conceptual casting, stylized battle scenes, trapeze, prop recycling and ghostly reappearance to create thematic coherence across the plays, Doran's Henriad was comparatively lean on concept, offering conspicuously few moments of design-driven staging and instead staking its fortune on character and ensemble acting.[3] Apart from Tennant's pop-culture caché, the productions felt slightly out of vogue in their relatively low-tech, simply designed style. It is precisely for this reason, however, that Doran's Henriad provides a useful site for testing the claims of recent character criticism, itself making a comeback in Shakespeare studies after being long out of fashion.

In their introduction to *Shakespeare and Character*, Paul Yachnin and Jessica Slights defend the study of character by observing that Shakespearean drama inverts Aristotelian principles that subjugate character to plot. They quote this key passage from Aristotle's *Poetics:* 'Dramatic action ... is not with a view to the representation of character: character comes in as subsidiary to the actions. Hence the incidents and the plot are the end of a tragedy; and the end is the chief thing of all. Again, without action there cannot be a tragedy; there may be without character'.[4] Yachnin and Slights argue that Shakespeare's intervention in conventional dramatic genres reverses this basic hierarchy of character and plot:

> Shakespeare tends to overturn the Aristotelian ranking of plot and character by reworking traditional narrative types such as revenge tragedy, romantic courtship, struggle for mastery between husband and wife, or the story of growth-into-adulthood so that character displaces plot as the center of interest in ways that determine the kinds of elements we find in the plays and how those elements are organized.[5]

How does this claim of Shakespeare's privileging of character over plot apply to the history plays, which are anchored – albeit loosely at times – in the plots of historical record? How does the performance of multiple, formally diverse histories as a unified cycle complicate our understanding of the relationship between Shakespearean plots and characters? Can Doran's consistent emphasis on characterization work for all four plays, or do the plays take disparate approaches to characterization that call for diverse directorial styles, acting methods or staging concepts?

In addressing such questions to Doran's Henriad, we may be tempted to fall back on the literary hermeneutics that underlie much of our scholarly and pedagogical engagement with Shakespearean performance. For example, we might trace how the productions synthesize broad concepts into pivotal, representative moments; observe how they impose thematic coherence across disparate texts; or suggest how they dramatize patterns and motifs to create a sense of authorial (or directorial) genius. But as performance scholars like W. B. Worthen and Andrew James Hartley have argued, staged Shakespeare cannot be understood simply as a dramatization of the Shakespearean text that can be analysed through textual hermeneutics. Worthen notes that literary-critical approaches to performance tend to describe 'correspondences' between a theatrical production and its textual source, focusing on how performance offers an 'interpretation' of the text.[6] This approach has marked limitations, he argues, because 'the significance of the [theatrical] event can't be reduced to mere communication, the transmission of an "interpretation" of Shakespeare's play'.[7] In a complementary analysis, Hartley specifically addresses the role of performance in constructing Shakespearean character. 'Character', he writes, 'is the hybrid production of actor and scripted role, something that cannot inhere merely in the material document (the play in the book) and requires the equally material conditions of the stage in order to come into being. ... Character is an embodied phenomenon'.[8]

By foregrounding characterization, resisting overarching interpretive claims and eschewing design-forward staging concepts, Doran's Henriad illustrated the inadequacy of conventional literary-critical hermeneutics for describing theatrical performance. The cycle invites literary scholars of Shakespeare to expand our analytical vocabularies beyond the textual and the readerly to include terms by which theatre practitioners constitute character. If we lack this vocabulary, many of the more subtle elements of the productions elude discussion. But the cycle also demonstrated the degree to which embodied character is indeed a 'hybrid production', to borrow Hartley's phrase – an 'embodied phenomenon' produced through the actor's engagement with spoken text. As Doran's cycle moved into the reign of Henry V, actorly method precluded connections between embodied character and the script from which that character claimed verbal and physical agency. In its mixture of achievement and flaw, 'King and Country' suggests how a mutually informing conversation between theatre practitioners and literary critics can advance our understanding of character in Shakespeare's history plays.

Conveying both the subtle contours of human psychology and the character's histrionic skill, David Tennant presented a significantly different Richard II from the one played by Jonathan Slinger in Boyd's 2007 cycle, which used programme notes, costuming, makeup and a curly red wig to analogize Richard to Elizabeth I. Over the course of Boyd's play, the king was gradually stripped of his elaborate finery to reveal the diseased mortal body underneath. By contrast, Tennant's Richard was costumed elegantly but simply, though his prim intonation and much-talked-about wig similarly characterized him as effete and haughty. Unlike in Boyd's production, however, these attributes did not accrue into an articulable plot arc or 'reading' of the play. For example, one of the most arresting moments of the production occurred during the exchange between Richard and Aumerle (Sam Marks) when Aumerle begins to weep on the battlements of Flint Castle ('Aumerle, thou weep'st, my tender-hearted cousin' [*R2* 3.3.159]).[9] Sitting next to each other on a scaffold spanning the stage, legs dangling beneath them as they mourned their unfolding catastrophe, Richard and Aumerle kissed. Richard then cradled Aumerle's head against his chest, consoling the weeping younger man in a gesture at once protective, fraternal and romantic. While it has become somewhat commonplace to represent Richard's court as a gay playboy coterie, as in the recent BBC miniseries *The Hollow Crown*, Doran's production had not explicitly pursued this reading. The kiss was therefore not integral to a broader concept governing the production. Rather, it was the expression of a complex, singular impulse that suggested an imbricated set of identities for Richard at this particular moment in the play: patriarch, matriarch, object of desire, desiring subject, friend, man, woman.

One is tempted to extend such a moment into a grand plot, extrapolating from it precisely the kind of 'interpretation' Worthen warns against. Charles Isherwood's *New York Times* review of 'King and Country' did precisely this, asking of the scene, 'Are we to believe that Richard's growing awareness of his vulnerable humanity, the growth into spiritual dignity that makes him a near-tragic figure, is a direct result of his sexual awakening? This seems reductive, and has a modestly deflating effect on both a fine performance and a fine production'.[10] Isherwood is right: this seems reductive. It deflates. But I would argue that the production neither invited nor pursued this interpretation. The desire for the kiss to produce something 'we are to believe' about Richard's arc towards 'spiritual dignity' – a phrase to which I will return – emerges from critical habit, in this case a theatre critic's expectation that the kiss should correspond legibly to his reading of the text. There is nothing textual about the content of this moment, as Worthen might remind us. It eludes critical interpretation, exposing what we lose when we press subtle moments of embodied characterization into the service of a totalizing 'reading'.

If the kiss can be plotted on a developmental arc, it was a much shorter one that primarily affected the immediate thirty lines exchanged on the main stage when Richard emblematically 'c[a]me down' to the 'base court' (*R2* 3.3.181). Before the kiss, Richard seemed to languish in the self-epitaphing imagery of his impending death. But his intimate contact with Aumerle – particularly as a response to Aumerle's naked expression of vulnerability, need and fear – generated in Richard a palpable resilience that buoyed him into the de facto resignation of his kingdom to Bolingbroke twenty-five lines later. In a talk about the play during its run at the Barbican, Tennant remarked how the exchange with Aumerle was, to him, an exceptional 'moment of human contact [that] sort of gave him the strength to surrender' at Flint Castle. The confidence gathered from this moment built into his dignified management of the deposition scene, in which Richard 'shames Henry's court', as Tennant put it.[11] Rather than treating homoerotic contact as a revelation of underlying desires – desires that would account for either Richard's troubled kingship or his dignified death – the spontaneous kiss resisted absorption into the tidy 'growth into spiritual dignity' that Isherwood describes. It located Richard's rhetorical confidence in an erotic form of contact, one that generated what would more rightly be described as the explicitly embodied dignity that arises from another person's desire.

As my discussion here suggests, the content of this moment is difficult to articulate and therefore impossible to preserve from the effects of time that render performance ephemeral. Although the subtle dynamics of the scene may be somewhat legible in the RSC's video recording, it cannot be summarized by a neat 'interpretation', expressed as a statement of character ('In Doran's Henriad, Richard was a king who ____'), or captured in still photos of the production. This wonderfully ephemeral quality marks one of the principal ways that Doran's Henriad differed from Boyd's. Much can be gleaned about Boyd's treatment of *Richard II* from an emblematic RSC production still of Jonathan Slinger in a tattered gown, sores on his closely shaved scalp and a fine stream of light and sand pouring down on his head. Like the many explicitly iconographic tableaux of *The Hollow Crown*'s production, such images are almost more painterly than they are theatrical.[12] By contrast, the most substantive content of Doran's production is not visible in press photos and is likely to be glimpsed only incompletely from what is preserved in the RSC archive.[13] Relying solely on such material to account for theatrical content reproduces what Rebecca Schneider describes (with Jacques Derrida and Diana Taylor) as a privileging of archival evidence over 'other ways of knowing', such as those generated by performance.[14] What remains of live theatre as the object of critical analysis is often design or concept, which is preserved intact in production archives. In the case of Tennant's Richard, the ephemeral, emotive present constituted the essential content of the production.

In contrast to the subtle character work that animated the Richard-Aumerle kiss scene, the production's later treatment of the two characters fell into a less compelling, more plot-driven mode that was indeed bound to the sort of interpretive gesture that troubled Isherwood. Like a number of prominent productions of the play, including *The Hollow Crown*, this one did away with the character of Exton and made Aumerle Richard's murderer. The production set this ending up by combining 5.3 and 5.4, so that Henry spoke Exton's line, 'Have I no friend will rid me of this living fear' directly to Aumerle rather than Exton asking two unnamed men if they 'mark[ed]' the words Henry spoke (*R2* 5.4.1–2). By eliminating 5.4 and having Henry speak his wish directly on the heels of Aumerle's pardon, Doran's production eliminated the ambiguity of will and intention so central to its backstory of Woodstock's murder and to its representation of Bolingbroke's rise. The broader effect of these revisions, particularly in concert with the earlier kiss moment, was to contract the political scope of Richard's murder into a romantic drama centred on him and Aumerle. While the elimination of Exton made Aumerle a more complex, interesting character, its overall effect was to enlist what had been a subtle character moment into a plot. The typological parallels Richard drew between his deposition scene and Jesus's betrayal – especially via the long, white gown he wore in the deposition and his reference to Judas's kiss – were likewise transformed into a plot.

Tennant remarked that the play felt incomplete without making these adjustments – that 'it feels like Shakespeare meant [the murderer] to be Aumerle' but may have been forced to a hasty revision by Aumerle's descendants, just as the descendants of Oldcastle are believed to have intervened against Shakespeare's early Falstaff. With Exton as the murderer, 'the whole scene with the King and the Yorks doesn't really go anywhere', Tennant argues.[15] But Shakespeare imported Exton straight from Holinshed's *Chronicles*, along with the detail of Exton overhearing Henry's remark.[16] The company's collective dissatisfaction with the written ending – and the production's resulting revision to make the play more 'complete' – privileges plot over character in the manner described by Aristotle, a privileging that is inverted, Yachnin and Slights argue, in Shakespeare's plays. In other words, the decision to make Aumerle the murderer expresses an Aristotelian value that Tennant describes as more authentically Shakespearean. Further, his remarks replace the emotional authority of performance with the authority of an original text, albeit an imagined one. The decision to make Aumerle the murderer arose from a performance-based, actor-experienced 'Shakespeare' that unfolded in rehearsal, but Tennant's reference to forced revisions suggests how even for actors, performative authority is ideally underwritten by textual or historical authority. While critics may misguidedly pursue correspondences between texts and their subsequent performances, as Worthen notes, the same can happen in reverse, as when an actor wrests the author's text to correspond to the 'truth' of performance.[17]

The cycle's production of *1 Henry IV* was largely true to Doran's non-conceptual style, with the exception of a striking transitional moment: in Act 2, between Scenes 4 and 5, Hotspur and Hal appeared together in a surreal on-stage face-to-face (the Folio text delays their meeting until the penultimate scene of the play). Creating a long cross-fade effect, Hotspur remained downstage centre at the end of his scene with Lady Percy, where he was then joined by Hal as the company reset the scenery behind them for the tavern. The two young men stood looking at each other from a few feet apart in a character-foil tableau. As in *Richard II*, however, the most compelling elements of their contrast emerged in subtle characterization rather than conceptual intervention. Alex Hassell's Prince Hal was wiry, energetic, outgoing and, above all, good humoured, particularly in comparison to Tom Hiddleston's recent Hal in *The Hollow Crown*, who is more sober and aloof. His desire for discretion seemed genuinely overcome by the spirit of fun, such as when he at length agreed to the Gadshill robbery. The conviviality of his tavern life, especially the companionship of Poins (Sam Marks again), was represented as authentically seductive rather than merely a strategic ploy for setting off his later reformation. The production created a stark contrast between this Hal and a taut, humourless Hotspur played by Matthew Needham. Although his penchant for hyperbole and outrage occasionally provoked laughter from the audience, Needham's Hotspur found no humour in himself and took no perceptible pleasure in his own rhetorical flights of fancy. He was unusually intense, especially given that the character is often played as likeably impetuous, if not charming and sexy. (Boyd's Histories emphasized Hotspur's youthful chivalric heroism by doubling him with John Talbot of *1 Henry VI*, and in *The Hollow Crown* both the scene with Lady Percy and the scene at Glendower's castle end with Hotspur taking his wife to bed.) In Needham's rendering, the character seethed with an intimidating rage, his awkward physical stiffness suggesting a sociopathic temper kept tenuously under control. The contrast between the two young men figured by the cross-fade tableau was thus elaborated most compellingly at the level of vocal and physical character work that set Hal's playfulness, wiry energy and expressive pleasure against Hotspur's humourless, bristling tension.

In its representation of the relationship between Hal and his father in *1* and *2 Henry IV*, the cycle partnered with the audience to fill out dramatic character. At the start of his 'I know you all' soliloquy at the end of 1.2, the house lights came up and Hal playfully addressed the audience as though we were the idle 'all' whom he claimed to know (*1H4* 1.2.192–93). Initially this looked like simply the standard, comic audience-address gambit that has become so popular through the rise of Original Practices staging. The full effect of Hal's soliloquy was not realized until *2 Henry IV*, when we were again addressed directly, this time in a scene that could have no comic implications. In the speech to Hal that is usually delivered from his deathbed, Henry IV (Jasper Britton) rose and directed his dreadful apocalyptic vision to us, as though we were the nation of England: 'O, thou wilt be a wilderness again', he thundered, 'Peopled with wolves, thy old inhabitants' (*2H4* 4.3.265–66). The same audience Hal had light-heartedly invoked as confederates in his future reformation were here summoned by Henry IV as witnesses to the doom of Hal's succession. The effect was to shame Hal – to expose his son to the very audience Hal had trained to his confidence. Hal's cover was blown. By disgracing him before the audience and inviting us to view him as an object of horror, Britton's Henry IV undid his son's capacity to perform. It was this exposure *to us* that motivated Hal's plea for forgiveness, 'O pardon me, my liege!' (*2H4* 4.3.267).

The effects created by Henry's direct address to the audience were sharpened by Doran's reversal of staging conventions in both this scene and the scene in *1 Henry IV* when the king chastises Hal at court (3.2). Although Henry prefaces his reprimand with an order for privacy – 'Lords, give us leave – the Prince of Wales and I / Must have some private conference – but be near at hand' – the exchange between them is often staged with the lords falling back to the periphery rather than exiting altogether, as in both Boyd's rendering and *The Hollow Crown* (*1H4* 3.2.1–2). In Doran's *1 Henry IV*, these lines were cut and the scene took place entirely in private, with father and son sitting side by side on a bench centre-stage. The blocking created an unexpected filial intimacy between Henry and Hal that was then palpably compromised in the next play. The deathbed scene in *2 Henry IV* begins with Henry's more explicit demand for privacy: 'Depart the chamber; leave us here alone' – and is customarily staged with the two men alone together and Henry in bed (*2H4* 4.3.219). The decision for Henry to rise from bed and directly address the audience multiplied rather than eliminated spectators to the scene. Through the simple reversing of staging conventions for these two key scenes, Doran's productions provocatively altered the dynamic between father and son. Instead of moving from an open chastisement to a private confrontation, as conventional blocking has it, the reversal of public and private characterized Hal's profligacy as a growing threat, not merely to the father-son relationship or to Hal's inherited crown but to civilization itself.

If the strength of the first three plays lay in their range of strategies for building and communicating character, the weakness of its treatment of the career of Henry V was likewise tied to characterization. From the outset of *1 Henry IV*, Antony Sher's Falstaff was out of breath with weight and age, making it difficult for the cycle to communicate a tonal shift from his playfulness in *Part One* to his melancholic sickliness in *Part Two*. Several of Falstaff's key speeches, such as the 'catechism' on honour that concludes 5.1, were delivered with Sher standing still at centre-stage, and during Hal's climactic rejection speech at the end of *2 Henry IV*, he was turned completely upstage, obscuring any facial expression. These blocking choices contributed to a conspicuously flat end to the Hal-Falstaff relationship, which had itself never fully gotten off the ground. As fellow audience member Alan Farmer summarized it, Sher's 'glacial delivery allowed the audience to understand Falstaff's verbal humour, but it did little to help suggest a deep relationship with Hal. Nor did it make Falstaff seem especially dangerous, to Hal or to the nation, thereby making Hal's rejection of him seem unnecessary and rather random. Neither the plot nor the character seemed to require this rejection'.[18]

Hassell's performance as the newly crowned Henry V likewise contributed to a disappointing ending for *2 Henry IV*. He delivered the 'I know thee not' monologue to Falstaff as if he couldn't get through the lines quickly enough, blazing through its several full stops at a dizzying clip (*2H5* 5.5.47–71). The aim of this delivery seemed to be to suggest Hal's discomfort with what needed to be said, as though it had been devised in advance, rehearsed meticulously, and then uttered in one breath lest he should fail to perform the unaccustomed character of authority. While this may have been psychologically realistic, it was not dramatically compelling, nor did it create a satisfying conclusion to the *Henry IV* plays. Moreover, as another audience member remarked to me after the show, it wasn't entirely clear whose memorization, rehearsal and breathless utterance we were watching: the actor's or the character's. Borrowing a formulation from Stanislavskian method to describe the illusion of theatrical character, Cary M. Mazer has described how '"doing real things in imagined circumstances[,]" the actor is perceived by the audience to be the character'.[19] What, then, caused the illusion of the Henry V character to break down? Hassell's performance of Hal dismissing Falstaff as though he (which he?) were completing a rehearsed, artificial and uncomfortable act proved to be a particularly fraught interpretive choice, given that it was the first public scene of Henry V's reign; in the context of the cycle, the actor and the character were both playing new roles. When the actor played the new role as rehearsed or artificial action – not as 'doing real things' – the audience failed to perceive the actor as the character. Henry's uncomfortable mimicry of kingship wasn't sufficiently distinguishable from an actor's uncomfortable mimicry of Henry.

Acting method likewise troubled *Henry V* – or it did for me; much of the audience appeared to find the production compelling. As in the climactic scene of *2 Henry IV*, Hassell flew through many of the key monologues of *Henry V*. Here too, his frenetic style of delivery seemed intended to indicate Henry's discomfort with the role of king. But Doran's play script had not been correspondingly adapted to reflect this understanding of the character. For instance, as in the Folio text, Doran's Canterbury described Henry V in the opening scene not as an ill-fitting, unconvincing king persona but as a seemingly innate role expressed through mastery of a wide range of rhetorical domains (*H5* 1.1.39–60). In the subsequent tennis ball monologue of Henry's first scene, the character was played as though out of his element, uncomfortable with the regal performance required. This characterization jarred against the spoken script of the monologue, a more or less unedited version of the Folio text and a tour de force of political confidence, one that figured Henry in complete rhetorical control. In Hassell's performance, Henry was at once tentative and hurried, as though arriving at each turn of metaphor by accident with neither a clear sense of the effects he intended to create nor pleasure in the kind of improvisational challenge that had energized him in the earlier plays. At the end of the scene, the messenger's exit was punctuated by a relieved sigh from Henry as he momentarily dropped the act, sinking exhausted into his throne before his peers and clergy.

If, as both Worthen and Hartley suggest, the phenomenon of theatrical performance is generated through cooperation of text and non-text (body, space, voice, time), Doran's *Henry V* manifested a lack of coordination between these different constituent elements. The discontinuities between the production script and the actor's performance of it seemed to emerge from the desire for psychological and temporal realism. In an interview about the play, Hassell remarked, 'The question of what has happened in between *Henry the Fourth, Part Two*, and *Henry V* is a very interesting one. It seems that some time has passed, but we, I think, have decided – sort of emotionally –

to feel like it was five minutes ago, so that Henry hasn't yet acclimatized to his new position, essentially'.[20] Hassell's reflections point to the central importance of 'feeling' in his process of generating the character of Henry V. As he notes, the emotion that motivates this character was not indicated by the play script but was, on the contrary, at odds with it: 'it seems [*from the script*] that some time has passed, but we...'. The purpose of this counter-textual feeling was to create a sense of immediacy that motivated the character's utterances in *Henry V*, in which he was presented in the ongoing process of acclimatizing to his position – of acclimatizing *now*, in the time in which the play was unfolding. In Mazer's terms, Hassell's performance 'fetishize[d] "spontaneity" [by] invoking "the illusion of the first time"'.[21] It illustrated what he calls 'the cliché of method acting – ... that the actor is always "in the moment". This creates the apparent truthfulness of the performer's and the performance's existence in the perpetual present tense. The actor, doing real things in imagined circumstances, does them in "real" – i.e., in the audience's – time'.[22]

Hartley traces this style of acting-as-spontaneity not just to method training but, more specifically, to Shakespearean actor training such as that illustrated by Patsy Rodenburg's influential guide, *Speaking Shakespeare*. Describing Hal's soliloquy at the end of the first act of *1 Henry IV* (discussed above), Rodenburg calls the moment an 'epiphany', a realization in the now: 'Now he understands that he has been mixing with villains and will have to change. He is growing up'.[23] As Hartley points out, this reading puts the 'actorly method' ahead of the meaning of the text, which suggests, rather, that Hal is disclosing his plans to us, not discovering them now. Hartley goes on to explain how this prioritizing of method – this reading of actorly work as textual work – can create an illusion of immediacy:

> Rodenburg treats the moment as epiphanic because it raises the stakes for Hal, makes him more immediate and honest in his presence and utterance. Above all, it puts him in the state of readiness that foregrounds and enacts the character's agency. Though a dissembling Hal confessing his methods to the audience would still be in control, a Hal coming to a discovery and using that energy to drive him forward into a new course of action (however much it looks suspiciously like the old one) is more vivid, more active. For Rodenburg and many actors of Shakespeare, Shakespearean characters are self-possessed subjects who speak their minds and direct their own course, and

it is not mere coincidence that for Rodenburg the word 'character' can be used of the scripted role alone. The actor brings into being a character that, for her, has ontological presence in the text, the actor's agency asserted and contained by the script in ways that lend urgency and authority to the performance. The resulting personation is seen to 'work' because the creative agency of the performer is subsumed within the cues perceived to be inherent in the text.[24]

Hartley describes precisely the problem of Doran's *Henry V*. Doran eschews 'clever' concept because it intervenes artificially between the Shakespearean text and the audience. For him, actor and director working together without the interference of concept can communicate Shakespeare's work more faithfully – can follow what Hartley calls 'the cues perceived to be inherent in the text'.[25] The performance of epiphany – of Hal figuring it out in the moment – creates an approximation of agency and therefore spontanaeity, presence, realism and coming-into-being. While this illusion of presence may (and did) please the audience, the construction of character-discovering-*now* did not cohere with the representation of character-as-already-realized in Doran's script. Further, although acting method inculcates a view of the character as a 'self-possessed subject', the script's Henry V was not that kind of character. While *1* and *2 Henry IV* explored the various roles Hal might choose for himself – how he might 'direct [his] own course', as Hartley puts it – self-direction was not the focus of Doran's script for *Henry V*, which depicted the character's fulfilment of an already-plotted role.

That role was not being formed in the present. As in the Folio text, it was dictated by generations – not only by the 'ill' Henry described himself inheriting through his father's usurpation but by the ancestral models other characters repeatedly invoked (*H5* 4.1.301). In a typological description that was echoed across the production, for example, Canterbury urged Henry,

> Look back into your mighty ancestors.
> Go, my dread lord, to your great-grandsire's tomb,
> From whom you claim; invoke his warlike spirit,
> And your great-uncle's, Edward the Black Prince,
> Who on the French ground played a tragedy,
> Making defeat on the full power of France,
> Whiles his most mighty father on a hill
> Stood smiling to behold his lion's whelp
> Forage in blood of French nobility. (*H5* 1.2.102–10)

In Canterbury's formulation, the development of Henry into the figure of his great-grandfather or great-uncle is not principally character development so much as it is the fulfilment of role and plot: will Henry succeed in replicating the conquests of his ancestors? Providence, which Henry described as bringing the traitors to light in Act 2 and leading the English to victory in Act 4, similarly worked as a form of plot-fulfilment. The 'tragedy' referenced by Canterbury that was 'on the French ground played' was not the Shakespearean tragedy Yachnin and Slights describe, which prioritizes character over plot. It was an Aristotelian tragedy, a bloody war in which Edward III, a plot-function more than a character, won France.

This is not to say that Doran's script for *Henry V* wasn't interested in the character of Henry V. But he was not the same kind of character as Richard II, as Doran's casting alone suggests: Richard II was played by an international star and Henry V by a relatively unknown younger actor. The directorial choice to foreground Henry's psychological process, however immediate, was fundamentally a mismatch with the character scripted by the production. Unlike *Richard II*, in which the king took over a political drama to become its central tragic focus, the spoken text of *Henry V* was not occupied with Hal's interior psychological state. Employing acting method to construct emotional immediacy – but with a script that did not constitute character in these terms – created dissonance between actor and script, even if it also generated appreciation for the visibly hard work of acting.

By emphasizing immediate character motivation but not significantly cutting, revising or reorganizing the Folio source, the production lost sight of the play's distinct strategies for constituting character, such as its dialogic structure for suggesting Henry's smooth deflection of moral responsibility. This tactic was not something the script represented Hal 'coming into discovery of', to borrow Hartley's phrase.[26] Rather, it was a strategy the character deployed with complete success in the very first scene of the play, where Henry manoeuvred the clergy into accepting responsibility for war (Canterbury: 'The sin upon my head, dread sovereign' [*H5* 1.2.97]) and then again as he cited the Dauphin's insult as the retroactive cause for a war he had already declared ('This mock of his / Hath turned his balls to gunstones, and his soul / Shall stand sore charged for the wasteful vengeance / That shall fly from them' [*H5* 1.2.281–84]). By suggesting Henry's spontaneous discovery of his role, the production attempted to sanitize the character of premeditation or strategy, although premeditation and strategy were features of the spoken text in nearly every major episode: Henry's staged drama of killed mercy in his confrontation with the traitors (2.2); the Harfleur speech, which diverted responsibility for rape and murder to the potential victims (3.3); his deflection of moral responsibility for battle deaths onto divine justice and the souls of his individual soldiers (4.1); his killing of the French prisoners, ordered before, not after, he learned of the luggage boys' murder (4.6). Even his 'idol ceremony' soliloquy after talking with Williams in disguise revealed Henry's characteristic shiftings; contrary to the conventional description he invokes of 'vacant-mind[ed]' commoners in deep slumber, his soldiers had in that very scene glimpsed 'horrid night, the child of hell' as they sat awake anticipating the violence only he could prevent (*H5* 4.1.237, 266, 268). With the exception of the Harfleur speech, Henry's habitual moral deflection was revealed through the form of the play – through the relationship of one event to the next in a structure at once linear and recursive. As in the Folio text, for example, Henry's chastisement of the traitors took on the cast of hypocrisy through two structural juxtapositions: first, through the juxtaposition between the traitor's betrayal of Henry and Henry's betrayal of Falstaff, whose death was unfolding in a simultaneous-yet-sequential, contrapuntal subplot; and second, through the juxtaposition between Henry's condemnation of the traitors for their deception and the calculated theatricality with which he managed their arrest. The production's focus on Henry's immediate, in-the-now psychological process constituted a basic disparity with how the play otherwise made meaning and character structurally and diachronically – not immediately and synchronically – through accumulation and recursion rather than revelation in the present.

By consistently suggesting that Henry was figuring out his warrior-king role on the fly, the production simply wanted too much for Henry to be a good guy. This desire came to function as the kind of concept that Doran describes negatively – a concept that 'get[s] between Shakespeare', by which he means the Shakespearean text, 'and the audience'.[27] There is evidence that this character-concept for Henry was developed when the production was sutured to the rest of the cycle after first being performed as a stand-alone play. In a promotional video by RSC Live before the plays were combined into 'King and Country', Hal performs the 'I know you all' speech from

1 Henry IV with cynical menace.[28] This quality was altogether absent when the plays were staged as a cycle, where Henry instead wept mournfully as he read the names of the French dead, having killed them with reluctance ('The names of their nobles that lie dead' [*H5* 4.8.91–112]). The dissonance between Hassell's nice-guy portrayal of Henry V and the production script, which seemed to have undergone little concomitant revision, rendered moments like Fluellen's Alexander the Pig analogy – another typological, not psychological, depiction of character – unintelligible.

This characterization of Hal also sapped the final scene in *Henry V* of many of its darker undertones. The exquisite *Te Deum* sung at the end of Act 4 brought the entire cast on stage and into the side balconies, including the murdered luggage boy and Monsieur Le Fer, Pistol's unfortunate prisoner. In a non-realistic style reminiscent of Boyd's cycle, both dead men appeared with gaping, bloody neck wounds to suggest their throats had been cut off-stage, and they sang the dirge, faintly spotlighted, along with the rest of the company. Although appropriate to the script's sustained meditation on the toll of war, this gruesome spectacle was then gradually abandoned in the giddily staged courtship of Act 5. The *Te Deum*'s sombre mood was picked up briefly by Queen Isabel (Jane Lapotaire), who was assigned Burgundy's long speech about the far-reaching losses of the war (*H5* 5.2.23–67). This assignment of the monologue to the Queen effectively resonated the play's broader interest in how gender organizes the roles and reasons for war. But these darker undercurrents were all but lost in Henry's wooing of Katherine (Jennifer Kirby), which again presented Henry as innocent of his own rhetorical effects. The interaction between them registered no broader consciousness of how the scene extended either Katherine's earlier lesson in English sexual colonization or Henry's rape threats at Harfleur.

I found myself wondering if such resonances can only be communicated through a design-heavy conceptual gambit such as the one employed by Boyd's production. During his *Te Deum*, the company dragged some dozen or two wooden coffins onto the stage and arranged them in the form of a Union Jack. A second stage floor was then laid on top of the coffins, so that the entire final scene took place on a low scaffold-stage built upon the dead. The effect was to temper the romantic discourse of the courtship scene with a visible reminder of the real terms of the alliance. Eschewing concept, Doran's production staged the scene as unmitigated romantic comedy, and as a consequence, its playful energy had no resonance with the more troubling content of its own script. It was fun to watch – at one moment Henry invited the audience to encourage Katherine into accepting him – but it posited Henry as an innocent despite all that had come before. Here, as in other places I have described, the production failed to situate the characterization of Henry within the script's broader representation of morally compromised conquest. This discrepancy need not have been addressed through a design-heavy move like Boyd's, but neither could it go ignored.

The weakness of Doran's *Henry V* was not its resistance to conceptual staging or even an over-investment in Shakespearean character above other elements of the play. What hampered the cycle's presentation of Henry was its prioritization of emotional immediacy over the production script's built-in formal mechanisms for constituting character, such as typology, structural juxtaposition and the diachronic accretion of habitual action. Although each of the four plays was developed separately, the performance of 'King and Country' as a cycle disclosed a consistent directorial approach to characterization that the scripts could not support. Doran indeed may be right that Shakespeare can be trusted to do much of the work for theatre practitioners if only they would let him.[29] His Henriad illustrates how varied that work is – how the character of Henry V is a different kind of construct than the character of Richard II, one that exposes the limitations of acting method to convey the full diversity of Shakespeare's English kings.

Alice Dailey is Associate Professor of English at Villanova University. She is author of *The English Martyr from Reformation to Revolution* (Notre Dame, 2012) and has published articles on a range of literary, dramatic and material artifacts, including photographs of Richard II, the skeleton of Richard III, the RSC's complete Histories cycle, and the self-destroying martyr sculptures of Michael Landy. Her current project is a book on Shakespeare's history plays titled *How to Do Things with Dead People: Temporal Conjecture and the Shakespearean History Play*.

Notes

I wish to thank fellow audience-members Alan Farmer, Elizabeth Zeman Kolkovich and Cary Mazer for sharing their insights about the productions and for their thoughtful comments on earlier drafts of this chapter.

1. Gregory Doran in conversation with James Shapiro, 'King and Country: Learning to Direct', Brooklyn Academy of Music, 18 April 2016, https://www.youtube.com/watch?v=JpGP6fECS3U (accessed 3 May 2016).
2. I discuss these productions in Alice Dailey, 'The RSC's "Glorious Moment" and the Making of Shakespearean History', *Shakespeare Survey* 63 (2010): 184–97.
3. The term 'conceptual casting' is from Alan Dessen, 'Conceptual Casting in the Age of Shakespeare: Evidence from *Mucedorus*', *Shakespeare Quarterly* 43 (1992): 67–70.
4. *Aristotle's Poetics*, trans. S. H. Butcher, intro. Francis Fergusson (New York: Hill and Wang, 1961), 62–63, quoted in Paul Yachnin and Jessica Slights, eds., *Shakespeare and Character: Theory, History, Performance, and Theatrical Persons* (New York: Palgrave, 2009), 7.
5. Yachnin and Slights, *Shakespeare and Character*, 7.
6. W. B. Worthen, *Shakespeare Performance Studies* (Cambridge: Cambridge University Press, 2014), 5. Worthen borrows the word 'correspondence' from Hans-Thies Lehmann, *Postdramatic Theatre*, trans. Karen Jürs-Munby (London: Routledge, 2006), 5.
7. Worthen, *Shakespeare Performance Studies*, 11.
8. Andrew James Hartley, 'Character, Agency and the Familiar Actor', in Yachnin and Slights, *Shakespeare and Character*, 159.
9. All references to Shakespeare's plays are from William Shakespeare, *The Complete Works*, ed. Stanley Wells, Gary Taylor, John Jowett and William Montgomery (Oxford: Clarendon Press, 1988).
10. Charles Isherwood, 'Review: Royal Shakespeare Company's "King and Country" at BAM', *New York Times*, 4 April 2016, http://www.nytimes.com/2016/04/05/theater/review-royal-shakespeare-companys-king-and-country-at-bam.html (accessed 3 May 2016).
11. David Tennant and Jonathan Slinger in conversation with Emma Smith, The Barbican, London, 16 January 2016, https://soundcloud.com/thersc/king-and-country-talk-richard-ii (accessed 10 May 2016).
12. *The Hollow Crown* refers to painted iconography repeatedly, especially images of Saint Sebastian.
13. Barbara Hodgdon's recent book, *Shakespeare, Performance, and the Archive* (New York: Routledge, 2015), tracks 'lost' elements of performance through surviving promptbooks, actors' scripts and production photos. She devotes particular attention to the elaborately annotated and illustrated scripts of Antony Sher, who played Falstaff in Doran's 'King and Country'.
14. Rebecca Schneider, *Performing Remains: Art and War in Times of Theatrical Reenactment* (New York: Routledge, 2011), 15. See also Jacques Derrida, *Archive Fever*, trans. Eric Prenowitz (Chicago: Chicago University Press, 1995); and Diana Taylor, *The Archive and the Repertoire* (Durham, NC: Duke University Press, 2003); as well as Alice Rayner, *Ghosts* (Minneapolis, MN: University of Minnesota Press, 2006), xiii–xiv. For a fuller discussion of the relationship between per-

formance and the archive in Shakespeare's history plays, see Alice Dailey, 'The Talbot Remains: Historical Drama and the Performative Archive', *Shakespeare Bulletin* 35.3 (2017): 373–87.

15. RSC *Richard II* Q&A, 8 January 2016, https://www.youtube.com/watch?v=-Z3pV7Pc1B0 (accessed 13 May 2016).
16. Holinshed writes: 'king Henrie, sitting on a daie at his table, sore sighing, said; Haue I no faithfull freend which will deliuer me of him, whose life will be my death, and whose death will be the preseruation of my life? This saieng was much noted of them which were present, and especiallie of one called sir Piers of Exton. This knight incontinentlie departed from the court, with eight strong persons in his companie, and came to Pomfret'. See Raphael Holinshed, *The Chronicles of England, Scotland, and Ireland*, 2nd edition, 3 vols (1587), 3.78.
17. The Q&A at the end of the Tennant/Slinger conversation at the Barbican (see note 11) is especially interesting in this regard. Several audience members pose intricate historical questions to the two actors, who valiantly attempt to answer them. The exchange demonstrates how the work of historians and actors appears interchangeable in popular understandings of theatrical performance.
18. Email exchange.
19. Cary M. Mazer, 'Historicizing Spontaneity: The Illusion of the First Time of "The Illusion of the First Time"', in *Shakespeare's Sense of Character: On the Page and from the Stage*, ed. Yu Jin Ko and Michael W. Shurgot (Burlington, VA: Ashgate, 2012), 88.
20. 'Alex Hassell on *Henry V*', Royal Shakespeare Company promotional video, https://www.youtube.com/watch?v=AbsC0tQ-5PY (accessed 11 May 2016).
21. Mazer, 'Historicizing Spontaneity', 87. Mazer traces the phrase 'the illusion of the first time' first from William Gillette's 1913 lecture, 'The Illusion of the First Time in Acting', through Lee Strasburg, to Don Weingust and the Original Practices movement (86–89).
22. Ibid., 89.
23. Patsy Rodenburg, *Speaking Shakespeare* (London: Palgrave Macmillan, 2004), 23, quoted in Hartley, 'Character, Agency', 161.
24. Hartley, 'Character, Agency', 162.
25. Ibid., 162; and Doran, 'Learning to Direct'.
26. Hartley, 'Character, Agency', 162.
27. Doran, 'Learning to Direct'.
28. '*Henry IV I* and *II* Official Trailer', RSC Live, published 8 April 2014, https://www.youtube.com/watch?v=aYKeN8ep6Dc (accessed 23 April 2016). The dates for the two RSC videos featuring Hassell suggest that the combination of plays into 'King and Country' may have affected the interpretation of Hal's character. The video that features his performance of the soliloquy from *1 Henry IV* was published in April 2014, in advance of *1* and *2 Henry IV* being broadcast worldwide via RSC Live, and the one in which he describes the decision to stage *2 Henry IV* and *Henry V* as temporally continuous was published on 30 November 2015, just before 'King and Country' began its tour.
29. Doran, 'Learning to Direct'.

Index

A

Aeschylus, 5, 27, 38, 40, 42
Afghanistan, war in, 13
Agamben, Giorgio, 15
alazōn (impostor), 110–11
Alito, Samuel, 106
alkē. *See* valour
All's Well That Ends Well (Shakespeare), 85–86, 94–97, 112
andreia. *See* courage
Antony and Cleopatra (Shakespeare), 12, 89
Aquinas, Thomas (St.), 71–72
Aristotle, 18, 21, 84–85, 109–10, 117n32, 138
Augustine (St.), 12–13, 16–17, 21–22, 71, 83–84, 97
authority
    delegation of, 55–56, 66n50, 66n53
    2 Henry IV, negotiation with Northern rebels in, and, 55–56, 66n53
    legitimate, 72–73, 79
autobiography, *El diario de Hamlet García* as, 130

B

Bacon, Francis, 53
Bakić-Hayden, Milica, 44n14
Balaguer, Víctor, 121, 133n13
Baliani, Marco, 37, 39, 45n32
Balkanism, 31, 37, 44n14
Balkans War, 4–6, 26–27
Ballard, John, 108–9
Barker, Roberta, 90
Barker, Simon, 71
Barton, John, 43n6
Bayley, John, 77–78
Beaumont, Francis, 115n11
Beckett, Samuel, 33–34, 38, 45n35
Bergamín, José, 19, 119–21, 124
Bergson, Henri, 85
Berlin Wall, fall of, 1
Bielmeier, Michael, 77
Billington, Michael, 37
Blades, John, 65n23
Blasted (Kane), 5, 27–28, 44n18, 44n22
    Beckett and, 33
    blinding ritual in, 33–34
    Macdonald, J., producing, 36
    mortar bomb in, 32, 34–35
    rape in, 32–35
    reception of, 31–32, 36–37
    storm scene in, 35
Bogdanov, Michael, 43n6
Botelho, Keith, 52, 65n32
Boyd, Michael, 20, 43n6, 138, 140, 142, 152–53
braggart soldier. *See miles gloriosus*
Bruster, Douglas, 92–93
Bryskett, Lodowick, 51

Buffery, Helena, 136n66
Bush, George W., 19

C
Caballé, Anna, 129
Cade, Jack, 3
Cahill, Patricia, 6–7
Cairns, Douglas, 115n8
Calderón de la Barca, Pedro, 123, 134n25
Calvin, John, 21
Canino, Catherine G., 67n68
Carter, Jimmy, 17
casus belli, 10–11, 75
character
    Aristotle on, 138
    audience perception of, 144–47
    in Doran's Henriad, 20–21, 137–53
    performance embodying, 139–40, 147–49
chivalric code, 8, 77, 90–91
Christianity, 16–18, 21
Christian morality, laughter at war and, 9–10, 83–84, 87–89, 92–97
Cicero, 51, 71
civil wars as unjust, 70–73. *See also* Hamletism during Spanish Civil War
clowning, 92–93
Cole, Douglas, 77, 82n42
Congressional Medal of Honor, 102–4
Conte, Rafael, 129
contrariety, 92–93
Corbalán, Pablo, 127, 129
Coriolà (Balaguer), 121, 133n12
Coriolanus (Shakespeare)
    Coriolà as adaptation of, 121, 133n12
    honour and, 12
    ignorance in, 87–89
    laughter at war and, 87–89, 96–97
    sine dolore in, 87–89
    valour in, 116n17

costume design, *3 Henry VI*, Mitchell staging of, and, 31
Council of the North, in England, fifteenth-century, 48
counterfeits
    alazōn as, 110–11
    Aristotle on, 110, 117n32
    honour and, 15, 101–13
    public records of, 107
    public ridicule of, 107
    satire as response to, 113, 117n33
    Stolen Valor Act and, 15, 102–3, 106, 113
    United States vs. Alvarez and, 15, 102–3, 105–7, 113, 115nn15–16
    See also miles gloriosus
courage, Aristotle on, 109–10
cowardice, Aristotle on, 109–10
creditworthiness, 58
Cultural Materialism, 3

D
Daldry, Stephen, 32
delight, laughter versus, 93
El diario de Hamlet García (Masip), 125–32, 135n56
dissimulation, *2 Henry IV*, negotiation with Northern rebels in, and, 58
Doran, Gregory, 20–21, 137–53, 155n17, 155n28
dysōpia (fecklessness), 18, 70

E
Eliot, T. S., 127
Elizabeth (Queen), 10–11, 55
Ellis, Steven, 47–48
Elton, W. R., 78
Elyot, Thomas, 51
England, Northern, fifteenth-century, proxy rule in, 47–48
ennoblement in England, 1558–1641, 106–7
equity, Calvin on, 21
Erasmus, 69, 74–75

escapism, *Rehearsal for War* and, 5, 41
Every Man in His Humour (Jonson), 111–12, 117n29
excellence, 115n9

F

Faber, Sebastiaan, 128, 130
Farmer, Alan, 146
fecklessness. *See dysōpia*
Fenton, Geoffrey, 54
Foakes, R. A., 71, 77
forever war, 13
Foucault, Michel, 3
Franco, Francisco, 118, 124
Freud, Sigmund, 13, 84–85
Fukuyama, Francis, 1, 14–16, 18, 24n47, 25n62

G

Garrard, William, 85
Gibbon, Edward, 16–18
Globe-to-Globe project, 26
good faith, 50
    2 Henry IV, negotiation with Northern rebels in, and, 51–53, 58–60
Grady, Hugh, 76
Graeber, David, 114n7
Gray, John, 14
Greenblatt, Stephen, 4
Gregor, Keith, 133n12
Grene, Nicholas, 71
Grey, Arthur, 60, 67n68
Gulf War, 1–2

H

Hadfield, Andrew, 61
Hale, J. R., 69
Hamlet (Shakespeare), 18–19, 74, 79, 97. *See also El diario de Hamlet García*
Hamlet, Valencia theatre production of, 121–25, 133n12, 134n15
Hamletism during Spanish Civil War, 122–23
    Bergamín and, 119–21, 124
    El diario de Hamlet García and, 125–32
    international resonance of, 124–25
    Masip and, 119–20, 125–32
    in periodicals, 119–21
Hands, Terry, 43n6
Hardyng, John, 48
Hartley, Andrew James, 20, 139, 147–50
Harvey, Gabriel, 108
hasina, honour and, 114n7
Hassell, Alex, 20, 144, 146–48, 152, 155n28
Hattaway, Michael, 71
Hazlitt, William, 4, 10
hearing, 65n32
    2 Henry IV, negotiation with Northern rebels in, and, 52–53
Hegel, G. W. F., 14
Henriad, Doran directing, 155n17, 155n28
    character explored in, 20–21, 137–53
    1 Henry IV in, 20–21, 143–46, 151–52
    2 Henry IV in, 145–47
    Henry V in, 147–53
    plot in, 139–43, 149–50
    Richard II in, 20, 140–43
    spontaneity in, 148–49
1 Henry IV (Shakespeare), 99n29
    chivalric code in, 91
    Doran directing, 20–21, 143–46, 151–52
    honour in, 85, 90–94, 103, 105–7
    ignorance in, 90
    laughter at war in, 85, 87, 90–94
    miles gloriosus in, 102
    rhipsaspis in, 92
    Rumour in, 51–52
    sine dolore in, 90–92
2 Henry IV (Shakespeare)
    Doran directing, 145–47

honour in, 107
just war theory and, 73
Rumour in, 51–52, 56, 65n23
unjust war in, 73
2 Henry IV, negotiation with Northern rebels in, 7–8, 46, 62–63, 65n29
   authority, delegation of, in, 55–56, 66n53
   creditworthiness and, 58
   dissimulation in, 58
   good faith in, 51–53, 58–60
   hearing in, 52–53
   1 Henry IV, antecedents in, 51–52
   honour in, 54–61
   infidels, rebels as, in, 60–61
Henry V (Shakespeare), 8–9, 69
   Bush and, 19
   Doran directing, 147–53
   dysōpia and, 18
   Hazlitt on, 10
   honour in, 10, 14, 16–17, 107–8, 112–13
   just war theory and, 72–74, 79
   Te Deum in, 152
   unjust war in, 73–74
Henry VI (Shakespeare), 16–18, 26–27, 70–71, 78
1 Henry VI (Shakespeare), Milivojević directing, 26
3 Henry VI, Mitchell staging of, 5, 27
   anti-mimetic approach of, 28–30
   Balkanism and, 31, 37
   costume design of, 31
   media spectacle of war and, 29
   medievalism of, 29–31
   nationalism and, 28
   set design of, 30
3 Henry VI (Shakespeare), just war theory and, 72–73
Henry VII (King), 48–49
Hiddleston, Tom, 144
Hiscock, Andrew, 6
Hobbes, Thomas, 13

Hodgdon, Barbara, 154n13
Holderness, Graham, 4–5
Holinshed's Chronicles, 48–49, 61–62, 143, 155n16
The Hollow Crown, 140, 142, 145
Homer, 92, 104–5, 115nn8–9
Honneth, Axel, 15
honour, 9, 115n8
   Aristotle on, 109–10
   Congressional Medal of Honor and, 102–4
   Coriolanus and, 12
   counterfeits and, 15, 101–13
   ennoblement in England, 1558–1641, and, 106–7
   Fukuyama on, 14–16, 25n62
   hasina as, 114n7
   1 Henry IV and, 85, 90–94, 103, 105–7
   2 Henry IV, negotiation with Northern rebels in, and, 54–61
   2 Henry IV and, 107
   Henry V and, 10, 14, 16–17, 107–8, 112–13
   Henry VI and, 16–17
   Iliad and, 104–5
   inflation of, 106–7
   King John and, 11
   The Knight of the Burning Pestle and, 115n11
   nationalism and, 104–6, 113
   recognition and, 15–16, 19, 25n62
   as social capital, 106
   thymos and, 14, 16, 18–19
   Troilus and Cressida and, 11, 76–78, 81n34
   valour versus, 103–4
Hooker, John, 49
Huntington, Samuel, 16, 24n47

I
ignorance
   All's Well That Ends Well and, 95–97

Antony and Cleopatra and, 89
Coriolanus and, 87–89
1 Henry IV and, 90
laughter and, 86–87
Iliad (Homer), 92, 104–5
impostor. *See alazōn*
infidels, negotiations and, 60–61
Ireland, sixteenth century, 55, 67n68
  negotiations in, 47, 50–51, 53–54
  presidential councils in, 49–50
  proxy rule in, 48–50, 64n21
  Second Desmond Rebellion in, 60, 64n22
  surrender and regrant policy in, 49
Isherwood, Charles, 140–41
Islam, Huntington on, 16, 24n47
isothymia, 16

J
James, Heather, 77, 81n34
Jonson, Ben, 111–12, 117n29
Jorgensen, Paul A., 5, 13–14
Julius Caesar (Shakespeare), 12
jus ad bellum, 9, 72–73, 76
jus in bello, 9, 72–73, 91
just cause, 72, 79
just war theory, 8–9
  Aquinas and, 71–72
  Augustine on, 71, 83–84
  Cicero and, 71
  Hamlet and, 74, 79
  2 Henry IV and, 73
  3 Henry VI and, 72–73
  Henry V and, 72–74, 79
  just cause in, 72, 79
  legitimate authority in, 72–73, 79
  proportionality in, 72–76, 78–79
  Richard III and, 71–73, 79
  right intention in, 72–73, 79
  Walzer on, 71–72, 75

K
Kane, Sarah. *See Blasted*

Kant, Immanuel, 2
Kastan, David Scott, 102
Kennedy, Anthony, 103–4
Kerrigan, John, 58–59
Kesselring, K. J., 49
King, Ros, 85
"King and Country: Shakespeare's Great Cycle of Kings." *See* Henriad, Doran directing
King John (Shakespeare), honour in, 11
King Lear (Shakespeare), 35, 39. *See also Blasted*
The Knight of the Burning Pestle (Beaumont), 115n11

L
laughter
  Aristotle on, 84–85
  Bergson on, 85
  clowning and, 92–93
  criticizing, 84
  delight versus, 93
  Freud on, 84–85
  ignorance and, 86–87
  Maggi on, 86–87, 90
  Plato on, 86–87, 99n20
laughter at war
  All's Well That Ends Well and, 85–86, 94–97
  Christian morality and, 9–10, 83–84, 87–89, 92–97
  Coriolanus and, 87–89, 96–97
  1 Henry IV and, 85, 87, 90–94
La vida es sueño (*Life's a Dream*) (Calderón), 123, 134n25
Leal, Milagros, 121, 123–24
Lee, Steven, 72, 75–76
Lefebvre, Henri, 3
Leggatt, Alexander, 90
legitimate authority in just war theory, 72–73, 79
libido dominandi (lust for dominion), 12–13
Llidó, Noelia, 123
Lluís Sirera, Josep, 134n25

Love's Labours Lost (Shakespeare), 112
lust for dominion. *See libido dominandi*
Lynch, S. J., 77

M

MacDonald, Alastair, 48
Macdonald, James, 36
Machiavelli, Niccolò, 50–51, 69
Maggi, Vincenzo, 86–87, 90, 99n13
Marañón, Gregorio, 120
marcher lords, proxy rule and, 47–48
Marlowe, Christopher, 61
Marrast, Robert, 123
Martone, Mario, 39. *See also Rehearsal for War*
Marx, Karl, 15
Marx, Steven, 9, 21, 69, 74–75
Mary (Queen of Scots), 108
Masip, Paulino, 19, 119–20, 125–32
Mattox, John Mark, 71
Mazer, Cary M., 146, 148, 155n21
McAlindon, Tom, 7, 77
McDonough, Christopher, 92
McKeown, Adam, 101
McMahan, Jeff, 76
media spectacle of war
　3 Henry VI, Mitchell staging of, and, 29
　Rehearsal for War and, 37
medievalism, *3 Henry VI*, Mitchell staging of, and, 29–31
megalothymia, 16, 18
Meron, Theodor, 8–9, 70
Merriam, Thomas, 91
microthymia, 18
miles gloriosus (braggart soldier), 15, 113, 116n26
　All's Well That Ends Well and, 94, 112
　Ballard as, 108–9
　Every Man in His Humour and, 111–12
　1 Henry IV and, 102
Miles Gloriosus (Plautus), 110–11

Military Revolution, 1560–1660, 6–7
Milivojević, Nikita, 26
Miola, Robert, 94–95
Mitchell, Katie. *See 3 Henry VI*, Mitchell staging of
Molina, Antonio Muñoz, 131
Morandini, Morando, 39
Morgan, Hiram, 50, 54–55, 64n14
Morreall, John, 85
Muir, Kenneth, 70, 77
Muldrew, Craig, 58
Mundi, Francisco, 133n12

N

nationalism, 28, 104–6, 113
Needham, Matthew, 144
negotiations
　good faith in, 50
　infidels in, 60–61
　Ireland, sixteenth century and, 47, 50–51, 53–54
　See also 2 Henry IV, negotiation with Northern rebels in
New Historicism, 2–6
Nietzsche, Friedrich, 4, 18
Nine Years War (1594–1603), 47, 50
Noble, Adrian, 43n6
Nora, Eugenio de, 126, 129
Northern Rebellion. *See 2 Henry IV*, negotiation with Northern rebels in

O

Oates-Smith, J., 77
Obama, Barack, 17–19
Oliva, César, 133n12
O'Neill, Hugh, 50–51, 53–54, 60, 62, 64nn21–22
Othello (Shakespeare), 121

P

pacifism, 69, 74–75, 79
　Christianity and, 21
　Henry VI and, 70–71
Pašović, Haris, 38
Patterson, Annabel, 67n77

Patterson, Lee, 3
performance, character embodied in, 139–40, 147–49
Phialas, Peter, 21
Pilgrimage of Grace, 7–8
Plato, 14, 16, 86–87, 99n20
Plautus, 110–11
plot
 Aristotle on, 138
 in Doran's Henriad, 139–43, 149–50
Plutarch, 18
Pommercy, Mario, 123
presidential councils in Ireland, 49–50
proportionality
 Erasmus on, 74–75
 Hamlet and, 74
 just war theory and, 72–76, 78–79
 Troilus and Cressida and, 9, 74, 76, 78–79
proxy rule
 England, Northern, fifteenth-century, and, 47–48
 Ireland, sixteenth century, and, 48–50, 64n21
 marcher lords and, 47–48
public records of counterfeits, 107
public ridicule of counterfeits, 107
Pugliatti, Paola, 8–9, 71

Q
Quabeck, Franziska, 9, 91, 99n29

R
Rabkin, Norman, 4, 9, 69
rape, in *Blasted*, 32–35
Rapple, Rory, 108
recognition, 15–16, 19, 25n62
Rehearsal for War (*Teatro di guerra*), 5, 27–28, 37–42, 45n32, 45n37
relative painlessness. *See sine dolore*
remembrance, *El diario de Hamlet García*, 131–32
rhipsaspis (shield-tosser), 92, 99n28

Richard II (Shakespeare)
 Doran directing, 20, 140–43
 Martone directing, 39
Richard III (Shakespeare), just war theory and, 71–73, 79
right intention in just war theory, 72–73, 79
Roberts, Michael, 6
Rodenburg, Patsy, 148
Romeo and Juliet (Shakespeare), 27
Rossiter, A. P., 76
Rumour, 51–52, 56, 65n23

S
Sacharoff, Mark, 77
Sartre, Jean Paul, 3
satire as response to counterfeits, 113, 117n33
Schneider, Rebecca, 20, 142
Second Desmond Rebellion, 60, 64n22
September 11, 2001, 2–3
set design, *3 Henry VI*, Mitchell staging of, and, 30
The Seven Against Thebes (Aeschylus), 5, 27, 38, 40, 42
Shakespeare, William. *See specific topics*
Shapiro, James, 91, 137–38
Shelley, Rudi, 138
Sher, Antony, 146, 154n13
shield-tosser. *See rhipsaspis*
Sidney, Henry, 93
sine dolore (relative painlessness), 9–10, 85
 All's Well That Ends Well and, 96–97
 Coriolanus and, 87–89
 1 Henry IV and, 90–92
 Maggi on, 86
Sivan, Emmanuel, 131
Slights, Jessica, 138, 143, 150
Slinger, Jonathan, 140, 142, 155n17
Smith, Rae, 30
Snyder, Jon, 58
social capital, honour as, 106

Soler, Salvador, 121–25
Somogyi, Nick de, 2–3, 6
Sontag, Susan, 33–34, 38, 45n35
Spanish Civil War, 19
Spanish Second Republic, 118–19
Spenser, Edmund, 60, 67n68
spontaneity, acting as, 148–49
Stanihurst, Richard, 48
St. Leger, Antony, 49
Stolen Valor Act, 15, 102–3, 106, 113
Stone, Laurence, 106–7
Suleiman, Susan, 131
Supreme Court, US, 114n3. *See also United States vs. Alvarez*
surrender and regrant policy, in Ireland, 49

T

Tamburlaine, Part Two (Marlowe), 61
The Taming of the Shrew (Shakespeare), 27, 39–41, 121, 123–24. *See also Rehearsal for War*
Taunton, Nina, 6
Teatro di guerra. See Rehearsal for War
Te Deum in *Henry V*, 152
Tennant, David, 20, 137–38, 140–43, 155n17
thymos, 14, 16, 18–19
Tillyard, E. M. W., 91
timē. *See* honour
Todorova, Maria, 44n14
Troilus and Cressida (Shakespeare), 82n42
  honour in, 11, 76–78, 81n34
  proportionality in, 9, 74, 76, 78–79
  unjust war in, 68–69, 76–79

Tronch, Jésus, 19
Trump, Donald, 2, 13

U

Unamuno, Miguel de, 127
United States vs. Alvarez, 15, 102–3, 105–7, 113, 115nn15–16
unjust wars
  civil wars as, 70–73
  Erasmus on, 69
  2 Henry IV and, 73
  Henry V and, 73–74
  Troilus and Cressida and, 68–69, 76–79

V

valour, 103, 104–5, 116n17
Vicary, Thomas, 52–53
Villanueva, Sanz, 129

W

Waiting for Godot (Beckett), Sontag production of, 33–34, 38, 45n35
Walsingham, Thomas, 61–62
Walzer, Michael, 71–72, 75
Weimann, Robert, 92–93
West, Thomas, 77
White, R. S., 9, 69, 78
Wilcox, Helen, 94
Winter, Jay M., 131
Worthen, W. B., 20, 139–40, 148

Y

Yachnin, Paul, 77, 138, 143, 150

www.ingramcontent.com/pod-product-compliance
Lightning Source LLC
Chambersburg PA
CBHW072158100526
44589CB00015B/2273